FIFTH EDITION
BUSINESS BASICS
AND PERSPECTIVES

AHMED RACHDI   GAIL RATHBUN

Kendall Hunt
publishing company

Cover image courtesy of James Whitcraft.

Kendall Hunt
publishing company

www.kendallhunt.com
Send all inquiries to:
4050 Westmark Drive
Dubuque, IA 52004-1840

Dedication

I dedicate this textbook to the memory of my beloved son, Naseem, whose name means "gentle breeze" in Arabic.

He was listening to me once over the phone, helping a student. He came to me and whispered, "I wish I were your student." This is how the idea to write a textbook was born.

Naseem possessed outstanding attributes, including a charming smile, intelligence, and a wisdom beyond his years. He had a very sweet and pleasant personality and was loyal to his friends and family. His love greatly affected all who knew him.

I am both the happiest and luckiest man on earth, for I have many Naseems in my classrooms. I thank them for all I have learned from them. I dedicate this textbook to all my students from Al Akhawayn University in Ifrane, Morocco, and those at my home university, Purdue University Fort Wayne. May God bless them all and shower them with many successes.

Ahmed Rachdi

Table of Contents

CHAPTER 1

The World of Business and Economics

What Is Business?

Business is a part of everyone's life. To what extent it is so, is a matter of perspective. We are all consumers of products and services. Many of us invest in homes, cars, and education with the expectation of a return on our investments. You may be considering starting your own business, or you may already count yourself among the 28 million small business owners in the United States. It is even more likely that you work for a small business or for a corporation. No matter what perspective you adopt, however, you need an understanding of the basics of business to be able to survive and prosper, and to ensure the health and well-being of your family and the global community of which you are a part.

Put simply, a business is the organized effort of a group of individuals that strives for a profit by providing goods and services that satisfy the needs and wants of its customers. The last part of this definition—creating value for people and enabling them to fulfill their needs for food, clothing, shelter, security, and entertainment, for example—is the most important aspect of the definition. A business that provides a product or service that people do not want or need will not be sustainable. Products are tangible objects such as computers, food, cars, and appliances. Services are intangible. Services use processes, products, and equipment to fulfill customer needs. Education, healthcare, insurance, and recreation are all examples of services.

What Is Profit?

Profit *What's left after subtracting all of the operating and production costs from revenue.*

Profit is the amount of money remaining after costs have been subtracted from revenue. Revenue is the total amount of money that the business earns from providing goods and services to its customers. Costs are all of the expenses that a company incurs from making, selling, and distributing its product or service. Profit can also be considered the reward that the owners receive for taking risks, because a business may experience a loss when costs are more than revenue. If losses continue over time, the business may have to close. In the United States approximately 600,000 businesses close every year. The profits of a business go to its owners or to its shareholders. In the case of not-for-profit organizations, the goal is not to generate profit, but to ensure that operating costs stay low in order to make the maximum amount of its resources available to those it serves. Government is the largest category within the nonprofit classification.

Factors of Production

Factors of production *The resources that are used to make a product or service.*

To generate profits, a business makes effective use of four types of productive resources (**factors of production**): natural resources, labor, capital, and entrepreneurship.

Natural resources are naturally occurring elements of the physical environment, such as crude oil, forests, minerals, land, water, and even air.

Human resources (also referred to as labor or human capital) refer to the input of people, such as managers, employees, or volunteers, to the production process.

Capital is another way to refer to the money, or funds, used to pay employees, to buy materials, and to generally keep the business going. Capital includes investments in activities such as upgrading production facilities, expanding to new geographic areas, or introducing a new product. Profit may become capital if it is retained and invested back into the business.

Entrepreneurship is an intangible resource but every bit as essential as the other three types of productive resources. Entrepreneurship entails the willingness to take the risks necessary to create and operate a business. An entrepreneur is a person who risks time, effort, and money to start and operate a business.

Types of Economic Systems

Economics is the social science that examines how societies make choices in the face of scarce resources to satisfy their unlimited wants. To address the problems presented by scarce resources, societies must answer the following questions:

1. *Which* **goods** and **services** will be produced?
2. *How* will they be produced?
3. *For whom* will they be produced?
4. *Who* owns and controls the major factors of production?

Economists usually study these questions from two perspectives, microeconomics and macroeconomics.

Microeconomics is the study of the decisions made by individual units of the economy, such as consumers and firms. It focuses on price, profits, wage markets, the gasoline market, demand for labor, and other factors of production.

Macroeconomics studies the performance of the national economy as a whole. It focuses on, for example, the causes of inflation and unemployment, the effect of the national debt on economic growth, the analysis of national economic patterns and trends, and the relative performance of the government's fiscal and/or monetary policies.

"Pure" economic systems such as communism, socialism, and capitalism do not exist in the real world. **Communism** is an economic system in which production facilities are communally owned by the public, as represented by a government, and the output distributed to consumers equally or according to need. **Socialism** professes egalitarianism, that is, equal distribution of income and social services, such as retirement benefits, health care, and education. In a socialist system the government may also own banks and run transportation services. The degree to which the government owns and controls the factors of production may vary. The state may also control rents, wages, and taxes. People are free to choose the work they will do. They may be self-employed or may opt for jobs in government-owned industries. In a **capitalistic economy**, the role of the government is to support private ownership and encourage entrepreneurship. Individuals choose where to work, what to buy, and how much to pay for goods and services. Likewise, producers of goods and services choose whom to hire, what to produce, and how much to charge.

In order to systematically study economic behaviors anywhere, economists classify the economic systems of the world into three major types: command economies, mixed economies, and free market economies (see Figure 1.1). These classifications are based on the answers to the four questions that form the foundation of economics, listed in the beginning of this section. You should understand, however, that most economic systems are mixed economies, although one type of system may be dominant in a particular region or country.

In **command** or **planned econom**ies a central government makes all of the decisions about which goods and services will be produced, how they will be produced, and for whom they will be produced. The government owns and controls the major factors of production. Cuba is one example of a command economy. The government controls 90 percent of the economy. There are signs, however, that Cuba's command economy is unsustainable. In order to soften the effect of laying off more than a million workers who were on the government payroll, it announced in 2010 that opportunities for self-employment would be broadened.

North Korea is another notable example of a command economy. Like Cuba, North Korea initially experienced great success under a command economy, harnessing natural resources and activating a largely idle workforce. However, starting as far back as the early 1960s, North Korea started to experience economic problems due to lack of productivity and its continued emphasis on heavy industry. The North Korean government continues to insist on centralized control of the economy in spite of widespread famine and malnutrition, due, in part, to collectivized agriculture.

Microeconomics
Economic perspective that focuses on the decisions made by individuals or firms.

Macroeconomics
Economic perspective that focuses on the decisions made by governments.

At the opposite end of the spectrum are free market economies. The **free market economy**, also known as the "private enterprise system" and "free enterprise," is based on competition in the marketplace and private ownership of the factors of production. Singapore is often singled out as an example of a true free market economy. This tiny island located at the southern tip of Malaysia depends entirely on international trade and the sale of services, pushing it to adopt economic openness, free trade, and free markets. At the same time, however, the government of Singapore does tightly control factors of production and compels its citizens to save 25 percent of their salaries in a government controlled pension fund.

The **mixed economy** combines elements of the other two types of systems. The United States is often called a free market economy (see below) but in truth, it is a mixed economy. The role of the government is limited to regulation and promotion of the welfare of all citizens. The government provides services that might not be provided by private businesses—for example, national defense, police and fire protection, education, and the building of transportation infrastructure. The government, at all levels, collects taxes and fees to defray the costs of these services. In the United States' mixed economy, individuals decide on the type of work they want to do, items they want to purchase, and the price they want to pay. Producers decide what to produce based on the needs and wants of consumers, industry, and the government.

The modern application of socialism produces a mixed economic system. Sweden, France, Canada, and India are often cited as examples of socialistic systems. Recently, however, the costs of maintaining social entitlements for retirement, health care, and education—all hallmarks of socialism—have outstripped the ability of socialist nations to pay for them. It is likely that these nations will shift toward the adoption of a greater number of free market system practices such as privatization and abandoning governmental oversight.

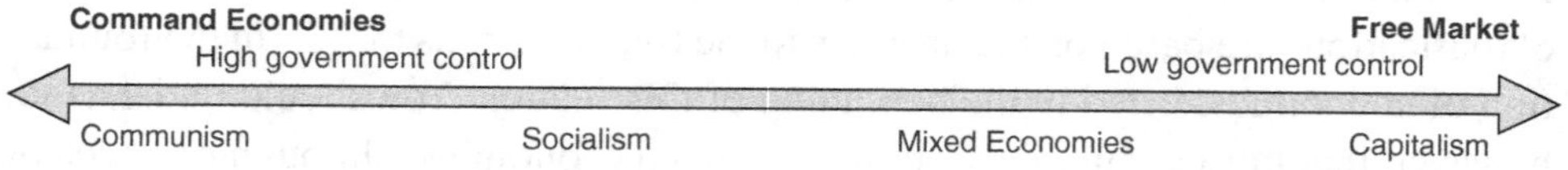

Figure 1.1 Types of economic systems

Economics of the Market Economy

Law of supply and demand Relationship between what people want to buy and what producers are willing to make.

The relationship between what people and organizations want to buy and what producers are willing to produce is governed by what is known as the **law of supply and demand** (see figure 1.2). This economic law describes the relationship among demand for a product, supply of the product, and an equilibrium (market) price. Buyers will purchase (demand) more of a product as its price drops and less of a product as the price increases. Producers of the product will offer (supply) more of a product as its price rises and less of a product as its price drops. The **equilibrium price**, or market price, is the price at which the quantity of goods demanded and the quantity of goods supplied are equal.

In the real world of economics, it is very seldom that the demand exactly equals the supply. **Surpluses** of a product or service occur when the quantity exceeds the amount demanded. Such a situation causes losses, as when U.S. farmers produce too much wheat, corn, or milk, driving prices down to levels where it is difficult to make a profit. The U.S. government has often stepped in with subsidies to pay farmers for not producing beyond a certain quantity of a crop. **Shortages**, in which the quantity demanded is greater than that supplied, also cause lost profits and invite increased competition. Government subsidies and increased competition serve to bring prices back toward equilibrium, following the law of supply and demand.

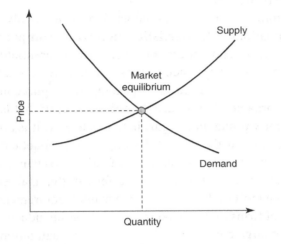

Figure 1.2   Law of supply and demand

Degrees of Competition

In a **free market system**, buyers are free to buy what they want at whatever price they wish to pay, and producers provide the goods and services needed and wanted by prospective buyers. This situation gives rise to competition, an intentional effort to win sales from potential customers. Economists have identified four degrees of competition (see figure 1.3). It is important for a business person to understand which of these market situations exists for the product or service offered, in order to compete successfully.

Perfect competition
Market situation where
every seller is offering
exactly the same product
or service.

   Perfect competition is the most highly competitive market situation. A commodity product such as wheat illustrates the characteristics of perfect competition. Every seller of wheat is offering the same product. There are many buyers and sellers, no individual seller can influence the price, and no seller can monopolize the market. They also have complete information about prices, suppliers, and other facts relevant to the buying and selling of this product. The sellers are "price takers," which means that they will have to accept the market or equilibrium price arrived at through the law of supply and demand.

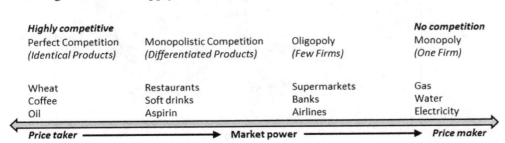

Figure 1.3   Continuum of competition

The opposite of perfect competition is **monopoly**, a situation in which a single firm accounts for all industry sales. An example of a **natural monopoly** is a gas or electric company, a rail system, or telecommunication system. A limited or **legal monopoly** is created when the federal government issues a copyright, patent, or trademark. In a monopoly the firm controls the price and the supply. Consumer choice is limited. New firms encounter barriers in entering and obstacles in competing with the existing firm.

Far more common than perfect competition or monopoly are monopolistic and oligopoly situations. **Monopolistic (imperfect) competition** exists when there are many buyers and sellers, products are differentiated, and the firms have some control over price. Each of these firms may hold a tiny "monopoly" because of differentiation of products. For example, a yogurt company might have a "monopoly" of organically produced probiotic yogurt; that is, no other yogurt company is currently producing yogurt in that category. It is also relatively easy for a firm to enter or exit the market. Examples of product categories in which monopolistic competition exists are aspirin, soft drinks, vacuum cleaners, and shoes.

Oligopoly means competition among a few. In this market situation, a few large firms produce most of the supply. Large capital requirements or other factors limit the number of firms in the marketplace, so that the industry is dominated by a small number of large companies. Because of the small number of companies, the action of one firm can have a significant impact on the sales of every other firm in the industry. Like a monopoly, barriers to entry for new firms are high. Examples of product and service categories in which only a few firms compete are supermarkets, banks, oil, medicinal drugs, auto and airline industries, and broadcasting.

The Business Cycle

A nation's economy does not grow at a steady rate. It expands and contracts depending on the interaction of a complex set of variables. These recurring economic "ups and downs" are known as the **business cycle**. Economists have identified four states of a business cycle: the **peak** (also known as "prosperity"), **recession**, the **trough**, and **recovery** (see figure 1.4).

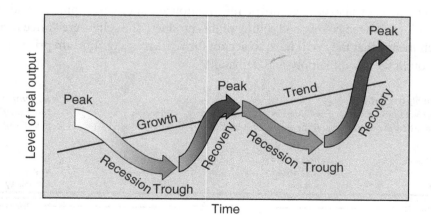

Figure 1.4 The business cycle

During the *peak* period, unemployment is low, total income is relatively high, and consumers are willing to buy products and services. Businesses often expand and offer new products and services. Economists define a *recession* as two or more consecutive three-month periods of decline in a country's gross domestic product. Unemployment rises during a recession and total buying power declines. Economists define a *depression* as a severe recession that lasts longer than a recession. The third phase of the business cycle, the *trough* of a recession or depression, is the phase in which the nation's output and unemployment bottom out and reach their lowest levels. *Recovery* is the movement of the economy from depression or recession to prosperity, resulting in a greater demand for products and services.

To offset the effects of recession and depression, the federal government uses both monetary and fiscal policies. **Monetary policies** are the Federal Reserve's decisions that determine the size of the supply of money and the level of interest rates. The government can also use **fiscal policy** to influence the amount of savings and expenditures by altering the tax structure and changing the levels of government spending. Fiscal and monetary policies are coordinated in order to smooth fluctuations in output and unemployment and to stabilize prices. Although the federal government collects US$3 trillion in annual revenues, it often spends more than it receives, resulting in a **federal deficit**. In 2016 the federal deficit decreased to $552 billion from a high of $1.47 trillion in 2010. The total of all federal deficits is called the **national debt.** By the end of 2018 the national debt was nearly $22 trillion, equal to 78% of the gross domestic product (GDP). To track the national debt from day to day, you may visit http://www.usdebtclock.org and view the U.S. National Debt Clock.

Economic indicators such as the **gross domestic product (GDP)** or the **gross national product (GNP)** show whether an economic system is strengthening, weakening, or remaining stable. The GDP and GNP are called growth indicators, while the inflation and unemployment rates are called stability indictors. The gross domestic product is an aggregate output measure of the total value of all goods and services produced within a given period by a national economy through domestic factors of production. If GDP is in a state of increase, it implies that the nation is experiencing economic growth. GNP is the total value of all goods and services produced within a given period by a national economy, regardless of where the factors of production are located.

Peak (prosperity) Unemployment is low, income is high, consumers willing to buy.

Recession Two or more consecutive periods of decline. Unemployment rises and buying power declines.

Depression Severe, long-lasting recession.

Trough The lowest point of a recession or a depression.

Recovery Movement of economy from recession or depression to prosperity.

The External Business Environment

The preceding section describing the business cycle took a macroeconomic perspective. In this section, you will learn about the factors in the **external business environment** that shape the behavior of a single business or of a particular industry. The organization has no control over factors in the external environment, often called **general environmental factors**. (See figure 1.5 below.)

The **technological environment** is dynamic and challenging. Technology daily transforms business processes such as manufacturing, automation, purchasing, distribution, customer services, and dissemination of information. Funding research, development, and implementation of technological innovations in order to avoid

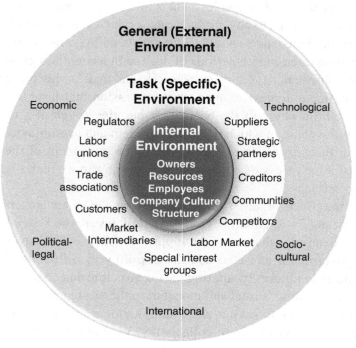

Figure 1.5 Factors in the business environment

obsolescence is essential for even the smallest of companies to remain profitable and competitive.

The **economic environment** must be considered carefully when making business decisions. For example, if an economy is doing well enough for most people to have jobs, a growing company might find it necessary to pay higher wages and offer more benefits in order to attract workers from other companies. On the other hand, if many people in an economy are looking for jobs, a firm may be able to pay less and offer fewer benefits. Factors such as consumer confidence, disposable income levels, inflation and unemployment rates, availability of low-cost energy, loan interest rates, and business cycle phase must be taken into account when deciding, for example, whether to fill vacancies, to expand the business, or to borrow money to meet the payroll.

The **political-legal environment** can both limit and permit business decisions. Local zoning requirements affect almost every business, as do environmental, health, employment, and safety regulations. Other factors in this category include international trade regulations and restrictions, advertising practices, the pro- or anti- business sentiment of local government, consumer protection laws, and armed conflicts.

The **socio-cultural environment** shapes the size, needs, wants, and location of the market for goods and services. Included in this environmental factor are population diversity, levels of education, labor and social mobility, religion, attitudes toward foreign products, the changing roles of men and women in society, increasing life expectancy, better living conditions, a greater consciousness of the physical environment, a heightened focus on maintaining a healthy lifestyle, fashion trends, entrepreneurial spirit, and changing attitudes toward marriage and gender. The attitudes, values, and lifestyles encompassed in these factors influence the products that people will buy, the effectiveness of product promotions, and how, where, and when the products will be purchased.

The **international environment** offers a global marketplace for goods and services, increases competition, provides opportunities for product innovation and adaptation, and expands the available labor market. A greater variety of products at lower prices becomes available. Workers may lose jobs when employers use offshore labor. When an organization does business in other countries, cultural differences must be considered. Ethical concerns, such as the acceptance of bribery as a standard business practice, the employment of children in factories, use of prisoners as free labor, and abuse of the natural environment, are a few of the complex issues that must be deliberated when contemplating operations in a global context. Last, each foreign setting has its own technological, economic, political-legal, and socio-cultural environment that must be taken into account.

Task (Specific) Environment

The **task (specific) environment** is a part of the general business environment that contains factors that directly interact with the company and which in turn influence the company's actions and operations.

Significant task environment factors include suppliers, customers, competitors, regulators, and the labor market, discussed below. Additional factors are shown in figure 1.5.

- Suppliers provide the inputs a company needs in order to produce its goods and services. The quality and cost of these inputs has a significant effect on the company's profit and reputation.
- Customers' demands put pressure on the firm to satisfy them. The customer is the "real boss."
- Competitors' actions and the company's response are critical to profitability and help shape tactics and strategy. Today the competitive environment includes global competition, as well, no matter what the size of the company is, or where the company is located. To be competitive, businesses must research suppliers, distributors, labor, markets, and other resources beyond their immediate borders. The growth of e-commerce has played an enormous role in increasing the intensity of competition experienced by U.S. businesses.
- Regulators, particularly in the immediate region in which the company operates, can greatly influence the cost of doing business. For example, companies ask for and receive tax abatements from local governments in return for locating or expanding their business. In 2015, General Motors announced its decision to invest US$1.2 billion to expand its Fort Wayne, Indiana, truck plant after Allen County granted the manufacturer a $15 million 10-year tax abatement in order to secure nearly 4,000 jobs.
- Labor supply close to the site(s) of a company's operations is essential to its success. The right mix of skilled, qualified labor enhances operations, delivers high value to customers, and builds the company's reputation. If an adequate supply of workers is not available, the firm must invest additional resources to acquire it.

The Internal Business Environment

The **internal business environment** refers to factors within the company that will affect business decisions. See figure 1.5. A key internal factor is the knowledge, skills, and abilities of the business owners, and the resources available to them. Business owners must also clearly understand the competitive advantage that they hold so that they can be strategic in their decision making. A skilled, motivated, and loyal workforce is another internal factor that can help overcome business obstacles, or become the impetus for growth. The organizational culture—shared values, norms, traditions, and beliefs—affect and guide the company's productivity, performance, and attitudes toward the customer and the environment. The structural design of the organization is another internal factor that shapes how the parts of company will coordinate their efforts to achieve its mission. (Organizational culture and structure will be discussed further in Chapter 6.)

APPLY YOUR KNOWLEDGE

Downsizing the National Debt

When the government takes in less revenue than it spends, a deficit occurs. The total of all annual federal budget deficits is called the national debt. The total amount of the national debt was over $22 trillion by the end of the second quarter of fiscal 2019. (The federal government's fiscal year 2019 started on October 1, 2018.) The national debt grew by 10 percent between 2016 and 2018, and by 100 percent during 2009-2016, largely due to the Great Recession, tax cuts, and measures taken by the Obama administration to protect the economy after the worldwide financial collapse of 2008. To put the national debt in perspective, the US Debt Clock (https://www.usdebtclock.org/) shows that the current debt amounts to about $68,000 per citizen and $182,000 per taxpayer.

The United States has always had a national debt. The financial affairs of the United States were in disarray after the Revolutionary War, 1775-1783. The new country had massive debts, and there was an economic crisis at the time the Constitution went into effect in 1789. Secretary of the Treasury Alexander Hamilton presented a plan whereby the federal government would pay the debts that the states had incurred from the war and would raise revenue from taxes on imports. In the years between 1796 and 1835 there were 14 budget surpluses and 2 deficits, one of which occurred as a result of the War of 1812. Andrew Jackson paid off the national debt in its entirety in 1835.

Most experts agree that too much debt is detrimental to the economy because of the impact it has on borrowing money and interest rates. A budget deficit means that the government must borrow money, but at the same time, lenders may be hesitant to loan money to an entity that is having trouble balancing its budget. To compensate for the risk, the lenders will increase their interest rates, and people who buy treasury securities will earn more money on their investments. To pay the higher interest to investors, the government will have to divert tax revenues from projects such as infrastructure renewal. Just as the interest rates on loans to the government and the yields on treasury securities rise, so do mortgage interest rates because they are tied to the rates set by the Federal Reserve and the treasury securities. Lastly, the high rate of return on risk-free treasury securities makes investing in corporations less attractive. This is called the "crowding out effect."

The main contributors to the mounting national debt are Social Security, the Bush-era tax cuts (2001-2008), healthcare entitlements, the stimulus bill of 2009 (the American Recovery and Reinvestment Act and Troubled Asset Relief Program), and involvement in three Middle Eastern wars. According to the Congressional Budget Office (CBO), annual budget deficits will grow by $1.2 trillion between 2019 and 2029.

Knowledge Application Questions

How would you reduce the annual federal budget deficit? Go to the Committee for a Responsible Federal Budget (CRFB) web page called The Debt Fixer at www.crfb.org/debtfixer/.

1. Using the seven budget categories of The Debt Fixer, displayed as tabs across the top of the page, "fix" the federal budget by making choices based on the platform of the Democratic Party, available at https://democrats.org/where-we-stand/party-platform/. How much were you able to cut? Were you able to meet the goal set by the CRFB? Print your results on paper or as a .pdf file.

2. "Fix" the budget again, this time using the Republican Party platform at https://gop.com/platform/ to guide your budget choices. How much were you able to cut? Were you able to meet the goal set by the CRFB? Were you able to meet the goal set by the CRFB? Print your results on paper or as a .pdf file.

3. Look at the "Savings" bar chart for each budget. Which budget came closest to the target? In which budget category(ies) did you save the most money? How does your comparison of the two budgets suggest ways that legislators might reduce deficits in future budgets?

Sources

Chappell, W. 2019, February 13. "U.S. National Debt Hits Record $22 Trillion." Accessed October 30, 2019. https://www.npr.org/2019/02/13/694199256/u-s-national-debt-hits-22-trillion-a-new-record-thats-predicted-to-fall.

History of the Public Debt. https://en.wikipedia.org/wiki/History_of_the_United_States_public_debt.

Investopedia. 2019, May. "The National Debt Explained." Accessed October 30, 2019. https://www.investopedia.com/updates/usa-national-debt/.

QUIZ YOURSELF

Without looking back at the chapter, choose the best answer to each of the questions below. Answers are in the back of the textbook before the Index. Review the chapter to find out why you missed any questions.

1. Economists define a _____ as two consecutive three-month periods of decline in a country's gross domestic product.
    a. repression
    b. prosperity
    c. recession
    d. trough
    e. recovery

2. The ultimate objective of every firm, such as IBM, Hewlett-Packard, JCPenney, and Cengage Learning, must be to
    a. sell either to other firms or to consumers.
    b. satisfy the needs of its customers.
    c. pay out money to cover the various expenses of doing business.
    d. know that people generally buy a product and store it.
    e. make it impossible to satisfy customers.

3. Although all casual clothing ultimately provides the same purpose, companies such as The Gap strive to make their brand seem unique from the many other brands available in the market. The market for casual clothing can best be characterized as _____.
    a. pure competition
    b. monopolistic competition
    c. an oligopoly
    d. a monopoly
    e. a natural monopoly

4. Manar works at an institutional bakery and is paid a wage dictated by the government. She does not like her job but is not allowed other options. Manar must purchase necessities for her family at fixed prices. The country Manar lives in can be described as a _____ economy.
    a. demand
    b. command
    c. market
    d. free-enterprise
    e. capitalist

5. In the city of Westminster, market analysts have observed that all Christmas trees offered for sale will be purchased at a price of $20 and all demand will be satisfied. In this market, $20 is the _____.
   a. equilibrium price
   b. demand price
   c. supply price
   d. margin price
   e. supply schedule

6. Which of the following measures the market value of all final goods and services produced in the United States?
   a. Index of market valuation
   b. Microeconomic equilibrium
   c. Consumer surplus
   d. Consumer price index
   e. Gross domestic product

7. The following questions are ones that society must answer, EXCEPT one. Which one is it?
   a. Which goods and services will be produced?
   b. How will they be produced?
   c. Why will they be produced?
   d. Who will own the factors of production?
   e. For whom will the goods and services be produced?

8. Surpluses of a product in the marketplace often result in losses for the suppliers of the product because
   a. the increased supply tends to drive prices down resulting in less income for the supplier.
   b. surpluses drive demand downward so that fewer people buy the product.
   c. the government is too slow to offer subsidies to the suppliers.
   d. the surplus increases the demand and the suppliers can't meet it.
   e. None of the aforementioned options is correct.

9. Customers, competitors, suppliers, and the labor market are all part of the
   a. external business environment.
   b. internal business environment.
   c. economic environment.
   d. task environment.
   e. general environment.

10. According to economists, land and natural resources, labor, capital, and entrepreneurship are called
    a. free resources.
    b. competitive resources.
    c. factory resources.
    d. factors of manufacturing.
    e. factors of production.

mangostock/Shutterstock

CHAPTER 2

Small Business and Business Ownership

Small Business and the U.S. Economy

A **small business** is one that is independently owned and operated, with fewer than 500 employees. The Census Bureau classifies businesses as non-employer and employer. Non-employer businesses are usually self-employed individuals. There are by far many more non-employer businesses than employer businesses in the United States, but non-employer businesses account for less than 4% of all income received from business transactions. Businesses with employees, on the other hand, comprise 99% of all firms in the United States and account for 40% of all income from business. Half of the people employed by a business in the United States are employed by a small business. In Europe, the situation is almost exactly the same, with **small and medium-sized enterprises (SMEs)** making up 99% of all business enterprises and employing 53% of the business workforce, according to the European Commission.

The importance of small business in job creation is evident everywhere you look. Your favorite restaurant, the dry cleaner, and shoe repair shop in your neighborhood strip mall, your physician and your dentist are probably all operated as small businesses and employ anywhere from 2 to 30 people. Just over half of the small businesses employ 10 to 99 people. Because small businesses often have simpler

Small business An independently owned business with fewer than 500 employees.

structures and fewer people to coordinate, they are able to develop rapidly and promote innovation. For example, the Krankcycle®, an innovative, hand-driven exercise cycle that makes it possible for people with lower-body injuries to receive a cardio workout, is offered by Five Giri Inc., a California-based business with fewer than 10 employees. Within one year of its introduction, the Krankcycle® had received national attention. Small firms make big contributions to big business, too. B & R textiles, a family-owned company with merely a handful of employees, supplies clothing manufacturers with millions of yards of woven linings and nylon fabrics from its offices in the fashion district in New York City. Mutton Power Equipment, another family-operated small business in northeast Indiana, sells and distributes name brand lawn equipment such as John Deere, Toro, and Stihl. Large manufacturers need independent distributors to make sure their products are available to everyone who needs them.

Table 2.1 Industries with the largest number of small businesses

Industry Group	Number of Firms
Professional,scientific, and technical services	802,476
Other services (except public administration)	688,950
Retailing	648,729
Construction	682,292
Healthcare and social assistance	657,311
Accommodation and food services	525,323
Administrative, support, waste management, and remediation services	336,997
Wholesale trade	300,128
Real estate	298,838
Manufacturing	246,125
Finance and insurance	236,273
Transportation and warehousing	179,166

Source: 2016 County Business Patterns, U.S. Census Bureau, https://www.census.gov/data/tables/2016/econ/susb/2016-susb-annual.html.

Small businesses are involved in a wide variety of industries. Based on the data released in the last Economic Census, the industries with the largest number of small businesses are shown in Table 2.1.

Starting a Small Business

Three basic approaches to starting a small business are (1) starting "from scratch," (2) buying an existing business, or (3) buying and running a **franchise**. When starting a completely new business, the risk of failure is going to be higher, but the new business will not be saddled with the problems of an existing business. Before launching the venture, the new **entrepreneur** must carefully consider the profile and location of prospective customers, how much they will pay for the product or service offered, and how much of that product or service will be sold. It is essential that the new business owner understand who the competitors will be and why customers will be willing to buy the new product and service instead of the product or service of the competitor.

Entrepreneur Person who starts and runs a business, usually at considerable financial risk.

Buying an existing, viable business is less risky. Many of the questions that face a brand new enterprise have already been answered in such cases. An existing business already has a customer base and a known performance track record. There is usually an accumulation of data on which to base future business decisions.

The third option for starting a small business is to buy a franchise, an arrangement in which a buyer, the **franchisee**, purchases the right to sell the good or service of the seller or parent company, the **franchisor**. Some studies show that franchises have a success rate of approximately 90% as compared to only about 15% for businesses that are started from the ground up.

Franchisee Person or company who buys the right to sell a good or service from a seller or parent company.

In a franchise relationship, the franchisor supplies a known and advertised business name, management skills, training and materials, and a method of doing business. In return for a specified investment, the franchisee provides labor and capital, operates the franchised business, and agrees to abide by the franchise agreement. According to *Statista*, in 2017 there were 745,290 franchise establishments in the United States employing over 8 million people. Fast-food restaurants had the highest number of franchise establishments, followed by gas stations with convenience stores, and full-service restaurants.

The Growing Importance of Franchising

There are over 1,000 franchises available in the United States. The world's most popular franchisor is McDonald's fast-food restaurant. Other popular retail franchisors include 7-Eleven, Visiting Angels, and JiffyLube. Franchisors also provide opportunities to serve other small businesses. Examples in this category include Unishippers, supplying low-cost shipping to small and medium-sized companies, and Servicemaster Clean, a professional cleaning company serving commercial customers.

The Advantages of Franchising

The concept of franchising has undeniable appeal because it offers the prospective entrepreneur advantages of both starting a new business and buying an existing business. The franchisee is able to control important risks in the internal and external business environment. The new business starts with brand recognition and a developed product or service. The franchisee receives management training and access to the business expertise of the franchisor, usually without charge. Advertising and promotion materials come from the home office. Direct financial assistance may be available from the franchisor, and savings may be realized from purchasing advertising and other business needs as a group with other franchisees. It may not be as expensive to purchase a franchise as it would be to start a new business from scratch. The advantage of franchising to the franchisor is the opportunity to expand without the trouble or expense of opening a new location. Operational responsibility is delegated but controlled through a contractual agreement.

The Worldwide Growth of Franchising

Over 60% of McDonald's restaurants are located outside the U.S. The European Franchise Federation estimates that there are over 13,000 distinct franchise brands operating in the EU compared to about 2,500 U.S. brands. Franchising in Africa though, with the exception of South Africa, is still in its early stages. African countries seek to reproduce the success of Nigeria's Mr. Biggs restaurants and Kenya's bar and restaurant chain, Kengeles. In many parts of the world, governmental regulations prevent the easy establishment of this form of small business. Lack of financing, currency restrictions, and legal barriers also slow the growth of franchising. National franchise development committees drawn from government, finance, and industry are starting to play a role in creating a more receptive environment for expanding existing business through the franchise format.

Phillip Lange/Shutterstock

Niloo/Shutterstock

Dailin/Shutterstock

The Disadvantages of Franchising

The matter of operational control is also a disadvantage of franchising to both the franchisor and the franchisee. The franchisor has taken the initial risks of starting the business, building a reputable brand, and perfecting a business method. The franchisor naturally wants to preserve the brand's unique characteristics, the consistency of product or service delivery, and high-quality standards in order to fulfill customer expectations and to remain an attractive business opportunity to future franchisees. Franchisors may therefore "micromanage" all aspects of the business, from the way employees wear their uniforms, to how the table is set, to how forms are to be completed. These efforts to control may cause the franchisee to lose enthusiasm in running the business. In fact, well-known franchisors have been sued for exerting too much control over franchisees.

Although the startup costs for a franchise may not be as great as starting from scratch or buying an existing business, buying a franchise can be expensive. Initial fees can be as little as US$2,000, but may be as great as $2 million! Frequently, the franchisor will also demand a percentage of the profits or net sales, called a **royalty,** in addition to the startup fees. Royalties can vary from 0% to 12.5% or more.

The success of a franchisee is always tied to the success of other franchisees. If other franchisees are failing or giving the brand name a bad reputation, this can have a negative effect on the success of the rest. Too much of a good thing, as in the case of a "Starbucks on every corner," can take profits from the franchisee. Franchisors have also been known to run their own franchise in competition with another franchisee.

Read "Can Franchising Save Steak 'n Shake" at the end of this chapter to learn more about the advantages and disadvantages of franchising from a corporate point of view.

Evaluating Franchise Opportunities

When evaluating a franchise opportunity you must ask many of the same questions that you would ask when developing your own business plan, or if you are considering buying an existing business. This includes carefully researching franchises that match your budget, experience, and your financial goals. The Bureau of Consumer Protection, a unit of the U.S. Federal Trade Commission (FTC), recommends that you critically assess any business opportunity before investing. You should ask:

- What is the franchisor's reputation for quality? Does the company have consumer complaints against it?
- How much experience does the franchisor have in managing a franchise system?
- How much money will you have to invest and how much will you have to borrow?
- Do you already have the knowledge and skills to run the business or will you need training?

The FTC also recommends that you study the franchisor's disclosure document and that you thoroughly examine any earnings' claims. To learn more about franchising and how to find good franchise opportunities visit the International Franchise Association website at www.franchise.org. Franchising.com and The Franchise Handbook (https://www.franchisetimes.com/The-Franchise-Handbook/) also provide a wealth of information about franchising.

The Importance of a Business Plan

Regardless of the approach an entrepreneur takes to establish a small business, the key to success is to develop a **business plan** based on research. Writing a business plan is like writing a resume for your business. If you are going to seek additional funding to start your business, experts widely agree that you must develop a formal written plan that clearly explains every aspect of your business. Even if you do not plan to borrow money, you should develop a simple plan that outlines your mission and goals, your strengths and weaknesses, a market analysis, and a break-even analysis. Even prospective franchisees should understand how to create a business plan, and use this knowledge to carefully evaluate a franchise opportunity. Although a business plan does not guarantee success, studies have found that your venture is more likely to succeed with a plan than without one. More than one failed entrepreneur has commented after taking a business course in which writing a plan was required that they regret not having written a plan before starting their business.

Table 2.2 Common components of a business plan

Component	Description
Executive Summary	The executive summary gives the reader of your plan a concise overview of the nature and organization of your business, your rationale for opening it, and explains why your business will be a success. The summary should interest the reader in immediately exploring the details of your plan, rather than tossing it on a stack of plans to read later.
Business Description	An overview of the business purpose, the goals, and how you will achieve them. Includes the name and address of your business, contact information, business goals, an analysis of the industry you will operate in, form of business ownership chosen, customer profile, competitive advantage, anticipation of ethical issues and social responsibility. May describe challenges and opportunities in the global business environment.
Management and Operations Plan	This section develops more fully your mission, goals, and how they will be achieved. It should convince the reader that you have made a thorough assessment of threats, risks, and challenges, and developed strategies to address them. Includes mission statement, specification of business goals, a SWOT analysis, description of the management team and organization structure, physical layout and operational scenarios, detailed description of the materials, supplies, and equipment that will be needed to start up and carry on the business, plan for maintaining consistent high quality, description of what information technology will be required and how it supports the mission of the enterprise.
Human Resource Plan	This section sets out in detail the number and types of personnel who will be needed in order to achieve your mission and goals. At minimum, you should provide job descriptions and specifications along with proposed compensation and incentive schemes. You should try to include your approach to leadership, the type of

Component	Description
	corporate culture you will create, and your plans for the training and professional development of employees and the management team.
Marketing Plan	This section expands on the rationale for starting your business and provides evidence of a market need. This section should be well researched with sources indicated. It provides a description of the target market including location, size, demographics, and psychographics; product/service features and benefits; an analysis of the competition and how your product/service is different; the prices you will charge; how your product/service will be distributed; a promotion plan.
Financial Plan	This section should explain how much it will cost to do business annually, how much revenue you expect, and how you intend to finance the business. You should be realistic about the claims you make in this section. A startup balance sheet and income statement are required. You may wish to include a break-even analysis.
Appendix	Items commonly found in the Appendix include the resumes of the owners and management team, brochures, menus, promotional and advertising samples, and other supplemental materials that help support your plan, but that may be too unwieldy to include in the body of the document. A list of sources may also be included.

When constructing a business plan, it is important to keep in mind your purpose and your audience. Not only does the plan help you clarify your thinking and anticipate obstacles, but it serves as a communication tool among your partners and as a persuasive argument to convince investors and bank officers to fund your venture. The readers of your plan will not be experts in your field or industry, so you should take care to explain terminology and practices in detail, simply and directly. Your plan should clearly explain what your business will do, its mission, your short-term and long-term business goals, the business opportunity your company will exploit, and how much the venture will cost. There is no one format for business plans, but the essential elements are set out in table 2.2. If you know to whom you will be submitting a plan, it is a good idea to find out in advance if there is a preferred format. There are also many software applications that can help you craft a professional looking business plan.

Why Do Some Small Businesses Succeed and Others Fail?

Seven out of ten new small business employer firms survive at least two years, and about half survive five years, according to the Small Business Administration. Successful small business owners work very hard—often 12 hours a day and weekends, are internally motivated, and possess the drive to persevere when others might quit. They also usually possess previous managerial experience. These personal qualities cannot be underrated, but equally important are factors beyond the control of the business owner: market demand and luck.

Not unsurprisingly, business failure is frequently due to a lack of understanding of the marketplace and lack of managerial skill. In fact, incompetence and managerial blunders top the list of reasons why small businesses fail. Another key factor in the failure of small businesses is a poorly chosen location. Even a well-managed small business cannot survive a bad location. Availability and cost are often the major factors used in determining a location, leading to a decision that dooms the business even before it opens. For a retail outlet, it is critical to know the characteristics of prospective customers and to locate where these customers are during the time that the business is open. The store location should be in the path of either foot traffic or auto traffic, easily accessible from the sidewalk or from roadways, and have adequate parking and lighting. Ideally, few, if any, competitors will be located nearby. The condition and safety of the building should be considered, too. The business owner should check to see if there are local incentive programs for business startups in specific targeted areas. Zoning laws should be researched, and the history, community flavor, and receptiveness to a new business at a prospective site should be investigated.

Insufficient capital to start, maintain, and grow the business is the other major reason why small businesses fail. At least half of all small businesses start with less than US$30,000, according to Census Bureau and Federal Reserve surveys, and the money usually comes from the business owner's personal savings. In many cases, this funding proves to be insufficient to start and sustain the business until it establishes itself. Compounding the problem of insufficient funding is poor control over cash flow and expenses, problems that can be attributed to the previously mentioned problem, lack of managerial experience.

Financing the Small Business

The first step in successfully financing a small business is to have a realistic idea of how much will be needed to start the business and operate it on an annual basis. The new business owner must also have an evidence-based estimate of expected near-term and longer-term revenue. Developing a formal business plan based on thorough research into the size of the market, the competition, local costs, and recurring expenses is extremely helpful in determining the amount of capital needed. Banks, venture capital companies, and other lenders require a detailed business plan in order to consider lending money to a business.

Aside from savings, loans from family and friends, and local commercial banks, there are other sources of capital that a small business can seek out. A **venture capital company** is a group of investors that pool their capital to invest in companies with rapid growth potential in return for owning part of the company, also called an "equity position." Venture capital firms will ask for sizable ownership in a firm just starting up to compensate for the risk of investing in an untested enterprise. Venture capital companies do not invest in the typical small business, but in companies with high profit potential. The amount of the investment will be from US$500,000 to $10 million, which can be used, for example, for research and development or to expand the production of a proven profitable product or service. A small business may be fortunate to find an **angel investor,** a wealthy individual who will provide a business with capital in exchange for equity in the company or the option to later convert the investment into shares or cash.

The federal government runs loan and grant programs specifically to assist small businesses with their near- and long-term financing.

Small Business Investment Company (SBIC) is a government-regulated investment company that borrows money from the Small Business Administration (SBA) to invest in or lend to a small business.

Minority Enterprise Small Business Investment Company (MESBIC) is a federally sponsored company that specializes in financing businesses that are owned and operated by minorities.

Microloans are loans in amounts ranging from US$100 to $35,000 made to people such as single mothers and public housing tenants.

CDC/504 loans are designed to provide long-term, fixed rate financing to small businesses for expansion or modernization. A Certified Development Company (CDC) is a private, nonprofit corporation that works with the SBA to support community development through its loans to small businesses.

Through the SBA, the federal government also runs a number of programs that provide general assistance to small businesses. These programs include:

Service Corps of Retired Executives (SCORE): A program in which retired business executives volunteer to work with small businesses. SCORE maintains an excellent website containing valuable resources for the small business owners.

Active Corps of Executives (ACE): A program similar to SCORE but staffed with volunteer executives who are currently employed.

Small Business Institute (SBI): A program in which college and university students and their instructors work with small business owners to help solve specific problems.

Small Business Development Center (SBDC): Another SBA program designed to consolidate information from various disciplines and make it available to small businesses.

The small business person should not overlook state and local government programs, similar to those operated by the federal government. Some localities operate business "incubator" programs or innovation centers. These local programs help new companies grow during the startup phase by providing managerial advice and access to financing, among other support services. If available, shared space and office services help reduce expenses for the first two or three years of the business. State and local grants, tax credits, and exemptions may also be available.

Why People Start Their Own Business

The appeal of being one's own boss, of not taking orders from anyone, and of having control over one's time motivates most who decide to start a business. The satisfaction of knowing that the rewards accrued are due to one's own efforts is another powerful motivator. Others may inherit the family business or may decide to carry on the family's tradition of producing a particular product or service. For others, starting a business may provide the opportunity to do enjoyable work, perhaps using skills from a hobby, and at the same time realize income from it.

The typical small business owner enjoys the advantages of being and staying small. Small retailers, for example, have close personal relationships with customers, employees, and their suppliers. These relationships are not only satisfying, but are a major competitive advantage. It is very difficult for a larger retailer or chain retailer to render the level of personalized service that the small retailer can. Closer relationships with employees help the small business owner retain employees, sometimes compensating for lower pay or lack of benefits. Through this network of relations, the small business becomes an integral part of the community, which is good for sales and provides a support mechanism in difficult times. A small business owner does not need approval to respond to the changing needs and wants of customers. Changes in pricing, store hours, products, and services can all be made fairly quickly, allowing the small business to stay competitive. Another major advantage of small size is simplified recordkeeping. It is, of course, important to keep good records of costs and expenses, but adequate records can be kept with a checkbook and sales and disbursement journals.

One big disadvantage of small business size is the risk of failure, due for the most part to lack of financial resources. As mentioned earlier, small business startups tend be underfunded to begin with. Small size means that the capacity to generate revenue is limited, which makes it difficult to attract new investment capital that may be needed to sustain and grow the business. Even a successful longstanding small business is vulnerable to economic downturns because its size limits the depth of its financial reserves and its capacity to borrow money. Another disadvantage of staying small is obvious—by deciding to stay small, the business owner limits the potential of the business. It could be that the owner's goal is simply to generate enough income to support a family, or to just be employed doing something enjoyable. Running a larger business may entail increased risk that the business owner does not wish to take.

The Role of the Entrepreneur

In Chapter 1, entrepreneurship was listed as an essential factor of production. Unless someone is willing to take the risks necessary to create and operate a business, there can be no business. While it is true that the small business owners described above have indeed taken risks and share similar reasons for going into business, entrepreneurs are distinguished by their love of innovation, their vision, a strong desire to make money, the possibility of creating employment, and acceptance of a higher level of risk. Consider the characteristics of these first-generation entrepreneurs who appear on the Forbes 400 list of wealthiest Americans.

- Bill Gates and Paul Allen (founders of Microsoft)
- Phil Knight (founder of Nike)
- Michael Dell (founder of Dell)
- Sergey Brin and Larry Page (founders of Google)
- Mark Zuckerberg (founder of Facebook)
- Katie Rodan and Kathy Fields (founders of Rodan+Fields skin care company)

Most articles describing entrepreneurs state that certain characteristics, most of which can be developed, are essential to success. Entrepreneurs are alert to changes in their everyday environment and have the imagination to understand how these changes might give rise to business opportunities. Successful entrepreneurs believe wholeheartedly in their business ideas and that their ideas are important for the well-being and enjoyment of others. While entrepreneurs are not averse to risk, they leave nothing to chance – by purposefully finding out everything they need to know about bringing their ideas to life and making a plan. Entrepreneurs possess and exude self-confidence, but they are constantly looking for ways to improve themselves and their ideas. They are self- disciplined, task-oriented, and take pleasure in working hard, because their labor moves them toward a valued goal. Other traits include an orientation toward people, valuing collaboration and critique, and perseverance over time.

Women Entrepreneurs

As of 2018, women were at least 50% owners of 12.3 million firms in the United States, representing 40% of all privately held companies, according to a study conducted by American Express. The number of women-owned firms continues to grow at about one and one-half times the national average. Industrial sectors with the highest numbers of women entrepreneurs are healthcare/social assistance and educational services. According to the 2018/19 Global Entrepreneurship Monitor report, 14% of the adult female population of the United States was engaged in early-stage entrepreneurship, compared to 18% of the adult male population. (The difference between male and female engagement decreased by 2% since 2014.) The SBA cites access to capital, credit, and equity as challenges to women business owners; in the United States there is no gender difference in the business survival rate. Other factors that may hamper women entrepreneurs are lack of a business network that enables women to make useful business connections and discrimination based on gender. Many women-owned businesses are run from home, but one in five firms in the United States with revenue of $1 million or more is woman-owned. These million-dollar firms represent 4.2% of all woman-owned firms.

According to the 2018 American Express report, the number of startups by minority women grew at three times the rate of startups by non-minority women. Minority women-owned firms numbered 5.8 million. Examples of minority women entrepreneurs who have become successful include: Sonia Kapadia, CEO of Taste Savant, a web-based service that helps diners find fine restaurants; Nicole Sanchez, founder of VIXENN, a company offering human hair extensions; and Kina De Santis, 19-year-old co-founder of MotorMood, a manufacturer producing an automotive accessory for thanking drivers.

Internet-based Small Business

The ease and low cost of starting an online business makes it an appealing alternative to establishing a business at a physical location. A web-based small business is especially appealing to entrepreneurs who want the flexibility of being able to stay home with their children while pursuing a career or contributing to household income. Doing business online offers the small business person the opportunity to participate in the global economy. These benefits and advantages of doing business on the Internet have contributed to an annual sales growth rate of 15% for "e-tailing."

Starting a virtual business is much like starting and running the traditional "brick-and-mortar" small business, but there are some special considerations that the online entrepreneur should make, according to the Small Business Administration. Because the online customer must provide personal and financial information in order to complete transactions, the online business owner must take steps to protect the customer by following federal privacy laws enforced by the Federal Trade Commission. The online customer may be located anywhere. Thus, the online business owner must understand how to properly collect the sales and use taxes that are in effect in different states, as well as what the rules and regulations are for exporting to locations beyond the borders of the United States.

The inherent anonymity of the Internet has given rise to dishonest advertising and marketing practices, which the federal government has addressed by passing additional laws designed specifically to encourage fair and truthful online advertising. The small businessperson should become familiar with these laws.

The conversion of different types of media to a digital format has also facilitated copyright infringement. Online entrepreneurs must follow the provisions of the Digital Millennium Copyright Act (DMCA), which protects the copyright of intellectual property owners whose work is transmitted or used via the Internet.

Online businesses fail for many of the same reasons traditional small businesses do. In particular, the online entrepreneur should pay special attention to analyzing the costs of acquiring new customers, customer behavior at the website, and the design of the website itself. When the business has a physical location, conducting these tasks is fairly straightforward. When the business is online, however, it may be wiser to invest in consultants with a specialty in online retailing.

Uses of Social Networking for Small Business

A common strategy for increasing sales and customer loyalty is to reward customers for referrals, called **affiliate marketing**. Customers copy small pieces of software from the retailer's web page that put a widget (a small software application) on the customer's social networking pages. A friend of the customer can buy from the retailer by clicking on the widget. When this happens, the retailer is automatically notified and the customer receives a small commission.

Another strategy for using social networking, called **content marketing,** is to engage current and potential customers in conversation about a product or service and to provide relevant information that would assist a customer in making decisions regarding a purchase. The social networking site may also be used to identify future employees or to network with others in the same industry or profession. Well-planned activity on a social networking system can help a small business gain visibility that a traditional business cannot. A disadvantage of this tactic is the significant amount of time that must be spent attending to the website. If the responsibility is delegated, it should be given to someone who fully understands the technology as well as the goals of the small business owner.

Choosing a Form of Business Ownership

In our discussion of small business so far, the focus has been on the business owner as an independent entrepreneur who seeks the satisfaction and rewards of being "the boss," and who also shoulders all of the associated risks. There are, however, a variety of ways in which the ownership of a business can be set up to expand opportunities to raise capital and to control the amount of risk to which an individual business person is exposed.

Sole Proprietorship

Sole proprietorship is a form of business ownership in which an individual owns and operates the business. This form of ownership is the easiest to establish, has a simple structure, and the owner can maintain a high degree of control over each aspect of the business. Income from the business is taxed once, as part of the owner's income taxes, which may result in lower taxes than are incurred by the other forms of business ownership, as shown in table 2.3.

However, one of the primary disadvantages of this form of ownership is the limited access to funding, as noted in the previous discussion on why small businesses often fail. Another serious disadvantage is the owner's exposure to risk. The owner's personal assets may be seized in order to settle debts, sometimes leading to personal bankruptcy and permanent damage to the individual's credit history. In addition to these major disadvantages, the sole proprietor may lack skills and experience in certain areas of running a business. There can also be problems with maintaining the continuity of the business should the owner die or become incapacitated. In spite of these significant disadvantages, and because of the simplicity and opportunity for reward commensurate with one's own efforts, over 70% of U.S. businesses are operated as sole proprietorships.

General and Limited Partnership

The form of business ownership known as **general partnership** addresses some of the disadvantages of the sole proprietorship. If each partner contributes financially, the amount of investment capital available will clearly be greater than that available to an individual owner. Any financial losses are shared. Partners share the work and management responsibilities and may bring skills and expertise to the venture that any single partner may not possess. As with the sole proprietorship, income from the business is taxed only once, as part of the personal income of each partner. As with a sole proprietorship though, each partner has unlimited liability and can potentially lose much more than was invested. It is even possible for a single partner to be sued for payment of the debts of the entire partnership. Profits must be shared, and major conflicts among partners can easily develop. If the ability to raise more money is the reason for considering a partnership, a corporation might be a better ownership strategy. As with sole proprietorship, problems in the continuity of the business may arise if one or more partners want to sell his or her interests in the business, or if a partner dies.

The **limited partnership** is a variation on the general partnership. In this form of business ownership, some of the partners have limited liability, but do not actively manage the business. One of the partners is designated as the "general partner" and manages the company. The general partner has unlimited liability, gets a salary, and participates in the profits and losses. In the limited partnership, the limited partners give up control over management of the company in return for reduced risk and protection from the negligence of the other partners. The limited partner is liable only for the amount of money he or she has invested.

Three Reasons General Partnerships are Liability Nightmares[1]

A general partnership may turn into a creditor or plaintiff's dream and a partner's liability nightmare. Consider three hidden dangers of a general partnership:

1. Partners Have Unlimited Liability for Partnership Debts

When you engage in a general partnership, you in effect personally guarantee every partnership debt and assume the risk for malpractice, accidents, and all other sources of liability for the entire partnership. Many businesspeople and other professionals fail to fully understand this unfortunate characteristic of general partnerships. In this type of arrangement, your liability as a partner is *joint and several* (a liability that allows a plaintiff to sue one or all) with other partners. As explained earlier, a plaintiff who successfully sues the partnership can collect the full judgment from any one partner. Here is an example:

Case Study: Jane and Ted's Real Estate Venture

Jane and Ted, long-time friends, decided to go into a real estate venture together to refurbish old three-family homes and sell them as condominiums. Events went well for a while, but their real estate market went sour and they defaulted on a $650,000 bank loan. Jane was much wealthier than Ted, so the bank pursued Jane for the full amount, ignoring Ted.

2. Partners Have Unlimited Liability for Their Partners' Actions

In a general partnership, if your partner loses a lawsuit, you could be personally liable for the full amount, regardless of your involvement in the actions that brought on the suit. You need not even have been aware of the incident. When a lawsuit arises from one partner's act or omission in the ordinary course of business, all partners are personally liable. The dreaded joint and several liability applies.

Consider the many ways a partner could get you into trouble: by committing malpractice; getting into a car accident while on partnership business; defrauding someone through the business; sexually harassing an employee; wrongfully firing an employee; etc. Multiply this risk by the number of partners in your partnership, and you have a lawsuit liability nightmare! A real-world example:

Case Study: Michael Gets Burned by His Partner

Michael founded a successful three-partner software development firm near Portland, Oregon. One of the firm's customers sued the firm when a program malfunctioned, causing a loss of valuable data. The lawsuit alleged breach of contract, product liability, and even punitive damages.

Settlement negotiations were unsuccessful and the trial jury awarded an extremely large verdict against the partnership, exceeding its liability policy limit. Since Michael was the wealthiest of the partners, the plaintiff's lawyer pursued him first, forcing Michael to pay the entire $250,000 amount (above the insurance policy limit) from his personal savings.

3. You May Be an "Unaware" General Partner

Unlike limited partnerships, general partnerships do not require a formal written agreement. You can verbally agree to start a venture with another person and unwittingly create a general partnership, with all of its liability problems.

Even if you make no agreement to partner with another person, the law may impose general partnership liability on you if the general public reasonably perceives you as partners.

Case Study: Roger Inadvertently Has Partners

Roger was one of four physicians using a common office arrangement. Each physician had his own patients, which they did not share. They did, however, share a common waiting area, support staff and accounting department. Each doctor had his own practice methods, set his own hours and was not otherwise accountable to the others.

When a client sued one of the doctors for professional misconduct, however, Roger and the other two had a rude awakening. Although only the client's physician was negligent, all four were defendants in the lawsuit. The court found that the patient could reasonably conclude the four professionals were partners because of their office set up and common support staff. Therefore, the court allowed the plaintiff to proceed with the suit against all four—as a general partnership, with each jointly and severally liable for the plaintiff 's losses.

(Continued)

So, if general partnerships are so dicey, what business form should you use? Consider a limited partnership, a C or S corporation, or a limited liability company. These entities have limited liability provisions for their owners.

If you do use a general partnership, each partner should set up a professional corporation (PC) and name the corporations as the partners in the general partnership. This model is followed by many medical professionals and attorneys using PCs. Structuring the partnership this way, the underlying corporate owner's personal assets remain protected from claims against the partnership. However, as with any corporation, the corporate formalities must be followed for asset protection.

From David B. Mandell and Richard DiPasquale,"Three Reasons General Partnerships are Liability Nightmares," *Gastroenterology & Endoscopy News* 58, (2007), Retrieved from http://www.gastroendonews. com/View Article.aspx? d_id=188&a_id=9760 Copyright © 2007 by McMahon Group. Reprinted with permission.

The Corporation

The **corporation** creates a legal entity that can act and have liability separate from the individuals who set it up. The owners are called stockholders and they are not liable for any more than the amount that they invested. A corporate form of business ownership allows many people to share in the ownership and profits of the business. Corporations are chartered by state government. They can be for-profit or nonprofit; they can be publicly or privately held. A publicly held corporation offers shares of its stock to the general public on stock exchanges, such as the New York Stock Exchange or Hong Kong's Hang Seng. Walmart and Exxon are examples of publicly held corporations. A privately held corporation does not offer its shares for sale to the public. Chrysler, IKEA, Credit Suisse, and Land Rover are examples of privately held corporations.

The primary advantages of incorporation are limited liability for the owners and the ease of raising capital through the sale of stock. Continuity of the business is enhanced, too. Since the corporation exists separately from its owners, it can persist beyond the lifetimes of the individuals who formed it. Ownership is easily transferred through the selling of stock. Setting up a corporation requires legal advice to set up a charter, and filing fees, expenses which the average entrepreneur may not wish to pay. Owners are taxed twice, once on the profits of the corporation and again when individual shareholders pay taxes on their dividends. Stockholders do not run the business and sometimes the interests of the managers may conflict with those of the owners (stockholders). Publicly held corporations must by law disclose more information about their operations than they might want to. Corporations are more likely than partnerships and sole proprietorships to become unmanageable in size, which can result in inflexibility and slow response to changing business conditions.

Table 2.3   Tax implications in various forms of business ownership

Profit Before Taxes = $500,000			
Form	**Sole Proprietorship**	**General Partnership (5 partners)**	**Corporation (100 shareholders)**
Tax rate	Individual rate = 20%	Individual rate = 20%	Corporation tax = 35% Personal dividend tax = 15%
Amount of tax paid	$100,000	5 x $20,000 = $100,000	$175,000 + ($487.50 x 100) = $223,750
Net profit	$400,000	5 x $80,000 = $400,000	$276, 250

The "S" Corporation

Subchapter S of Chapter 1 of the U.S. Internal Revenue Code creates a form of business ownership that provides the protection of a corporation but is taxed like a partnership. About 3 million U.S. businesses operate **S corporations**. The businessperson who uses this form of ownership must meet these conditions:

- Have no more than 100 shareholders
- Shareholders must be individuals (not companies) who are citizens or permanent residents of the United States
- Offer only one class of stock (such as common or preferred stock)
- Receive no more than 25% of corporate income from passive sources such as rent, royalties, or interest
- Submit Internal Revenue Service Form 2553 Election by a Small Business Corporation, signed by all shareholders

One disadvantage of this form of ownership is that it arises from the IRS tax code, which changes frequently. Another disadvantage is that some states may impose a corporation tax. When considering the S corporation, it is advisable to seek the advice of a lawyer who can go over the benefits and disadvantages of the S corporation for a specific business.

The Limited Liability Company (LLC)

A form of business ownership that has become increasingly common since the late 1980s is the **limited liability company (LLC)**. In the LLC there can be multiple owners, just as in a general partnership, but the liability of each owner is limited to the amount that each invests, as in a corporation or a limited partnership. Members of the LLC also have the option of being taxed like a partnership or a corporation. LLCs are not limited to a maximum number of members, and members may participate in the management of the business to the extent that they wish. Members of an LLC write an operating agreement in which they spell out their responsibilities, how decisions will be made, buyout options, and how profits will be shared. There are some disadvantages to this form of ownership. In some states, the LLC must be dissolved after 30 years. The death of a member of an LLC automatically dissolves the company. The flexibility of this form of business ownership has made it very popular among businesses large and small. Apple Computer started as a limited liability company.

Cooperatives

Another form of business ownership is the **cooperative.** The same people who buy and use the products and services of a cooperative are the people who own and run it. Members of a cooperative can include its producers, consumers, and workers. They pool their resources for mutual benefit in order to provide service to co-op members. The cooperative is run very much like a democratic government. Members elect a board of directors, who in turn, hire professional management. Surplus revenues are returned in proportion to a member's use of the cooperative, not to a member's investment in it. Co-ops are particularly popular in rural areas among farmers. Credit unions are organized as cooperatives, as are many childcare businesses, preschools, organic and "locavore" food retailers, and electric utilities.

Nonprofit Organizations

Nonprofit organizations are business organizations that exist only to provide some benefit to the public, not to make a profit for stockholders. Any funds remaining after expenses are paid are put back into operating the business. Nonprofit organizations are eligible for exemptions from local, state, and federal taxes. Nonprofit businesses must apply for incorporation with state government and must separately apply to the Internal Revenue Service in order to receive tax-exempt status. This status is available to organizations that engage in charitable, educational, scientific, religious, and literary work and that meet other criteria set out in the tax code. Examples of nonprofit organizations are cooperatives, churches, public universities, public hospitals, governments, charities such as United Way and Heifer International, and philanthropic organizations such as the Bill and Melinda Gates Foundation.

Growth through Mergers and Acquisitions

Sometimes the most cost-effective and profitable way to expand a business or to protect market share is by associating with another business. In a **merger**, two or more companies become a single company. In an **acquisition**, one company purchases the property and assumes the liabilities of another. The acquired company may retain its own identity. A company may only have to obtain a **controlling interest** in another, for example, Comcast's acquisition of 51% of the shares of NBC in 2011.

Mergers can be classified as vertical, horizontal, and conglomerate. (see figure 2.1). **Horizontal mergers** involve companies in the same industry or companies involved in the same phase of a production process, as illustrated in Figurue 2.1 by Companies C, G, and H. For example, a merger of Pepsi-Cola and Coca-Cola, both of which are in the soft drink production and distribution business, would be considered a horizontal merger. Horizontal mergers help reduce competition and can reduce production costs by eliminating duplicate facilities and realizing economies of scale. **Vertical mergers** occur when companies at different phases of the production process become one, as shown in Figure 2.1 by the consolidation of Companies A through E. An example would be an automaker acquiring its suppliers of auto upholstery or car batteries. A **conglomerate merger** results in a highly diversified company made up of two or more corporations in different industries as illustrated in Figure 2.1 by the merger of Companies C, J, and K. A well-known example of a conglomerate is Berkshire Hathaway, which includes subsidiaries as different from each other as GEICO (Government Employees Insurance Company) and Heinz, the U.S. food processing company purchased for US$23 billion in 2013. The diverse types of companies in a conglomerate protect the parent company from downturns and losses.

A term related to mergers and acquisitions is **leveraged buyout**, or LBO. A leveraged buyout simply means that the merger or acquisition is accomplished primarily with borrowed money. There was a leveraged buyout boom in the 1980s, led by investors who came to be known as "corporate raiders." One of these investors, Carl Icahn, came to symbolize their ruthlessness after his hostile takeover of TWA (Trans World Airlines) in 1985.

Horizontal merger Growth involving companies in the same industry or in the same phase of the production process.

Vertical merger Growth involving companies in different phases of the production process.

Conglomerate Growth involving two or more corporations in different industries.

Leveraged buyout Merger or acquisition accomplished primarily with borrowed money.

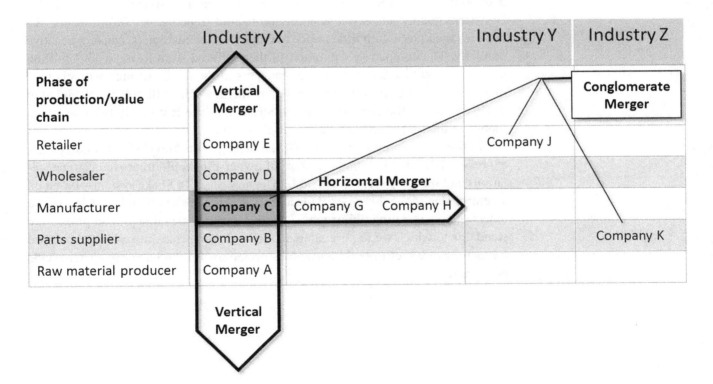

Figure 2.1   Comparison of growth strategies

APPLY YOUR KNOWLEDGE

Can Franchising Save Steak 'n Shake?

Steak 'n Shake is an Indianapolis-based family dining–quick service restaurant chain with 616 locations, 415 of which are managed by Biglari Holdings and the remainder operated by franchisees. Steak 'n Shake opened its first franchise in 1939, opening one franchise per year until 2010. The franchise business operated at a loss between 2010 and 2014. The chain has added more than 70 franchises since 2014. Sales from established locations (called "same-store sales") declined by 5.1 percent from 2017 to 2018, continuing a three-year trend. In late 2019, Steak 'n Shake announced plans to convert all company-managed locations to "franchise partnerships" as part of its strategy to combat the sales slump.

A Steak 'n Shake "franchise partner" will pay $10,000 for the rights to operate, not own, a Steak 'n Shake restaurant. In return, the franchisee will receive 50 percent of the profits with a guaranteed minimum of $100,000 in the first year. The franchisee is required to undergo 6 months of on-the-job training. Steak 'n Shake will also charge the restaurant up to 15 percent of sales to lease the restaurant and its equipment. Steak 'n Shake's traditional franchising arrangement requires an investment of up to $1.8 million dollars, depending on the size and location of the restaurant.

To carry out the 3-year conversion plan, in early 2019 Steak 'n Shake closed over 60 locations in St. Louis, Indianapolis, and Ohio to streamline processes for consistent quality and faster service, and to find franchisees. Unfortunately, the closures took place with little notice to employees or customers, causing negative publicity. The company's reputation further suffered from losing a $7.7 million lawsuit brought by Steak 'n Shake managers in the St. Louis area who claimed they were not paid for overtime hours. Another lawsuit in Illinois is scheduled in 2019. Adding to the company's woes, Steak 'n Shake lost nearly twice as much money in the first quarter of 2019 as it did in all of 2018.

In the 2018 annual report, CEO Sardar Biglari acknowledged missteps but expressed faith that building a culture of ownership would improve customer relations and speed up service. He said, "The new Steak 'n Shake system—based on an entrepreneurial culture—will place trust in those deserving of it ... Clearly, the tenets of our operating philosophy—quality, service, cleanliness, and price—are standards to which we require allegiance. By viewing franchise partners as equal partners, we expect to build harmonious relationships and achieve system-wide consistency."

Knowledge Application Questions

1. What are the main advantages of becoming a franchisor? What are the disadvantages?

2. Why do you think Steak 'n Shake did not accelerate the pace of converting more of its company-owned locations into franchises?

3. Learn more about becoming a Steak 'n Shake franchise partner at http://www.steaknshakefranchise.com/partner.html. Evaluate the opportunity using the "Selecting a Franchise" portion of the *FTC Consumer's Guide to Buying a Franchise* at https://www.ftc.gov/tips-advice/business-center/guidance/consumers-guide-buying-franchise. Research the answers to the questions the guide raises. Based on your research, would you consider becoming a Steak 'n Shake franchise partner?

Sources

Biglari Holdings, Inc. 2019. "2018 Annual Report." Accessed October 30, 2019. http://www.biglariholdings.com/financials/2018/Reports/Biglari%20Holdings%20Annual%20Report%202018.pdf.

Maze, J. 2019, February 2019. "Steak 'n Shake Wants to Speed Things Up." Accessed October 30, 2019. https://www.restaurantbusinessonline.com/financing/steak-n-shake-wants-speed-things.

Newman, J. 2018, August 14. "Steak n Shake offering 'Franchise Partnerships' for $10,000." *Indianapolis Business Journal.com*. Accessed October 30, 2019. https://www.ibj.com/articles/70071-steak-n-shake-offering-franchise-partnerships-for-10000.

Newman, J. 2019, May 6. "Closures at Steak n Shake hit 60 this year, Including Five in Indy Area." *Indianapolis Business Journal.com*. Accessed October 30, 2019. https://www.ibj.com/articles/73638-closures-at-steak-n-shake-hit-60-this-year-including-five-in-indy-area.

Patrick, R. 2019, May 20. "Steak 'n Shake gets $7.7 Million tab for St. Louis-Area Manager Overtime in Latest Blow to Chain." *St. Louis Post-Dispatch*. Accessed October 30, 2019. https://www.stltoday.com/business/local/steak-n-shake-gets-million-tab-for-st-louis-area/article_4dd9146a-10c5-54ac-b026-670e8c03193a.html.

Peterson, H. 2016, May 10. "Why Chick-fil-A's Restaurants Sell 3 Times As Much As KFC's." Accessed October 30, 2019. https://www.businessinsider.com/why-chick-fil-a-is-so-successful-2016-5.

QUIZ YOURSELF

Without looking back at the chapter, choose the best answer to each of the questions below. Answers are in the back of the textbook before the Index. Review the chapter to find out why you missed any questions.

1. Emilio owns a McDonald's franchise that is having some troubles. Where is Emilio most likely to go for advice and guidance?
   a. The franchisor
   b. The Small Business Administration
   c. Food and Drug Administration
   d. Restaurant consultants
   e. Chamber of Commerce

2. A local retailer calls its customers when it receives merchandise that they may be interested in, provides individual service to each customer, provides forms and phone numbers for complaints and comments, and has a 100 percent satisfaction guarantee. This business is working hard to
   a. make a profit.
   b. achieve low employee turnover.
   c. satisfy the needs of its customers.
   d. increase the owner's wealth.
   e. keep up with the current technology.

3. Michael organized his three-partner software development company as a general partnership. When a customer sued Michael's company for damages caused by a program that the company designed, Michael had to pay $250,000 from his personal savings to settle the lawsuit. How could Michael have avoided this outcome?
   a. He could have organized the business as a sole proprietorship.
   b. He could have obtained a loan.
   c. He could have organized the business as an LLC or S Corporation.
   d. He could have countersued because he did not design the faulty program.
   e. There was nothing he could have done differently.

4. Recently there have been several mergers involving large accounting firms. One such merger involved the firms of Arthur Young and Ernst & Whinney, who combined to form Ernst & Young. This is an example of a
   a. joint venture.
   b. horizontal merger.
   c. vertical merger.
   d. syndicate.
   e. conglomerate merger.

5. Your friend Ella has just inherited $50,000 and is eager to buy a small café near her suburban neighborhood that her mother used to take her to. She tells you that she will make an offer tonight. You know that she has not prepared a business plan. What reasons do you give her for writing a plan before making an offer?
   a. The plan will communicate her vision and help her business run more smoothly.
   b. The Small Business Administration will want to see her plan before loaning her any money.
   c. She needs to test the feasibility of the café.
   d. The plan will make her look competent and prepared to be a business owner.
   e. All of the above.

6. Jawad would like to start his own retail computer repair shop. He has $20,000 in savings and just completed a business plan in BUS 10001. All of the following are ways that he can finance his business, EXCEPT one. Which one is it?
   a. A commercial loan from Chase Bank
   b. A loan from his grandfather
   c. Selling shares on the NY Stock Exchange
   d. Convincing Chuck Surack, the wealthy owner of Sweetwater Sound, to be an angel investor
   e. Taking out a second mortgage on his house

7. ABC corporation has just purchased XYZ company in its entirety. All of the XYZ employees will now become ABC employees, that is, the two companies are now one. This is an example of
   a. a merger.
   b. a conglomeration.
   c. a vertical supply chain.
   d. a leveraged buyout.
   e. None of the above.

8. All of the following are special considerations that the online entrepreneur should make when starting a web-based business, EXCEPT one. Which one is it?
   a. Providing a means to safeguard the customer's identity and financial information
   b. Understanding the tax laws that apply in different states
   c. Being careful to abide by intellectual property laws
   d. Making sure that the customer does not feel anonymous
   e. Becoming familiar with exporting rules and regulations

9. Maya has a web page on which she has installed an icon linked to
    Ticketmaster so that visitors to her page can purchase tickets after
    reading her music reviews. Ticketmaster pays Maya for every referral.
    This is an example of
    a. collusion.
    b. franchising.
    c. personal selling.
    d. dishonest advertising.
    e. affiliate marketing.

10. Entrepreneurs are different from small business owners in that they
    a. tend to be innovators.
    b. have a high tolerance for risk.
    c. have a strong desire to make money.
    d. often do extensive research before implementing their ideas.
    e. All of the above.

iQoncept/Shutterstock

CHAPTER 3

Business Ethics and Social Responsibility

We commonly think of **ethics** as a system for deciding between what is right and what is wrong to do. In a social context, ethical behavior is regulated and controlled by the enforcement of laws. Being an ethical business person means, among other things, obeying pertinent laws, being truthful in advertising, charging fair prices, and fulfilling all contracts completely and fairly. In this chapter you will learn that ethical business behavior is defined as more than simply obeying laws and being honest. There is an ethical dimension to almost every decision made in the course of doing business, whether you are an owner, a manager, or an employee. In the 21st century context, the concept of business ethics includes fulfilling responsibilities to co-workers, to employers, to the local and global community, and to our environment. The concept of **social responsibility** often requires delicately balancing duty to shareholders and other investors with what is just for workers or for preservation of the environment. This chapter will sensitize you to the ethical and moral aspects of common business situations, help you understand their complexity, and provide you with the analytical tools that should help guide you toward sound, ethical decisions.

Influences on the Development of Ethical Behavior

An individual develops personal ethics over time. Parents and family are the earliest, and perhaps strongest, influence. They are the first role models and also the ones to introduce a child to religious beliefs that eventually shape ethical behavior. Social interactions with peers at school, on the playground, and at places of worship are also strong influences on a person's ethical development. Authority figures such as teachers, coaches, and religious leaders may affect moral development. The role of experience in solidifying a personal code of ethics cannot be underestimated. When ethical behavior is rewarded, it is likely to become a habit. Unfortunately, "doing the right thing" often does not have obvious benefits or direct positive consequences and can even result in a personal disaster. In such situations, the individual may have to be guided by basic teachings of parents and other beliefs acquired through study and experience as rationale for taking ethical actions.

When it comes to possessing a good "work ethic"—values based on hard work and diligence—it would seem that the parents of Millennials or those born after 1980, have not had significant influence on their offspring. In 2010 the Pew Research Center published a study that found that Millennials did not describe themselves in terms of a work ethic, unlike all other age groups. People in this age group acknowledged that their parents and grandparents had a better work ethic than they did.

Another study, however, conducted by the training and leadership development company Achieve Global, concluded that differences among the four age groups present in the workforce were overblown. Their report, *The Generational Divide: Crucial Consideration or Trivial Hype?*, claimed that looking at workers in terms of their ages helped promote stereotypical perceptions that could prove to be obstacles in effectively managing a multigenerational workplace.

Common Unethical Workplace Behaviors

An employee working in the quality control department of a small manufacturer inspects every tenth item moving past her on the conveyor belt instead of every third item. A security guard completes only two out of three required walk-throughs of a building during his shift. These workers are not fulfilling their obligation to perform the work they have promised to do in exchange for salary or wages. No matter what the reasons may be for these behaviors, these employees are engaged in one of the top five most common unethical behaviors observed in the workplace. Three of the five most common unethical behaviors have to do with lying. If the supervisors of the quality control worker and the security guard confront them about their unethical behavior, but the employees proceed to lie about or cover up their negligence, they have engaged in yet another unethical behavior. Calling in sick when the caller is not really sick is another extremely unethical behavior.

Lying to or deceiving customers is another common unscrupulous practice that affects the customer and damages the reputation of the employer as well. This type of behavior can also make the employee and employer vulnerable to legal action. Putting inappropriate pressure on a co-worker to achieve a personal or business goal is another type of unethical behavior that can have legal and financial consequences. In 2018 the U.S. Equal Employment Opportunity Commission received over 24,000 charges of sexual harassment and reported settlements totaling US$70 million. Giving gifts to co-workers or supervisors with the expectation of receiving something in return is another form of inappropriate pressure.

Causes of Unethical Workplace Behaviors

The causes of unethical behaviors in the workplace range from the simple to the complex. One common cause is poor communication. Employers frequently assume that everyone shares the same set of values and beliefs. In a diverse work environment, it is important for employers to clearly describe their expectations regarding employee conduct and the consequences of unethical behavior. Taking shortcuts, covering up mistakes, and lying on expense accounts are ways that workers manage pressure to meet production, sales, budget, or profit goals. Abuse of sick leaves or lying about working is often a result of trying to balance work and family obligations. Lack of recognition and personal financial worries also factor into workplace misconduct.

The 2009 National Business Ethics survey conducted by the Ethics Resource Center found that the tactics that companies employed in order to survive the recession beginning in 2007 were "related to significant increases in the number of employees observing misconduct." These tactics included adjusted work schedules, layoffs, compensation and benefit reductions, hiring freezes, early buyouts, production slowdowns, and plant closures. All of these tactics increased workers' concern about their financial future. This concern was a likely cause of increased misconduct in the workplace. Since then, however, observed instances of misconduct have started to decrease (see figure 3.1), due in part to a heightened sensitivity to ethics in the workplace, to widespread adoption of corporate codes of ethics, and to the ease with which misconduct can now be reported through social media. Retaliation for reporting misconduct is also a disturbing trend, according to the last available national ethics survey (see figure 3.2).

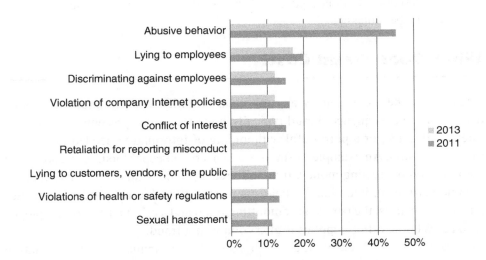

Figure 3.1   Percentage of U.S. workforce observing misconduct in 2011 and 2013

Source: Adapted from *2013 Business Ethics Survey®*, performed by the Ethics Resource Center.

Other less frequently observed misconduct includes breaking environmental and safety rules, falsifying records, using drugs and alcohol on the job, and stealing—behaviors that are punishable by fines and imprisonment.

Employee fraud costs billions 33.2% of retail shrinkage is due to employee theft.

Workers in the private sector who filed reports about misconduct who experienced some form of retaliation.

Proportion of tips that lead to the detection of fraud that come from employees

High school athletes who admitted cheating on an exam at least once in a year (based on survey of 5,000 student athletes)

How 800 adults living in the U.S. ranked the honesty and integrity of nurses

Figure 3.2   Surprising Facts About Ethical Behavior

Source: 2013 Business Ethics Survey ® performed by the Ethics Resource Center; *2016 Report to the Nations on Occupational Fraud and Abuse* by the Association of Certified Fraud Examiners; Josephson Institute report, 2007; 2016 Gallup poll "Honesty/Ethics in the Professions."

What Does Fraud Cost?

Fraud is deliberate action by an individual or entity to cheat another, causing damage as a consequence. Fraud typically involves a misrepresentation with the intent to deceive, or a purposeful withholding of information needed in order to make a decision. An example of fraud is when a bookkeeper falsifies records with the intention of stealing money. If an individual provides false information on an income tax return, intentionally neglects to report taxable income, or overstates business expenses, the person is committing fraud and a criminal act. An employee who takes home office supplies is also committing fraud.

Fraud costs U.S. corporations billions of dollars annually. The Association of Certified Fraud Examiners estimates that a loss of 5% of annual revenues is the amount that a company can expect to lose to employee fraud. A survey of U.S. retailers in 2018 showed that 33.2% of retail shrinkage – meaning the loss of products between manufacture and point of sale – was due to employee theft.

Steps in Making Ethical Decisions

Deciding between what is right and what is wrong to do is a complex and highly contextualized process. What seems correct in one instance may not be appropriate in another situation. Because making good ethical choices is so complicated, it can be helpful to use a set of questions when making **ethical decisions**. The decision-making process can be enumerated in five steps: recognize an ethical situation, get the facts, evaluate alternative courses of action, test your decision, and implement it.

Recognize an Ethical Situation

Ethical dilemmas arise in every field of endeavor, usually from competing "goods." For example, the individual's right to privacy (a good thing) seems constantly in conflict with the need to ensure personal security in public spaces (another good thing). The controversy over the implementation of full-body scanners in airports is an excellent example of the complexity and difficulty involved in trying to achieve these divergent desirable goals at the same time. Another example of competing positive values is the availability of drugs containing pseudoephedrine. This chemical is a key ingredient in the production of methamphetamine, which is a highly addictive, easy-to-make, illegal psychostimulant. Pseudoephedrine is a very effective antihistamine, but in order to control the production of illegal drugs, it has become more and more difficult for cold and allergy sufferers to obtain this drug over the counter. In these two examples of ethically challenging situations, it is important to ask how the decisions affected all stakeholders. What did these decisions do to people, their dignity, and their right to a better life?

Ethical dilemma
Situation in which no choice resolves the situation in an ethically acceptable way.

Get the Facts

Gathering all relevant information can take time, but it is an important step. Throughout the process, decision-makers must assess whether enough is known in order to make a decision. decision-makers can ask themselves which individuals or groups have an important stake in the outcome, and the response should guide data collection efforts. The relevance of some persons or groups may not be apparent at the beginning of the process, and for this reason, sufficient time should be allotted to fact finding to allow for all relevant parties to be consulted.

Evaluate Alternative Courses of Action

There are four major approaches to evaluating the ethical implications of a decision. Each approach is based on a different philosophical perspective. You will see that in order to apply each approach, a complete knowledge of all stakeholders helps the decision-maker select the approach.

Which Option Will Produce the Greatest Net Benefits?

The **utilitarian approach** is probably the most familiar and the most frequently used. This approach is associated with John Stuart Mill and Jeremy Bentham who, in the 19th century, developed this ethical reasoning to help English legislators examine the morality of laws. It states that ethical action is the one that will result in the greatest benefits for the greatest number of people. It is therefore implied that there will be a

Utilitarian approach
An ethical action is the one that will produce the most benefit for the most people.

few people who will not benefit from the decision and who may even be harmed by it. In such cases, decision-makers will usually find a way to compensate those who do not benefit. The utilitarian approach is favored by business managers and the military.

Will Everyone's Rights and Dignity Be Respected?

Moral rights approach An ethical action is the one that most dutifully respects the rights of all who are affected

In the **moral rights approach** to ethics, an ethical action is the one that most dutifully respects the rights of all who are affected. This perspective arises from the philosophy of the German thinker Immanuel Kant and his followers who said that everyone has the right to freely choose what to do in his or her life, and that this right should be respected. Rights associated with the right to choose are the right to the truth, the right to privacy so long as it does not harm others, the right not to be harmed unless we knowingly take risks or harm others, and the right to receive what has been agreed upon when we freely enter into a contract.

Which Option is Fair to all Stakeholders? Does It Treat Everyone the Same Way, or Does It Show Favoritism and Discrimination?

Fairness/justice approach An ethical action is the one that treats people fairly and impartially

Greek philosopher Aristotle said that "equals should be treated equally and unequals unequally." In the **fairness** or **justice approach,** ethical action is the one that treats people fairly and impartially. From this philosophy flows the belief that favoritism and discrimination are wrong.

Does the Action Respect the Relationships You Have With the People Who Depend on You?

Ethic of care approach A morally correct action is the one that appropriately cares for the people with whom you have a relationship.

The **ethic of care approach** to ethics is most closely identified with feminist Carol Gilligan and educator Nel Noddings, according to whom a morally correct action is the one that appropriately cares for the people with whom you have a relationship. This approach can be useful when faced with a decision in which applying the fairness approach will result in a decision that is actually unfair to one or more of those concerned. For example, from the perspective of the ethic of care, it may be ethical to make a special exception to rules when a person is in need and when the consequences of the exception do not harm others.

Test Your Decision

Once the ethical situation has been fully studied, an approach identified, and a decision made, it is time to test the decision by sharing it. If you told someone you respect your reasons for choosing this option, what would that person say? An even better test is to ask yourself if you would be comfortable explaining your decision on television or on YouTube. If you cringe at the thought, you should return to evaluating another course of action and test it.

Implement Your Decision

Once a course of action has been decided, the decision should be implemented with care and attention to all stakeholders. With decisions that involve significant change, moving in gradual phases is one way to show consideration for the stakeholders. Having a compensatory plan ready for those who do not benefit from a utilitarian approach is another way to demonstrate concern for the well-being of stakeholders. Since ethical decisions arise daily, it is likely that you will use this process again and again. By reflecting on your decision and how it turned out for all concerned, you can develop new options and improve your responses to future ethical situations.

Fostering Ethical Behavior

Ethical behavior should be considered as a factor in the strategic planning of every aspect of a business. This helps build ethical awareness throughout the company. Most importantly, leaders at every level of the organization should model ethical behavior in public and private life. Leading by example is probably the most powerful tool to foster ethical behavior across the entire company.

Codes of Conduct

Many companies have adopted ethical policy statements that inform employees of acceptable standards of conduct (or **codes of conduct**), further contributing to ethical awareness and guiding employees toward ethical behavior. The following are some examples:

Code of conduct
A company's ethical policy statement meant to guide employee decision-making.

Walgreens
Computer Security: As a general rule, we may not make unauthorized copies of any copyrighted material. Further, we may not install or distribute software products on company owned computers without an appropriate license.

Sunoco
Confidential Information, Disclosure and Insider Trading: Officers, directors and employees must maintain the confidentiality of confidential information entrusted to them by the Company, except when disclosure is authorized by the Legal Department or required by applicable laws or regulations as determined by the Legal Department. Confidential information includes all non-public information that might be of use to competitors, or harmful to the Company or its customers and suppliers, if disclosed.

Zimmer Holdings, Inc.
Record-keeping: Zimmer requires honest and accurate recording and reporting of information in order to make responsible business decisions. For example, only the true and actual number of hours worked by Zimmer personnel should be reported. You must ensure that all records for which you are responsible accurately reflect transactions and do not include any false or misleading information.

Ethics Training

Creating and publishing a code of ethics or code of conduct establishes a foundation for ethics training and helps employees maintain a high level of awareness. When employees see that time and resources are being devoted to this topic, they are likely to understand the value that the company puts on ethical behavior. Messages from top executives emphasizing ethical business practices support the goals of ethics training. Managers from all departments must in turn reinforce the goals of top management and formal ethics training in order to attain consistent ethical behavior across the organization. Another important aspect of ethics training is clearly communicating the procedures for discussing or reporting unethical behavior.

Social Audits

The idea of **social audit,** a systematic evaluation of a company's implementation of socially responsible policies, arose about 50 years ago. It is only in the last two decades, though, that the term and the practice have entered the mainstream. A social audit is a way of measuring, understanding, reporting on an organization's social and ethical performance. It helps identify gaps between the organization's social and ethical goals and what is actually occurring so that it can improve its social performance.

Ideally, both internal and external stakeholders should participate in social audits, cooperating in collecting data, evaluating it, and making recommendations to the company for changes or improvements. Internal auditors might comprise an ethics committee. External auditors might include union officials, customers, environmentalists, representatives of local government, and socially conscious investors.

Ethics assistance lines or help lines provide an important source of data for social audits. Employees are invited to ask questions regarding compliance with the law or with the codes of conduct, and to anonymously report incidents that violate codes, standards, or the law. For example, the University of Vermont has an Ethics and Compliance Reporting and Help Line where employees are encouraged to ask questions regarding compliance issues or to anonymously report incidents or situations that may involve violations of the University's Code of Business Conduct or other policy standards or legal requirements.

Whistle-blowing Policies and Procedures

Whistle-blowers
Employees who notify superiors of unethical or illegal behaviors they have witnessed.

Whistle-blowers are individuals who witness unethical or illegal behaviors that are tolerated or undetected and who decide to notify superiors of these behaviors, in other words, "blow the whistle" to attract attention to the wrongdoing. If not for the courage of the whistle-blower, these harmful behaviors would continue in most cases, damaging company reputation and employee morale. Failure to expose observed wrongdoing poses a severe threat to society and to the organization. Furthermore, the whistleblower runs the risk of being implicated as an accessory before or after the fact if he or she does not report the witnessed behavior.

It is therefore important to the well-being of a firm and its stakeholders to have a policy in place that encourages reporting of unethical conduct. To be effective, the policy should have visible support and involvement of top management. A key element of a whistle-blowing policy is the designation of an ethics officer or committee to whom an employee may anonymously report violations. Without the availability of such officially designated responsibility for dealing with reports of such behavior, the whistle-blower may hesitate to come forward with sensitive information. A meaningful procedure should be developed to deal fairly with reported violations, taking into consideration relevant federal and local laws and regulations.

Whistle-blowers, for obvious reasons, are vulnerable to retaliation. Hollywood films like *Silkwood* and *The Insider* have realistically portrayed two instances of extreme corporate reprisals against two individuals who publicly disclosed wrong-doing. Firing, blacklisting, transfer to undesirable locations, physical injury, and murder are all possible consequences. For optimal effectiveness of the whistle-blowing policy, it is important that those who come forward are assured of protection. The Sarbanes-Oxley Act of 2002 expanded the range of protection for whistle-blowers who are employees of publicly traded companies, in response to a string of financial fraud scandals in the 1990s. The law specifically states that no employer may "discharge, demote, suspend, threaten, harass, or in any other manner discriminate against an employee because of any lawful act done by the employee to provide information, cause information to be provided, or otherwise assist in an investigation regarding any conduct which the employee reasonably believes constitutes a violation of . . . any rule or regulation of the Securities and Exchange Commission (SEC), or any provision of Federal law relating to fraud against shareholders. . . ."

The Occupational Safety and Health Administration (OSHA) in the US runs the Office of Whistleblower Protection Program, which investigates complaints of retaliation against whistle-blowers. The Dodd-Frank Wall Street Reform and Consumer Protection Act of 2010 rewarded whistle-blowers and allowed them to report financial wrongdoing directly to the Securities and Exchange Commission (SEC).

Social Responsibility in Business

Social responsibility is the way in which a business attempts to balance its commitments to relevant groups and individuals – known as stakeholders – in its social environment. In a sense, social responsibility is the application of ethical decision-making at the level of an organization, an industry, field, or a nation. Organizational stakeholders are groups, individuals, and other organizations that are directly affected by the practices of an organization and, therefore, have a stake in its performance. Figure 3.3 illustrates the most common business stakeholders.

Responsibility toward the Environment

Today, responsibility toward our environment is summed up in a single word—"green." Environmentalism is not a new concept. Awareness of pollution dates back to the medieval period when the writings of Arab philosophers and scientists constituted an "agricultural revolution" in the Middle East. Activities of organizations such as Greenpeace, widespread publicity and research surrounding global warming, and binding international agreements such as the **Kyoto Protocol** and the **Paris Agreement,** have helped bring this form of social responsibility to the forefront of the public mind. Examples of responsibility toward the environment include controlling air, water, and land pollution; proper disposing of toxic waste; engaging in recycling; reducing or eliminating use of chemicals in raising livestock, vegetable, fruit, and other food (organic farming).

Kyoto Protocol
International agreement that sets targets for countries to reduce greenhouse gas emissions.

Responsibility toward Customers

A firm's responsibility to its customers falls into four major categories: guaranteeing consumer rights, pricing products fairly, advertising ethically, and providing quality products. Prior to 1965, only one federal law protected U.S. consumers from dangerous products or false advertising, and that was the Food, Drug, and Cosmetic Act of 1938. The rise of the consumer movement in the 1960s prompted President John F. Kennedy to propose a *Bill for Consumer Rights* to the U.S. Congress in 1962. Kennedy's bill rested on four rights, stemming in part from the Kantian approach to ethics mentioned earlier in this chapter: the right to safe products, the right to demand information about a product or service, the right to a competitive marketplace, and the right to redress from a manufacturer or distributor. Kennedy and his supporters believed that upholding consumer rights would preserve personal freedom and enhance business. In 1975 under the Ford administration and in 1994 under the Clinton administration, two other consumer rights were added: the right to consumer education and the right to courteous, convenient, and responsive service.

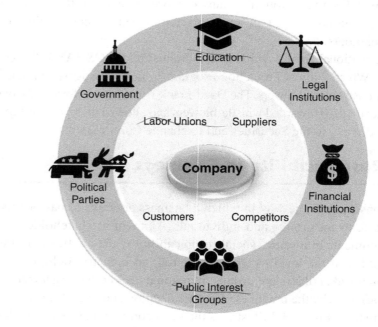
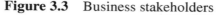

Figure 3.3 Business stakeholders

National Consumer Day March 15, the day that John F. Kennedy introduced his Bill for Consumer Rights to congress in 1962.

Consumer protection laws now exist in most industrialized nations, but they are not uniform in their policies, nor are the laws enforced consistently in all countries. In 1985 the United Nations adopted a set of 46 consumer protection guidelines that it hoped would provide an internationally recognized foundation for the implementation of consumer protection laws in its member nations. In 1989 India started observing March 15th, the day that Kennedy introduced his consumer rights legislation, as National Consumer Day.

The Right to Safe Products

The U.S. Consumer Product Safety Commission (CPSC) protects the public from injury resulting from the use of thousands of consumer products. The CPSC provides information to consumers and businesses about the many laws and policies relevant to product safety and their improvement. Most of us are familiar with recalls of products originating with CPSC, such as the recall of drop-side cribs and toys made in China containing paint with lead in it. Other agencies that ensure product safety through recalls, consumer education, and law enforcement are the Food and Drug Administration (FDA), the Food Safety and Inspection Service of the U.S. Department of Agriculture, the National Highway Traffic Safety Administration, the U.S. Environmental Protection Agency (EPA), and the U.S. Coast Guard, among others. OSHA has approved a number of private product safety and certification services to manufacturers. These Nationally Recognized Testing Laboratories (NRTLs) certify products that meet standards set by independent organizations such as the American National Standards Institute (ANSI). Probably the best known NRTL is the Underwriters Laboratories Inc. (UL), founded in 1894.

The Right to Be Informed

Consumers have the right to complete information about a product or service before they buy it. The FDA-mandated "Nutrition Facts" label on foods listing all ingredients is one example. The detailed information provided in magazine and television advertisements of prescription drugs is another example of providing complete information about not only the benefits but the risks of using a product. Borrowers must be informed about all costs when requesting a credit card or a home mortgage and the consequences of not fulfilling their obligations. Manufacturers and service providers can be prosecuted with severe penalties for not providing this information, which may have led to injuries suffered by the consumer, resulting from the use of the product or service.

On the other hand, the consumer has a responsibility for seeking out and heeding any information provided. In the age of the Internet, product information is readily available from a variety of sources. Manufacturers provide detailed information at company websites, customer ratings and reviews are available online, independent shopping guides teach consumers what to look for in specific products and services, and government regulations and policies regarding various product categories can be easily searched online.

The Right to Choose What to Buy

Genuine competition among manufacturers, service providers, and other sellers creates choice for consumers. Continuing advances in technology in all types of industries help companies offer products of high quality that satisfy consumer needs at affordable prices, creating competition in a market-driven economy.

The government plays a role in ensuring the right to choose through enforcement of laws prohibiting monopolies and through antitrust legislation. The Sherman Anti-Trust Act of 1890 was the first U.S. federal law that regulated competition, banning monopolies, contracts, mergers, or conspiracies to act in restraint of trade. The Clayton Act of 1914 and the Celler-Kefauver Act of 1950 added further provisions – for instance, provisions for all corporate acquisitions to receive prior regulatory approval. The Federal Trade Commission Act of 1914 banned unfair trade practices and created the Federal Trade Commission (FTC). The FTC is a five-member board that investigates complaints and can force companies to stop unethical trade practices. The FTC is a powerful and important federal agency.

Federal Trade Commission (FTC) A five-member board created in 1914 to investigate consumer complaints and stop unethical trade practices.

The Right to be Heard

The right to be heard means that sellers will take consumer complaints seriously and take action to correct problems. Soon after World War II (1939–1945) when manufacturing returned to the production of consumer goods, companies learned that listening to consumers could give them a competitive advantage. This change in attitude meant that answering complaints was not just good public relations, but a way of gathering vital marketing information. Today customers and companies find it easier than ever to exercise the right to be heard using various forms of electronic communication.

The Right to be Educated about Purchases

In 1975 President Gerald Ford added the right to consumer education because he believed that consumers would not be able to fully enjoy the first four rights without the training and knowledge needed to make informed choices. Surveys performed over the past 20 years show that even college-educated Americans have deficient consumer knowledge of credit, bank accounts, landlord–tenant obligations, and automobiles. Thirty states and the District of Columbia have statewide consumer education policies. Wisconsin and Illinois require consumer education and have model consumer education programs starting in middle school.

The Right to Courteous Service

The addition of the right to courteous service to consumers' rights coincided with the Clinton administration's 1994 National Performance Review of customer service in all governmental operations. The right to courteous service includes having things done right and done quickly, by knowledgeable and reliable people. Courteous service includes knowing where to turn when things go wrong or where to get answers to questions, and clarity in forms and explanations. Of course, courteous service includes dealing with friendly, respectful people who are willing to listen.

Unfair Pricing Practices

Collusion Companies that ought to be competing are actually collaborating to change the price of a good or service to their advantage.

Another way in which companies implement their responsibility to consumers is through ethical pricing. There are a variety of ethical ways to arrive at a selling price of a product or service, involving costs, profit margins, and market conditions. There are two pricing practices, collusion and "price gouging," notorious among oligopolists, that are considered unethical. **Collusion** is when the companies that ought to be competing are actually collaborating to change the price of a good or service to their advantage. Collusion occurs when two or more firms selling the same product or service agree to sell it at a price they establish, or "fix," rather than letting the price be set by market forces. The collaborating companies could act together to restrict the availability of a product in order to influence the price. Collusion is an illegal practice. **Price gouging** means that a required product or service is in short supply and sellers raise prices to take advantage of the situation. An example would be a grocery store raising prices on bread and milk prior to the arrival of a storm during which consumers would be unable to leave their homes. Another illegal pricing practice is **price discrimination**, which occurs when a company offers one customer discounts that are not offered to others who are buying under similar terms.

Price gouging A required product or service is in short supply and sellers raise prices to take advantage of the situation.

Ethics in Advertising/Sales

Ethically run businesses discourage overly aggressive sales tactics and do not use deceptive advertising. It is illegal to make claims in advertisements that are not truthful, are deceptive or unfair, and are not based on evidence. The Federal Trade Commission enforces laws related to truth in advertising. Aggressive or manipulative sales tactics and less than truthful advertising anger customers and ultimately discourage sales. Deceptive advertising also interferes with consumers' right to be informed. **Stealth marketing** is a recently introduced marketing technique in which consumers do not realize that they are being marketed to. Individuals, either employees of the marketing firm or consumers paid by marketers, interact with others to deliver a specific marketing message. Critics say that in this situation unaware consumers do not ask the questions they would be likely to ask if they knew what was actually happening. Another form of stealth marketing is when you see a branded product displayed as part of a film or TV setting. The manufacturer has probably paid for a "product placement."

Stealth marketing
Technique in which consumers do not realize that they are being marketed to.

The advent of online advertising has created even more opportunities for deception and given rise to new concerns over privacy and data security. Online advertisers can collect personal information such as the consumer's name, address, or social security number to use for marketing purposes, as long as they allow customers to "opt-out" of making this data available. Advertisers also collect information about a person's online browsing habits, search queries and website history, and use this information to present targeted content to the consumer, a practice called **behavioral advertising**. Although this technique cuts down on advertising that is of no interest to a customer, the convenience seems to come at a cost to individual privacy.

Behavioral advertising
Practice of using browsing habits and search history to target advertising content.

On the other hand, the Internet offers consumers and businesses the opportunity to make marketing communications a two-way conversation. Businesses now consider the addition of a social networking site a necessary addition to the company website to exchange ideas, suggestions, and criticisms, which in turn help advertise and sell the product or service. Companies, whether online or a storefront retailer, are also making use of **permission-based marketing**. They invite current and potential customers to receive specific information of interest to them, rather than be bombarded by general advertising. In business-to-business marketing, customers may be offered a research report or other information that may help them run their businesses.

Permission-based marketing *Current and potential customers are invited to receive specific information of interest to them rather than be bombarded by general advertising.*

Responsibility toward Employees

Motivated employees who are committed to the mission and the values of the company for which they work are essential in building and sustaining a firm's business performance. A corporate stance of justice and fairness toward all employees forms the foundation of policies and practices that encourage the enthusiasm of the workforce.

Although people from all over the world continue to choose the United States as a place to settle, to enjoy political freedom and seek economic opportunity, workplace discrimination based on race, religion, gender, ethnicity, or any other personal characteristic with no bearing on how one might perform a job persists. The historic Civil Rights Act of 1964, which established the Equal Employment Opportunity Commission (EEOC), was the first federal law to address job discrimination. The EEOC is empowered to monitor hiring practices and to investigate complaints. It can also file legal charges and oblige offending companies to pay compensation to wronged individuals or groups. In 1991, another civil rights act expanded the 1964 legislation so employees could sue companies and gave women legal tools to fight gender discrimination.

In 1990, people with mental and physical disabilities received legal protection from job discrimination when the Americans with Disabilities Act (ADA) was passed. The act defined *disability* very broadly, moving beyond physical disability to include people with cancer, heart disease, diabetes, alcoholism, and other conditions. Requiring people to pass a physical test as a condition of employment was outlawed. Under the ADA, companies must make reasonable accommodations for employees with disabilities.

Table 3.1 Median Household Income

	2016	2017	Percent Change in Real Median Income
	(estimated, in 2017 dollars)		
Race and Origin of Householder			
White	$63,188	$ 65,273	3.3
White, not Hispanic	$66,440	$ 68,145	2.6
Black	$40,340	$ 40,258	–0.2
Asian	$83,183	$ 81,331	–2.2
Hispanic origin (any race)	$48,700	$ 50,486	3.7
Nativity of Householder			
Native born	$61,066	$ 61,987	1.5
Foreign born	$56,754	$ 57,273	0.9
Naturalized citizen	$ 65,268	$ 65,859	0.9
Not a citizen	$ 49,100	$ 49,739	1.3

Source: "Income and Poverty in the United States: 2017" US Census Bureau. www.census.gov/library/publications/2018/demo/p60-263.html.

Affirmative action programs complement antidiscrimination laws. Affirmative action programs try to ensure the diversity and representativeness of a company's workforce. Affirmative action plans affect all aspects of human resource management: recruiting, hiring, training, promotion, and pay. A firm following an affirmative action plan would try to hire the same percentage of Native American carpenters as are present in the surrounding community. The same company would take care to train and promote its Native American workers in the same fashion as it trained and promoted its other workers. Employers that receive more than US$50,000 a year in federal contracts are required to have affirmative action plans.

Critics of affirmative action portray it as "**reverse discrimination**." The hiring quotas that resulted from early affirmative action efforts were indeed ruled unconstitutional by the courts. But the persistent differences in income levels among white males, women of any race, Hispanics, Asians, and African Americans indicate that inequalities in the workplace, based on these personal attributes, not on the individual's ability to do a job, remain. Evidently, stronger antidiscrimination laws and government agencies with the power to enforce these laws are still needed in order to close the earnings gaps (see table 3.1).

Providing a Physically and Socially Safe Workplace

According to the U.S. Bureau of Labor Statistics, nearly 5,000 workers die on the job every year in this country. In 2017, 2.8 million workers suffered serious injuries and illnesses while on the job. The combined direct and indirect costs of these work-related deaths, injuries, and diseases range from US$128 billion to $155 billion annually. The Occupational Safety and Health Act (OSHA) of 1970 set standards for workplace safety and health and established the Occupational Safety and Health Administration. OSHA's education and enforcement efforts have been a major influence in the significant decline of workplace injuries since its establishment.

A company's responsibility to provide a safe and healthy workplace can extend to workers employed by subcontractors, no matter where the subcontractors or suppliers are located. For many years, Nike received severe criticism for the conditions under which foreign laborers worked in order to produce its popular footwear. The company now has a model monitoring program to deal with labor issues at 900 subcontractor factories throughout the world. Nearly 100 Nike staff members visit these factories to evaluate them against company standards for health, safety, and fair labor practices.

In 1999 the Fair Labor Association (FLA) was founded by human rights groups and companies such as Nike, Reebok, and Liz Claiborne. It developed a Workplace Code of Conduct, based on International Labor Organization (ILO) standards, and created a practical monitoring, remediation, and verification process to achieve those standards. A growing number of companies have devised supplier codes of conduct to ensure that all companies involved in the production and distribution of their products respect the basic rights of their workers. For example, clothing retailer Gap inspectors travel the world to make sure that subcontractors adhere to its *Code of Vendor Conduct*. The Carrefour Group, which owns a chain of hypermarkets in Europe, has since 2006 obliged its subcontractors to sign its *Group Social Charter*.

Providing Opportunities to Balance Work and Life

By the 1990s "employee well-being" started to mean more to employees than feeling safe and fairly treated. Corporations observed that their current and prospective employees were seeking jobs that would not only provide financial security, but opportunities for growth, autonomy, and time to pursue personal interests outside of work. At the same time, employers had come to the realization that stress from unsuccessfully managing work and non-work commitments could have detrimental effects on worker health. This phenomenon came to be known as "work/life balance."

Occupational Safety and Health Administration
Federal agency that sets standards for workplace safety and health.

Safe Moving of Nursing Home Patients: A growing Issue

A study conducted in Australia in 2008 found that 37% of workplace fatalities involved design. Design includes the physical workplace, tools, equipment, machinery, substances, and work processes, including their construction, manufacture, use, maintenance, and final disposal or reuse. Prevention through Design (PtD) is an initiative of the National Institute for Occupational Safety and Health (NIOSH) that asserts that one of the best ways to prevent and control occupational injuries, illnesses, and fatalities is to "design out" or minimize hazards and risks early in the designing process. The PtD initiative promotes this concept and highlights its importance in all business decisions.

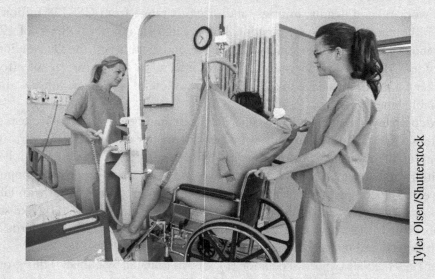

An example of PtD in action is the redesigning of a mechanical lifting device to be used in nursing homes.

Source: NIOSH [2006]. Safe Lifting and Movement of Nursing Home Residents. By Collins, J.W., Nelson, A., Sublet, V. U.S. Department of Health and Human Services, Centers for Disease Control and Prevention, National Institute for Occupational Safety and Health, DHHS (NIOSH) Publication Number 2006 - 177. https://www.cdc.gov/niosh/docs/2006-117/default.html

Companies wishing to attract and retain the best workers developed policies and programs that would help employees balance childcare, elder care, community involvement, continuing education, and other commitments and pursuits with job responsibilities. Examples of work/life initiatives include:

- on-site childcare
- elder-care initiatives (may range from referral programs, elder-care assessments, case management, to a list of local organizations or businesses that can help with information or products, or seminars and support groups)

- flexible working arrangements (alternatives to the 9–5, Monday–Friday schedule of work)
- family leave policies (e.g., Family Medical Leave Act provisions that allow leave for parents and to care for family members)
- other leaves of absence policies such as educational leave, community service leaves, self-funded leave or sabbaticals
- employee assistance programs (e.g., confidential, short-term counseling services for employees with personal problems that affect their work performance)
- on-site seminars and workshops on topics like stress, diet, smoking, etc.
- fitness facilities or assistance in obtaining fitness membership

Responsibility toward Investors and Shareholders

Companies are directly accountable to those who have funded them, regardless of the form of investment. Investors should feel confident that their money is being managed in a way that will provide them reasonable return on their investment and that financial transactions and performance are being communicated clearly and accurately.

The practice of "insider trading" is an illegal activity in which information known only to those close to decision-makers is used for trading stock to achieve large profits, usually for the individuals working inside the company, who have access to this nonpublic information. Insider trading clearly demonstrates a lack of responsibility toward investors and shareholders. A famous example of insider trading is the case of Martha Stewart, media personality and publisher, who was convicted of lying in 2003 to the Securities and Exchange Commission about her sale of stock in a cancer drug company one day before its main product was rejected by the FDA. A good friend of hers owned the company, and Stewart acted on the inside information he gave her, thus avoiding huge personal losses when share prices plummeted the next day.

Insider trading Using information known only to a company's executives to gain advantage in trading stock.

Responsibility toward the Community

Corporate social responsibility toward the community in which a company operates has become widely accepted as a business obligation not just in the United States but globally. The World Business Council for Sustainable Development, a global association of over 200 companies, has defined corporate social responsibility (CSR) as "the continuing commitment by business to behave ethically and contribute to economic development while improving the quality of life of the workforce and their families as well as of the local community and the society at large."

Corporate Social Responsibility (CSR) Commitment to behave ethically and contribute to economic development while improving the quality of life and society.

With regard to employment of workers, companies and communities enter into a mutually responsible, reciprocal relationship. Business, local government, and educational institutions must coordinate efforts to ensure that the workforce is equipped with the type of training that companies need. Businesses have a responsibility to consider how layoffs and closings will affect the community and should feel obligated to implement compensatory measures to soften the direct and indirect consequences of their actions.

The consequences of the layoffs of tens of thousands of General Motors workers in Flint, Michigan, during the 1980s is a striking example of what can happen when little coordination and communication exists between a corporation and its community. Within 20 years, Flint went from a prosperous and desirable city to one of the most troubled cities in the United States. Poverty and unemployment rates climbed, and only a little over half of high school students were able to graduate. By 2002, the city was US$35 million in debt. Today General Motors employs only 3,500 people, compared to 80,000 in the 1970s. After a brief period of recovery, Flint suffered a devastating water contamination crisis lasting two years as a result of an effort to reduce public water service costs.

Another vital aspect of a company's responsibility to the community in which it operates is to ensure a safe living environment for all who dwell there. Preserving clean air, water, and soil enhances the sustainability of a business, at the least by helping in maintaining the health and well-being of the local workforce. Every business generates pollution of some type and consumes natural resources. Even so-called "clean" businesses, such as web-based services, consume electricity. In the United States, over 70% of the fuel used in generating electricity is carbon-based, thus depleting a finite natural resource. Many companies today strive to conserve energy, especially if they use massive amounts of it. An example of such a company is Google, which says that it obtains most of the electric power for its data centers from nuclear and other renewable energy sources.

Preserve the Character of the Community

A company can further enhance its relations with the local community by supporting charitable organizations (see table 3.2). This support can take many forms, such as providing human, physical, and financial resources for community fundraisers and other events, by encouraging employees to participate in community activities, and making donations to public institutions like libraries

Table 3.2 Corporate charitable cash contributions of over $200 million in 2017

Company	Donation (in USD million)
Gilead Sciences	388
Wells Fargo & Company	287
Goldman Sachs	280
Google	255
JPMorgan Chase	250
Johnson & Johnson	227
Pfizer	210

Source: Business Insider. www.businessinsider.com/companies-that-give-the-most-to-charity-in-the-us-2018-9.

and hospitals. People respect businesses that participate in community life, and the positive public relations resulting from these activities is beneficial to the reputation of the company.

Implementing Corporate Social Responsibility (CSR) Programs

Although corporate social responsibility has become more widely accepted as a business norm over the past two decades, there remain potent arguments, against full implementation of CSR. One of the strongest arguments is that the cost of CSR threatens profits. It is obvious from the foregoing discussion of a company's obligation toward its stakeholders that enacting CSR costs money. For example, installing equipment that will prevent air and water from being polluted as a re-sult of production activities is expensive. Proponents of CSR argue, however, that viewed in a long-term perspective, reducing pollution will actually lead to profits. Another argument against CSR is that because businesses can pick and choose which responsibilities to act on and which to ignore, they may tend to choose only those that will be easy, inexpensive, or yield the highest boost in public relations. The opposing viewpoint relies on seeing corporations as citizens with a duty to help others. Some even believe that businesses lack the expertise to act effectively and appropriately in matters related to social responsibility. Those arguing for the pursuit of social responsibility say that CSR is simply a matter of companies solving the problems they create in the production of products and services that create value for consumers.

The **"B" (for "benefit") corporation** movement is an attempt to move the rationale for corporate social responsibility beyond the arguments presented herein. Proponents of B corporation certification aim to redefine business success in terms of social responsibility. The B corporation "declaration of interdependence" envisions "a new sector of the economy which harnesses the power of private enterprise to create public benefit." As of 2019, 36 states in the U.S. had passed legislation spelling out the requirements for certification as a B corporation, and 5 more states were considering passing similar laws. Ben and Jerry's – maker of ice cream and a leader in corporate social responsibility – gained B corporation status in 2012. For more information about B corporations, visit the B Lab website at www.bcorporation.net.

Another recent trend in corporate social responsibility is **"cause marketing"** in which a non-profit organization and a for-profit company cooperate for mutual benefit. The non-profit benefits from the ability to reach out to the customers of the for profit company while the for-profit company enhances its profile as a socially responsible entity, possibly gaining new customers. American Express is thought to have originated the concept in 1981 when it made a 2-cent donation to a list of non-profits every time someone used its credit card. More recently, yogurt brands such as Yoplait, Dannon ®, and Stoneyfield have helped raise money for breast cancer research through sales of their products. It is predicted that According to IEG, a sponsorship consulting company, cause sponsorship spending was predicted to keep growing at a rate of at least 4.5 percent in North America in 2018 and 4.9 percent globally, to US$65.8 billion.

Approaches to Social Responsibility

In light of the arguments presented, companies have been generally found to adopt four different approaches to their responsibilities to stakeholders (see figure 3.4).

An **obstructionist stance** describes the position of a company that does as little as possible to implement its responsibility and may even try to deny or cover up violations. The company chooses to meet only its economic responsibilities and to fight social demands. For example, an explosion in 2010 that killed 29 workers at Massey Energy's Big Branch coal mine in West Virginia was the result of adopting an obstructionist stance toward its responsibility to provide a safe work environment for its workers. Massey had previously been cited for many safety violations. Investigators found gas-detecting equipment that was not engaged properly, and workers testified that they had been asked to interfere with the operation of other devices. Company behavior was clearly at odds with Massey's public statement that safety was more important than profits and that they had taken all necessary precautions.

A company that does everything required of it legally, but no more than that, is taking a **defensive stance** toward social responsibility. Such a company meets only its economic and legal responsibilities. An example of a defensive stance toward social responsibility is when the government orders a manufacturer or service provider to comply with laws relevant to its product or service, usually through a product recall. Even company-initiated recalls of products that do not meet safety standards or that have already caused injury are usually the result of government intervention. In early 2010, the Consumer Product Safety Commission approved new rules that allow it to order a mandatory product recall. Mattel™ and Toyota have made frequent recalls of their products in the past.

An **accommodative stance** toward social responsibility means that the company considers its ethical responsibilities to stakeholders while meeting its legal and economic obligations to them. Top management feels an obligation to respond to social and environmental pressures because it is "the right thing to do." Companies taking an accommodative stance might develop codes of conduct that focus on different concerns, depending on industry type and country. For example, in the United States, codes of conduct focus on the well-being of the community and the environment, while in Europe codes of conduct might focus on producing quality products. In Asia and Africa, the focus of codes of conduct might include preventing corruption.

A company that actively seeks to contribute to the well-being of groups and individuals in its social environment by assuming leadership initiatives is said to be taking a **proactive stance.** The top management of this type of company seeks discretionary responsibilities because it understands the value that social responsibility creates and sees the organization as part of a complex and interrelated network of social, economic, and political relationships. Proactive companies act on their own, without social pressure. In 2010 the Palmer House Hilton became the largest Green Seal Certified hotel in Chicago, in recognition of its proactive stance on green initiatives. The management believed that sustainable, environmentally friendly practices were important in creating value to its customers and decided to submit the hotel to a science-based evaluation of its property.

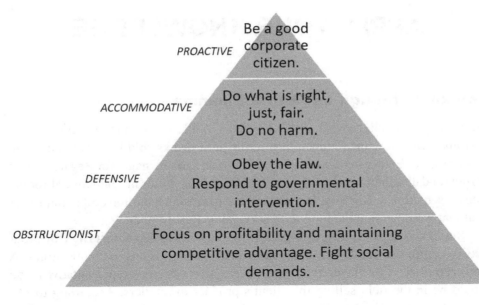

Figure 3.4   Approaches to corporate social responsibility

APPLY YOUR KNOWLEDGE

Thinking Through an Ethical Dilemma

Jamal could not believe what his boss, Warren Smith, was telling their prospective customer, Big Boy, Inc., a manufacturer of juice drinks sold in convenience and grocery stores everywhere. Jamal was an assistant sales manager for Regal Foods, a frozen food distribution company serving 500 grocery stores in southern California. The presentation to Big Boy, Inc. was critical to closing a million dollar, multiyear deal that would assure the long-term survival of Regal Foods.

Smith was explaining how Regal had the capacity to insure that Big Boy products were fully stocked at all times in optimal shelf positions in all 500 stores. A PowerPoint slide displayed the names of Regal Foods sales representatives who would be in the field selling the client's product to retailers. According to Mr. Smith there would be 10 sales representatives covering 500 retailers. The Big Boy representatives sitting around the table were clearly impressed, and so was Jamal because he knew that one representative was dead and the other had left the company two years before. Jamal sat through the rest of the meeting in a daze, rousing himself when his boss flipped the lights back on.

After shaking hands with everyone and showing them to the door, Smith turned to Jamal and asked, "Well, do you think they'll sign with us?"

"Sure, we have a lot to offer them," replied Jamal, trying to decide whether to point out the lie on the slide. He had only worked for the company for two months, and he liked his boss and his job, but this misrepresentation of the company bothered him. What would happen when the new customer found out that there were only 8 reps? Did this lie mean that the boss expected Jamal to "shade the truth" to make sales? On the other hand, had any harm been done by "padding" the number of people on the salesforce? What was the right thing to do?

Knowledge Application Questions

1. What courses of action can Jamal take? Evaluate two courses of action using the "Steps in Making Ethical Decisions." Explain the possible consequences of each course of action.

2. Which course of action would you take if you were Jamal? Justify your answer.

QUIZ YOURSELF

Without looking back at the chapter, choose the best answer to each of the questions below. Answers are in the back of the textbook before the Index. Review the chapter to find out why you missed any questions.

1. Socially responsible companies should periodically conduct social audits for all of the following reasons, EXCEPT to
   a. identify gaps between policy goals and what is really happening.
   b. enhance employee awareness of the company's codes of conduct and ethical rules.
   c. determine the effectiveness of socially responsible policies.
   d. improve the attractiveness of the company to investors.
   e. identify the source of any whistle-blowing activity.

2. Managers should behave ethically because
   a. they are role models for employees.
   b. they could damage the reputation of their employers by acting unethically.
   c. unethical behavior such as falsifying reports or other records could endanger workplace safety.
   d. unethical behavior could result in expensive litigation.
   e. of all the reasons listed above.

3. Companies project an image of being "green" for all of the following reasons, EXCEPT one. Which one is it?
   a. Controlling air, water, and soil pollution saves money in the long run.
   b. People consider "green" companies more trustworthy.
   c. It is a defensive stance toward corporate social responsibility.
   d. Employees feel safer working for companies that care about them and their environment.
   e. It increases the company's status in the business world.

4. Cargill Meat Solutions and the local Denver teamsters' union paid over $1.6 million dollars to resolve the company's violation of antidiscrimination laws when it refused to accommodate the requests of Muslim workers for prayer breaks. Cargill now allows the prayer breaks and has agreed to provide training to managers and union representatives. Cargill's approach to corporate social responsibility is
   a. proactive.
   b. defensive.
   c. accommodative.
   d. obstructionist.
   e. destructive.

5. The Environmental Protection Agency, Food and Drug Administration, Occupational Safety and Health Administration, the Equal Employment Opportunity Commission, and the Federal Trade Commission all regulate corporate social responsibility (CSR) through laws and federal policies. One argument against regulating CSR is that regulation
   a. limits people's freedom to make choices in their own self-interest.
   b. frees companies from producing safe products.
   c. decreases the federal deficit.
   d. gives whistle-blowers more to do.
   e. prevents demand and supply from reaching the equilibrium point.

6. In applying the utilitarian rule (utility), managers should look at how a decision will impact all stakeholders, then choose the action that
   a. benefits the manager most.
   b. benefits employees most.
   c. harms competitors most.
   d. maximizes stock price.
   e. provides the most benefit to the most stakeholders, or the one that does the least harm to the most stakeholders.

7. After Wells Fargo admitted in the fall of 2016 to creating as many as two million fake accounts, nearly half a dozen former employees told news media that they were retaliated against after they tried to stop these illegal sales tactics. Wells Fargo was in violation of which of the following laws?
   a. Sarbanes–Oxley Act and Dodd–Frank Wall Street Reform and Consumer Protection Act
   b. Truth-in-advertising laws
   c. Clayton Act and Sherman Anti-trust Act
   d. Laws against insider trading
   e. None of the aforementioned options

8. All of the following rights must be taken into consideration in applying the moral rights rule EXCEPT
   a. the right to life.
   b. the right to privacy.
   c. the right to maximize profits.
   d. the right to freedom.
   e. the right to free speech.

9. Business Insider reports that "Facebook can tell if you looked at a product on an ecommerce site and can use that information to serve you an ad for that product when you go on to browse your news feed later." This is an example of
    a. stealth advertising.
    b. permission-based advertising.
    c. behavioral advertising.
    d. deceptive advertising.
    e. "opt-in" advertising.

10. Causes of employee misconduct include
    a. the inability to balance personal commitments with workplace obligations.
    b. companies' attempts to reduce operating costs.
    c. workplace culture in which unethical behavior is tolerated.
    d. the lack of employee incentives.
    e. all of the above.

Toria/Shutterstock

CHAPTER 4

Exploring Global Business

Why Do Nations Trade?

The reasons for which nations trade today are essentially the same as Marco Polo's legendary expeditions to the Far East in the 13th century. At that time, the nations of Europe competed fiercely for political power and for new markets for their goods, and the merchants of Venice were among the most aggressive in their quest. Today as well, the quest for new markets for raw materials, goods, and services continues, facilitated by advances in communication and in transportation. As domestic markets shrink, or become saturated with certain types of goods, foreign markets provide new opportunities for profits, as shown in table 4.1. Emerging foreign markets such as China and India are growing faster than markets in Europe and Africa. Colonial conquests were once driven by the need to find new sources of raw materials such as oil, sugar, rubber, and lumber. The need for raw materials still continues. Today corporations seek new sources of labor from a variety of international sources. Modern companies look at global trade as a way to distribute and reduce overall risk. Besides, producing and distributing for an expanded market can help a company realize economies of scale, making manufacturing cheaper and enabling products to be offered at lower prices.

How Do Countries Decide Which Products to Trade?

Absolute advantage
The ability to produce
a specific product more
efficiently than other
nations.

Countries decide which products to make locally and which ones to buy elsewhere by considering their capabilities and natural resources compared with other nations. A nation that has the ability to produce a specific product more efficiently than other nations, or that has a natural resource that few or no other countries have, is said to have an **absolute advantage**. For example, the climate in Sri Lanka is very favorable for the production of tea, rubber, and coconut. These products can be cultivated much more efficiently there than in Europe or in China, where these products would probably not grow well at all. Sri Lanka has therefore focused its resources on producing and processing these agricultural products, in which it has an absolute advantage, so that it may trade them for products in which Sri Lanka has lesser or no advantage. A nation may also develop an absolute advantage that is not associated with natural resources. Japan, for example, is an importer of iron and coal, but has an absolute advantage in the production of steel because of the efficient processes that Japanese steel mills use. Obviously, an absolute advantage that depends on a natural resource lasts longer than one

Table 4.1   Market potential for US goods—2019

Countries Ranked by Market Size	Rank by Market Receptivity	Rank by Overall Market Potential
1. China	4	1
2. India	4	4
3. Japan	7	6
4. Russia	5	50
5. Brazil	2	51
6. Indonesia	3	32
7. Germany	17	7
8. Mexico	26	34
9. Canada	72	5
10. South Korea	19	12

Source: An indexing study conducted by MSU-CIBER that compares and ranks 87 markets on multiple dimensions. Market Size is determined from the urban population in millions in 2017 and electricity consumption in billions of kwh in 2016. Market Receptivity is computed from per capita imports from the United States in 2018 and trade as a percentage of GDP in 2017. See https://globaledge.msu.edu/mpi/2019.

that depends on a process. An acquired absolute advantage may disappear with increased global competition.

The theory of **comparative advantage** is based on the concept of opportunity cost. The opportunity cost refers to products that a country must decline to make in order to produce something else. Comparative advantage means that a nation should specialize in the production of a product for which it has a lower opportunity cost and trade for products that it cannot produce as efficiently. For example, conditions in the U.S. are not favorable for the efficient production of coffee. Declining to produce coffee thus has a fairly low opportunity cost—not much is being sacrificed. The theory of comparative advantage suggests that the U.S. should produce pharmaceuticals, which it does very efficiently, and trade to obtain coffee. Applying this theory to another example, we can say that since South Korea enjoys a comparative advantage in electronics, but produces furniture inefficiently, it should export electronics and import furniture from a country that produces furniture more efficiently. This way, both countries in this trade relationship are able to optimize their productive resources for mutual benefit.

Comparative advantage A nation should specialize in the production of a product for which it has a lower opportunity cost and trade for products that it cannot produce as efficiently.

How Is International Trade Measured?

An important measure of international trade is called the **balance of trade,** which is the difference between a nation's exports and imports. U.S. exports continue to lag behind its imports, creating a negative balance of trade, or **deficit** (see figure 4.1). The last time that the United States experienced a positive balance of trade, called a **surplus,** was in 1975.

Balance of trade The difference between a nation's exports and imports.

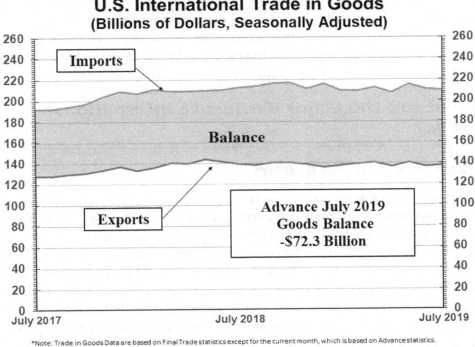

Figure 4.1 U.S. international trade in goods and services

Source: U.S. Census Bureau

Balance of payments
The difference between
the money flowing into
a country and the money
flowing out of it.

The **balance of payments** is another measure of international trade that refers to the difference between the money flowing into the country and the money flowing out of the country (see table 4.2). The balance of payments includes the balance of trade (exports minus imports) and other payments received and made, such as foreign investment, military expenditures, tourism, foreign aid, and other international transactions.

Table 4.2   Balance of payments

Monetary Inflows (+)	Monetary Outflows (−)
• Payments for *exported* goods & services	• Payments for *imported* goods & services
• Expenditures by foreign travelers	• Expenditures by residents traveling outside the country
• Income from foreign investments earned by domestic residents	• Investments by residents in foreign securities and real estate
• Investments from foreign sources	• Payments to foreign governments
• Payments from foreign governments	• Government spending
	• Military Assistance
	• Foreign Aid

Currency **exchange rates** are another way of measuring the comparative strength or weakness of a country's economy in a global context. The exchange rate is the value of one nation's currency relative to the currencies of other nations. When one country borrows from another, the debt must be repaid in the currency of the lender. The exchange rate is a "floating" system, meaning the rates are determined through the forces of supply and demand. Rates also change daily. A currency is considered "strong" if it buys more units of another country's currency than the currency of another country would. For example, the U.S. dollar would be considered "strong" if $1 bought more Japanese yen than 1 euro could buy.

What Are the Major Barriers to International Trade?

Social and Cultural Barriers

Language, cultural values, local customs, and religious attitudes may pose indirect barriers to international trade. **Ethnocentrism**, the belief that one's own culture is superior to other cultures, prevents businesspeople from understanding another culture on its own terms. Excellent market research and a high degree of sensitivity to foreign cultural norms are the best ways to reduce the obstacles that cultural differences may place in the way of doing business abroad. With additional market research, Coca-Cola and McDonald's both could have avoided the temporary setbacks they experienced when they put the Saudi Arabian flag on their packaging, which upset customers because in being crumpled and discarded, it implied disrespect for the Quran.

© granata1111, 2011. Used under license from Shutterstock, Inc.

The flag of Saudi Arabia displays a verse from the Quran. When used on packaging, the consumer will show disrespect for the Quran when the package is crumpled and discarded.

Economic Barriers

Economic barriers to global trade often stem from the relative value of a country's currency. When a nation's currency is strong in comparison to other world currencies, buyers in that country pay less for imports, and foreign investments are cheaper. Citizens of the country with a strong currency can travel to foreign countries on moderate expenses, while conversely, it will be expensive for others to visit from abroad. Domestic producers can be hurt because they must compete against cheaper foreign imports. These conditions result from letting the currency "float," that is, allowing the laws of supply and demand determine the value of the currency. Sometimes however, in order to bolster its domestic industries, a country will devalue its currency, making its products more affordable abroad, and restoring competitive prices to its own products compared to imports for sale to the country's consumers. Another country trying to export to a country whose currency has been devalued may consider the results of the devaluation a barrier to trade because fewer people will want to buy high-priced imports.

Members of the U.S. Congress have over the past 20 years accused China of intentionally undervaluing its currency, a practice they label as an unfair trade policy. By not letting its currency float, they say, China has kept the *yuan* (also known as *renminbi*) artificially weak, resulting in the domination of U.S. markets by cheap Chinese imports. Conversely, U.S. exports to China are more expensive to the Chinese consumer, reducing the level of U.S. exports there and consequently putting U.S. firms out of business.

Another economic barrier to global trade is government involvement in a country's economic system. A high level of government control, as in a command or socialist system, will usually result in a greater number of regulations, taxes, and laws that directly and indirectly restrict international trade.

How Do Laws, International Regulations, and Trade Restrictions Affect International Commerce?

It is clear that some countries enjoy significant advantages over others in the global marketplace. Emerging economies and young industries need support and protection in order to flourish. Trade restrictions of various kinds are designed to protect domestic industries and provide revenues that can be used to further develop and support a domestic economy.

Tariff A tax on imports for the purpose of protecting domestic industry or generating revenue.

The most common of these restrictions is the **tariff,** which is a tax on imports. It is imposed for the primary purpose of protecting domestic industry from foreign competition or for providing the government with more revenue. For example, in 2018 the Trump administration imposed tariffs on steel and aluminum imported from most countries in order to protect these industries. Nontariff trade barriers include the **quota,** which limits the amount of a specific product that can be imported into a country, and the **embargo,** which is a complete ban on the import of certain products or of all trading with a particular country. For example, U.S. companies are barred from trading with Cuba, Iran, and North Korea. In 2015 the Obama administration re-established economic and diplomatic ties with Cuba, but left the 50-year embargo in place.

"Dumping" Predatory pricing tactic in which imported products are sold at prices far below domestic market prices.

In the last few decades, countries have adopted **"anti-dumping" laws** to prevent foreign companies from selling goods at prices lower than domestic market prices. This predatory pricing tactic undermines domestic competition and can lead to the control of a market by foreign entities. Article VI of the **General Agreement on Tariffs and Trade** (GATT) requires a government to show that "there are dumped imports, [that there is] material injury to a domestic industry, and a causal link between the dumped imports and the injury" before imposing anti-dumping laws. The most well-known example of anti-dumping legislation in the United States was the government's 1998 imposition of a tariff on steel imported from Japan and Brazil in response to pricing that was 70% below the "fair market value" of steel in the United States.

There are various arguments to be made against trade restrictions. Tariffs raise the prices on imported goods that may be in high demand. Higher prices on imports restrict consumer choices. The enactment of tariffs, quotas, embargoes, and anti-dumping laws may cause retaliation of the same kind from other countries, limiting export opportunities for domestic businesses. After the US imposed tariffs on hundreds of goods imported from China in 2018, that country retaliated with tariffs on $75 billion worth of U.S. goods and raised duties on American autos. While trade restrictions might protect domestic jobs, they may also result in a loss of jobs that might be created through international business. Because of the opportunities that international trade offers, governments must carefully consider all of the implications of the various types of trade restrictions before making them law.

Foreign Corrupt Practices Act of 1977 law that prohibits payments in exchange for business.

The systems of laws and regulations in effect in different countries may also have the same restrictive effect as tariffs, quotas, and anti-dumping laws. For example, each country or region will have its own anti-trust rules, patent and copyright laws, taxes, product liability laws, and child labor laws, to name just a few of the types of legal issues that can impact business activities. Since U.S. businesses must also follow U.S. laws and regulations in conducting global activities, they can find themselves at a competitive disadvantage when it comes to the use of bribery or gifts to secure contracts. In many countries of the world, this practice is customary and not illegal, but the U.S. Foreign Corrupt Practices Act of 1977 prohibits the payments in exchange for business. In order to promote greater equality of access to global business opportunities, the Organization of Economic Cooperation and Development (OECD) and Transparency International have been working together to strengthen the implementation of anti-bribery measures through education, awareness campaigns, and self-monitoring.

Bureaucratic rules, procedures, and policies pose barriers to trade and can discourage companies from even attempting commerce outside their borders. For example, Mexican truck owners must apply for authority from the Federal Motor Carrier Safety Administration prior to crossing the border into the U.S. Products are frequently damaged during border inspections. Customs offices may be understaffed, which can cause expensive delays and spoilage if the goods are perishable. The sheer number of documents, such as bills of lading, inspection certificates, and other paperwork can make trade time consuming and frustrating. Companies often hire freight forwarders to deal with all of the paperwork involved.

Reducing Barriers to International Trade

In 1947 after the end of World War II, 23 nations signed the treaty called **General Agreement on Tariffs and Trade** (GATT) to promote free trade by reducing or eliminating trade barriers. GATT ensured nondiscrimination, outlined clear procedures, provided guidelines for the negotiation of disputes, and invited the participation of less developed countries in international trade.

The **World Trade Organization (WTO)** was established in Geneva, Switzerland, in 1995 in order to monitor GATT agreements and mediate disputes among its members. WTO has 164 member countries. The goals of WTO are to promote world trade, to settle disputes such as those that develop around product dumping, and to provide a framework for global trade negotiations.

World Trade Organization (WTO) In 1995 the GATT was absorbed by the World Trade Organization.

International Economic Communities

A number of regional economic communities sprang up after the end of World War II in 1945. The purpose of these supranational organizations, some of the largest of which are listed below, is to promote economic growth by removing barriers to trade among the member nations – for example, by setting share price ceilings on certain products and by removing tariffs.

Today's European Union (EU) evolved from the European Economic Community (EEC) of the 1950s. The EU was established by the Treaty of Maastricht in 1993. It includes 28 European nations that have eliminated most product quotas and set uniform tariff levels on products imported and exported within the group. EU member nations are shown in Figure 4.2. In mid-2016 citizens of the United Kingdom voted to leave the EU, also known as "Brexit." Voters felt that membership in the EU threatened national identity and independence.

In 1994 the **North American Free Trade Agreement (NAFTA)** was signed by the United States, Canada, and Mexico to break down tariffs and trade restrictions. NAFTA is a free trade area comprising about one-third of the world's GDP. According to the U.S. free trade representative, each day NAFTA countries conduct nearly US$1.7 billion in trilateral trade. In 2018 the three countries negotiated a new trade pact called the United States-Mexico-Canada Agreement (USMCA).

The United States-Dominican Republic **Central America Free Trade Agreement (CAFTA)** represents another step toward free trade in the western hemisphere. Under this agreement 80% of all tariffs on U.S. goods have been eliminated, with the rest to be phased out over several years. Costa Rica, the Dominican Republic, El Salvador, Guatemala, Honduras, Nicaragua, and the United States are members of the CAFTA, which was formed in 2005.

The **Association of Southeast Asian Nations (ASEAN)**, founded in 1967, is composed of 10 nations: Indonesia, Brunei, Malaysia, Myanmar (Burma), Singapore, Thailand, Philippines, Cambodia, Lao PDR, and Vietnam. The ASEAN group has a population of over 600 million and a GDP of about US$1.8 trillion.

The **Economic Community of West African States (ECOWAS)** was created in 1975 to integrate agricultural policies and facilitate the movement of resources, people, and capital among its 16 members, which include Benin, Côte d'Ivoire, Gambia, Ghana, Guinea, Guinea-Bissau, Liberia, Mali, Niger, Nigeria, Senegal, Sierra Leone, Togo, Burkina Faso, and Cape Verde.

The original goal of the Frontline States, which later became known as the **South African Development Community (SADC)**, was the political liberation of South Africa from white minority rule. In 1992 the purpose of the SADC shifted to include economic integration of the member countries, which had by that time become independent. Currently, SADC has a membership of 15 countries: Angola, Botswana, Comoros Democratic Republic of Congo (DRC), Lesotho, Madagascar, Malawi, Mauritius, Mozambique, Namibia, Seychelles, South Africa, Swaziland, United Republic of Tanzania, Zambia, and Zimbabwe. The combined GDP of the SADC is US$471.1 billion.

MERCOSUR Means Mercado Común del Sur or "Common Market of the South"

Argentina, Brazil, Paraguay, Venezuela (suspended in 2016), and Uruguay are the full member nations comprising **MERCOSUR**, which means *Mercado Común del Sur*, or "Common Market of the South." Founded in 1991, MERCOSUR is the largest trading bloc in South America. Like the other communities, its goals are to eliminate high tariffs, income inequalities, and conflicting technical requirements for bringing products to market.

The **Organization of Petroleum Exporting Countries (OPEC)** was founded in 1960 by Iran, Iraq, Kuwait, Saudi Arabia, and Venezuela to coordinate the policies of its members in order to ensure a steady supply of oil to consumers at prices that would provide income and a fair return on investment to member nations. Currently there are 14 members: Algeria, Angola, Ecuador, Equatorial Guinea, Gabon, Iran, Iraq, Kuwait, Libya, Nigeria, the Republic of the Congo, Saudi Arabia, United Arab Emirates, and Venezuela. Indonesia and Qatar left the group in 2016 and 2018, respectively. The United States and Russia, ranked first and third in oil production, do not belong to OPEC.

The **Organisation of Islamic Cooperation (OIC)** is an intergovernmental organization of 57 member states founded in 1969. Its general purpose is to strengthen political, economic, and cultural ties among member nations. The OIC Charter specifically calls for economic and trade cooperation leading to the establishment of an Islamic Common Market, a goal that has not been realized.

The **World Bank** and the **International Monetary Fund (IMF)** both provide financial assistance and advice. The World Bank is a United Nations agency that provides financial advice and lends money to support projects that build or expand infrastructure to less-developed and developing countries. The IMF promotes trade through financial cooperation, makes short-term loans to member nations to meet expenses, and operates as lender of last resort for troubled nations.

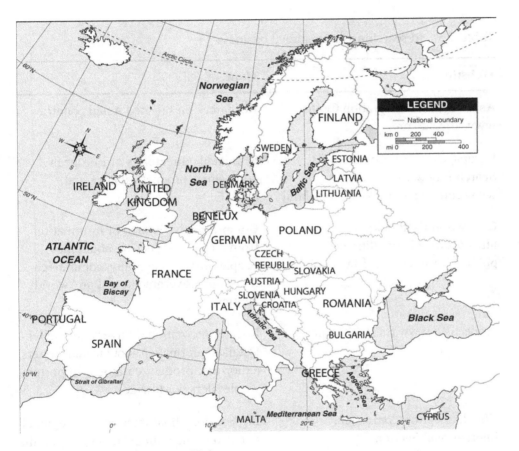

Figure 4.2 The European Union

Considerations in Going Global

While the benefits of expanding into foreign markets are very enticing, companies must carefully consider the decision to "go global" from a number of perspectives before proceeding. Two among the many variables to consider are assessing the demand for a product and adapting the product to the particular needs and culture of the customers in the target market.

A company must first consider whether there is a demand for its product in the host country. Determining international demand may require market research. Table 4.3 provides resources for starting this research. A company anticipating entry into a foreign market may even choose to observe the entry of competitors into that market to gauge demand for its own similar products.

The next consideration is to determine the type and extent of changes to the product that may have to be made in order to adapt to customer needs in the target country or region. Many times the adaptations are connected to culture, as in the case of restaurant offerings. In India, for example, where Hindus do not eat beef, McDonald's serves burgers of chicken, fish, and vegetables, alongside the

Table 4.3 Researching international business

Website	Content
Asia Regional Integration Center www.aric.adb.org	Resources on selected Asian countries
Europages–The European B2B Search Engine: www.europages.co.uk/catalogs.html	Searchable directories of European companies, product catalogs and classifieds
CIA World Factbook: https://www.cia.gov/library/ publications/the-world-factbook/	Comprehensive source of information from a U.S. perspective, about the people, history, economy, communications, and governments of 266 "world entities."
Tradeeasy: www.tradeeasy.com	Locate international buyers and sellers. Detailed information about manufacturers, exporters, product catalogs, importers, wholesalers worldwide
US Chamber of Commerce, International Section: www.uschamber.com/international	Information about international regional initiatives, international trade policies, the work of the U.S. Chamber of Commerce
US Commercial Service: http://trade.gov/cs	The U.S. Commercial Service helps companies get started in over 80 countries of the world with market intelligence, business matchmaking, trade counseling, and trade advocacy
World Trade Organization (WTO): www.wto.org	Trade statistics, economic research and analysis, international trade and tariff data

CIA World Factbook
U.S. perspective on 266 "world entities" at www.cia.gov

Maharaja Mac—two all-mutton patties, special sauce, lettuce, cheese, pickles, onions, on a sesame seed bun. In Saudi Arabia, McDonald's serves the *McArabia*, made with grilled chicken or grilled *kafta* (ground beef with spices) accompanied by tomatoes, onions, and garlic mayonnaise, wrapped in Arabic style pita bread. In Morocco McDonald's introduced the *Recette Moutarde* (mustard burger on *ciabatta* bread) in 2006.

Product modifications can also be linked to the type and level of technology in the target region. For example, some regions of the world, such as North Africa and France, use 220 volts as the standard electrical voltage. Products originating in countries where 120 volts is the standard must be wired differently and meet different safety standards. Products built to rely on electricity from wall current may have to be adapted for customers living in places where electrical power is limited to batteries. The literacy level of the typical customer may require a company to modify the design of a product or the instructions that accompany it. These and other factors have major implications for the costs of production, which may prevent a company from realizing the savings from economies of scale that expanding into global markets might produce.

A further consideration is the general business climate in the countries or region in which a company intends to do business. In some countries bureaucratic obstacles and high costs limit the number of registered businesses and provide fertile opportunities for corruption. The World Bank has found that when there are a large number of registered businesses, known as business density, the entire economy benefits. A government and legal system that is welcoming to domestic business is likely to be more open to global business opportunities. Table 4.4 shows ten countries with the most favorable conditions for new business startups. The World Bank Group ranked the United States 53rd out of 100 countries in 2018.

Ways of Entering the International Marketplace

A firm may enter the global marketplace at one of five different levels of involvement. A decision about which level to choose balances the size of the financial commitment required, the overall level of risk, and the degree of control the company will retain, with the potential for profit. Figure 4.3 illustrates that low-risk entry methods require less of a financial investment, little control, and a low level of risk, but do not offer the profit potential of riskier, more expensive methods.

Exporting or **importing** products represents a relatively low-risk method of entering international markets. The exporting firm manufactures its products in its home country and exports them for sale in foreign markets. In many cases, the firm opens its own sales offices in foreign countries. These offices or branches operate as extensions of the company's own distribution system. In this scheme of operation, the company is in complete control of production, distribution, and marketing, thus limiting its risk. The exporting company loses some control if it decides to sell its products to an export-import merchant, who acts like a wholesaler, or to an export-import agent, who sells the product to foreign intermediaries.

Table 4.4 Top Ten countries for business startups compared with United States

Country	Rank in 2018	Starting a business score	Procedures (number)	Time (days)	Cost (% of income per capita)	(Per capita income ($)
New Zealand	1	99.96	1	0.5	0.2	42,249.00
Georgia	2	99.34	1	2.0	2.0	4,345.52
Canada	3	98.23	2	1.5	0.3	43,045.61
Singapore	4	98.23	2	1.8	0.4	64,567.00
Hong Kong	5	98.15	2	3.0	1.1	48,684.28
Jamaica	6	97.35	2	3.0	4.4	5,617.66
Australia	7	96.47	3	2.5	0.7	57,821.51
Armenia	8	96.21	3	3.5	0.8	1,453.62
Azerbaijan	9	96.14	3	3.5	1.3	4,780.10
Ireland	10	95.91	3	5.0	0.1	79,500.00
The United States	53	91.23	6	6.5	1.0	59,484.00

Sources: World Bank at www.doingbusiness.org/en/data/exploretopics/starting-a-business and CEIC Data at www.ceicdata.com.

Procedures means procedures officially required, or commonly done in practice, for an entrepreneur to start up and formally operate an industrial or commercial business.

Time means median duration (in days) that incorporation lawyers or notaries indicate is necessary in practice to complete a procedure with minimum follow-up with government agencies and no unofficial payments.

Cost means percentage of the economy's income per capita. It includes all official fees and fees for legal or professional services if such services are required by law or commonly used in practice.

Per capita income means average income earned per person in a specified year.

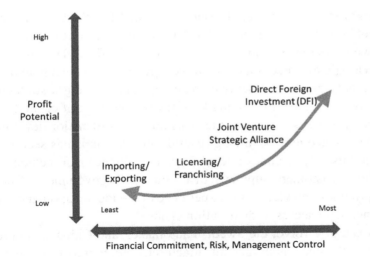

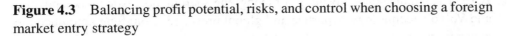

Figure 4.3   Balancing profit potential, risks, and control when choosing a foreign market entry strategy

Licensing is a contractual agreement whereby one company (the licensor) makes an asset available to another company (the licensee) in exchange for royalties, license fees, or some other form of compensation. In return for paying a licensing fee, the licensee may use the licensor's manufacturing process, its trademark, patent, and trade secrets. Licensing is also a low-risk method of entering foreign markets, but the licensor gives up more control over how the product is marketed and serviced, than in exporting. This loss of control can have a negative impact on an international brand name if the licensee cannot live up to the reputation of the brand. An unscrupulous licensee could steal trade secrets and create "knock-offs" or establish another competitive brand.

Pharmaceutical firms frequently use licensing as an efficient and profitable way to enter foreign markets, licensing the production and distribution of a patented drug to local firms. For example, a large U.S.-based drug company paid French BioAlliance Pharma US$20 million for a license to make and distribute its latest cancer drug. BioAlliance Pharma will receive royalties on all sales of the drug in the United States.

A **joint venture** is an entry strategy for a single target country in which the partners share ownership of a newly created business entity. The new company is co-owned to some degree by each of the partners and is formed to operate for a specific period of time. The challenge is to find a local partner in the host nation to share the operation costs of the business.

General Motors has been in a 50-50 joint venture with Russian automaker Avtovaz since 2001. GM-Avtovaz produces the Chevrolet Niva. The higher risk of the joint venture strategy is illustrated by the fact that in 2006 production was halted when the venture was taken over by a government-owned company, slowing planned expansion. Starbucks' joint venture with the Indian company Tata Global

Beverages is another example. The venture is called Tata Starbucks Private Ltd. and has 73 coffee shops throughout India. This has been a successful project, though it took two years longer than anticipated to open the first 50 shops.

Strategic alliance The Star alliance of 27 airlines is an example of a cooperative agreement among competitors to create competitive advantage.

A **strategic alliance** is a cooperative agreement between potential or actual competitors to create competitive advantage. By forming a strategic alliance, a company gains entry to new markets, takes advantage of capabilities that the other firm possesses, or shares the risks and costs of major development projects. The alliance may be among several foreign companies seeking to enter a market and usually includes a local firm. The alliance can include a variety of stakeholders: customers, suppliers, distributors, and governments. The local firm usually provides knowledge and experience of the local market and may provide the alliance with access to distribution channels.

For example, Volvo, the Swedish automaker, and China's Dongfeng Motor Group, a well-established truck manufacturer, entered into a strategic alliance in 2015. The alliance took advantage of Dongfeng's strong domestic market position and Volvo's technology expertise and global presence. Dongfeng announced its new generation of trucks in early 2019, noting that the new Dongfeng KL and KR models were products of five years of research and development. This successful strategic alliance has improved Dongfeng's product reliability and helped Volvo gain a foothold in the Chinese commercial vehicle marketplace.

In forming a strategic alliance among competitors, a company takes a higher risk than in other methods of foreign entry. Among these risks is loss of operational control, especially if other partners are considerably larger. Alliance partners must be willing to share considerable amounts of information and expertise. Twenty-seven airlines form the Star alliance. This strategic alliance sets standards for customer service, security, and infrastructure that must be met by all of its members, which include Lufthansa, United, Continental Airlines, Air Canada, and Air China. This alliance of international airlines integrates member schedules and mileage programs, helping the partners realize economies of scale and providing better service to customers.

It is vitally important for companies seeking to enter foreign markets through an alliance to select partners with care. Companies seeking to form alliances should become well acquainted with potential partners before commitment, and obtain as much information as possible about potential partners by collecting data from informed third parties, such as former partners, investment bankers, and former employees.

The most risky method, but one in which the company has complete control, is the **wholly owned overseas division** or **subsidiary**. This form of entry is also known as direct foreign investment (DFI). The parent company sets up an independent company in a foreign country. The parent company either buys an existing company and allows it to operate on its own, or starts a new company on foreign soil. A recent example is the Ford Motor Co. expansion into Morocco in North Africa. Citing Morocco's skilled labor force and excellent infrastructure, Ford now supplies its plants in Spain and Germany with parts from Morocco. Figure 4.4 shows where U.S. companies make direct foreign investments and compares this activity to the DFI of other countries in U.S. firms.

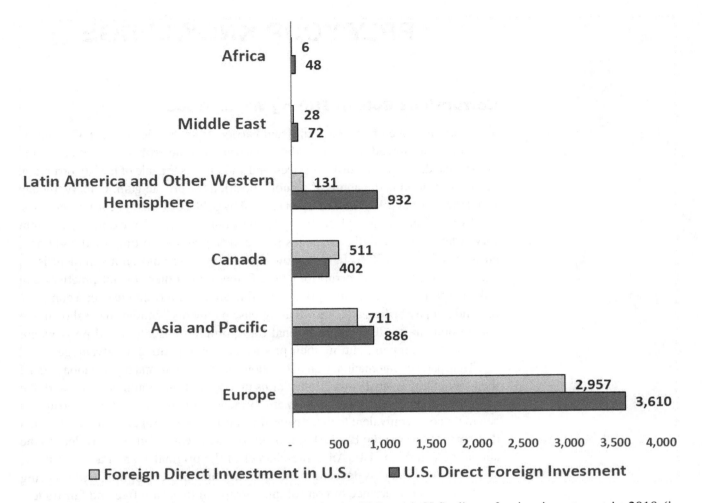

Figure 4.4 Comparison of foreign investment in the U.S. with U.S. direct foreign investment in 2018 (in billions of dollars)

Source: U.S. Department of Commerce Bureau of Economic Analysis, International Economic Accounts, http:www.bea.gov

APPLY YOUR KNOWLEDGE

Corruption's Role in Stifling World Trade

Tariffs are just one of several significant barriers to international trade. Corruption is another widespread factor that "deters international investment, stifles economic growth and development, distorts prices, and undermines the rule of law" (Corruption, n.d.). Corruption is the abuse of a public position for private gain. Bribery, money laundering, "kickbacks," and extortion enacted by public officials are corrupt activities.

Corruption can take place at any level of bureaucracy. For example, a freight forwarder (a company that arranges for importing and exporting goods) giving a customs official $100 to falsely show that duties were paid on a shipment is an example of a common corrupt practice. Bribery and other corrupt practices can reduce a company's costs and prices, creating an unfair advantage over a company that did not pay bribes, also known as "grease payments." Studies have shown that some companies will incur additional transportation costs to avoid ports where corruption is rampant, putting their products at a competitive disadvantage.

Transparency International, an international nongovernmental organization leading the global fight against corruption, claims that corruption should be addressed like any other trade barrier because it is an obstacle to open competition. Corruption can incur costs equivalent to those caused by tariffs. The European Union estimated that corruption cost the EU 120 million euros each year, a figure equivalent to the annual budget of the EU. An entire chapter of the original Trans-Pacific Partnership trade agreement is devoted to transparency and anti-corruption, underscoring the enormous importance of controlling corruption to ensure free and fair trade.

Transparency International further contends that any international trade agreement must fully disclose the processes that led to its conclusion, its anti-corruption clauses, and the means by which the pact will be implemented and enforced.

Knowledge Application Questions

1. Using Transparency International's web-based Corruption Perceptions Index for the most recent year, find an ethical country to compare with an unethical one, Denmark with Mexico, for example. Download the "Global map graphic and results table" at www.transparency.org/cpi2018#downloads

2. Research economic, legal, regulatory, and political barriers that would affect international trade in each country. The "Read More About This Country" feature at The Heritage Foundation's Index of Economic Freedom interactive web page will help you (www.heritage.org/index/ranking).

3. Write a brief report on what you found out about each country.

Source

Corruption n.d. Accessed October 10, 2019. https://www.export.gov/article?id=Corruption.

QUIZ YOURSELF

Without looking back at the chapter, choose the best answer to each of the questions below. Answers are in the back of the textbook before the Index. Review the chapter to find out why you missed any questions.

1. Why do companies engage in international trade?
    a. To find new markets for their goods and services
    b. To locate new sources of raw materials
    c. To reduce risk
    d. To realize economies of scale, which helps reduce prices
    e. All of the above

2. Which of the following statements is/are true?
    a. The United States cannot produce coffee efficiently, but it produces pharmaceuticals efficiently. Therefore, the opportunity cost of producing pharmaceuticals is lower than that for coffee.
    b. The United States has an absolute advantage in the production of plastic toys.
    c. Brazil has an absolute advantage in coffee.
    d. The theory of comparative advantage says that a country should specialize in the production of goods that it produces efficiently and trade for goods that it manufactures less efficiently.
    e. Statements a, c, and d are all true.

3. China's ability to produce steel more cheaply than almost any other country is an example of
    a. a comparative advantage.
    b. specialization.
    c. an acquired absolute advantage.
    d. predatory trade tactics.
    e. a command economy.

4. The _____ is a measure of international trade that refers to the difference between money flowing into the country and money flowing out of the country.
    a. balance of trade
    b. deficit
    c. balance of investment
    d. balance of payments
    e. None of the above

5. Jurgen must decide if he wants to be paid in dollars or euros for his new job in London. He wants to invest in a Japanese company, so he will have to make his investment in Japanese yen. A dollar will purchase 109.33 yen and the euro will purchase 124.93 yen. Jurgen should choose to be paid
   a. in dollars because the dollar is the world's standard currency.
   b. in yen because he will receive thousands of yen.
   c. in euros because it is the stronger currency.
   d. in dollars because the UK plans to leave the the European Union.
   e. in pounds because Jurgen will be living in London.

6. Ford purchased Volvo. What does this illustrate?
   a. Social responsibility
   b. Licensing arrangement
   c. Direct foreign investment
   d. Strategic alliance
   e. Joint venture

7. The idea that American-made goods are superior to goods of the same type produced in other countries is an example of
   a. specialization.
   b. a self-evident fact.
   c. ethnocentrism.
   d. the "most-favored nation" clause.
   e. eccentricity.

8. Ford Motor Company, Mazda Motor Corporation, and Matsushita Electrical Industrial Company formed a _____ to make heating and cooling units in Japan for Mazda cars beginning in 1988. The new company's heating and cooling units may also be used in Ford's cars.
   a. sales branch
   b. joint venture
   c. subsidiary
   d. licensing agreement
   e. sole proprietorship

9. One complaint that the United States has against China is that it will not let the value of its currency be determined by supply and demand as other countries do. Instead, the Chinese government frequently devalues its currency. The result is
    a. prices on domestic goods become lower than those of imported goods.
    b. Chinese exports become cheaper to foreign markets.
    c. visiting China becomes more expensive for foreign visitors.
    d. the balance of trade between China and the US becomes lopsided.
    e. all of the foregoing options.

10. The trilateral trade agreement between Canada, Mexico, and the United States that replaces NAFTA is
    a. the TPP.
    b. the GATT.
    c. OAS.
    d. the USMCA.
    e. the Kyoto Protocol.

Goal Setting
Specific
Measurable
Achievable
Realistic
Timely

Dusit/Shutterstock

CHAPTER 5

Perspectives on the Management Process

The Management Process

Management is a process that coordinates the activities of planning, organizing, leading, and controlling people, time, and other resources in order to achieve organizational goals effectively and efficiently (see figure 5.1).

Planning

Of the four management functions—planning, organizing, leading, and controlling— planning is the most important because the other functions depend to a great extent on having a good plan in place. Planning is the process of setting performance objectives and determining what actions should be taken to achieve them. It is looking ahead to chart the best courses of future action. Planning helps reduce uncertainty, maintain stability in the organization, and adapt to changes in the external environment. This way, the firm improves its time management in order to become more competitive. It is a continuous process.

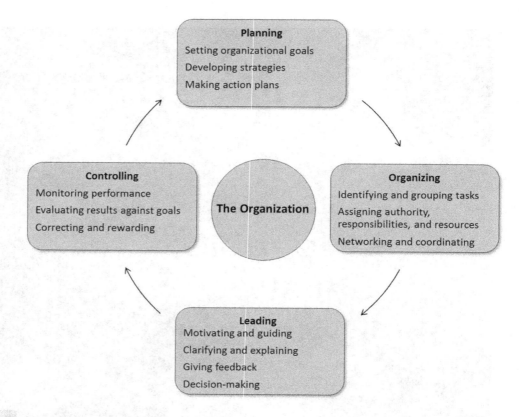

Figure 5.1 The management process

Management Process that coordinates planning, organizing, leading, and controlling people, time, and other resources to achieve organizational goals.

Setting Organizational Goals

Organizational goals are the broad, long-term accomplishments that, if attained, will help the organization achieve its vision. Goals differ from company to company, depending on the firm's purpose: businesses seek profits, universities seek to discover and transmit new knowledge, and government agencies seek to set and enforce public policy. Well-articulated and widely communicated goals are essential to effective management.

Although the terms *goals* and *objectives* are often used interchangeably, **organizational objectives** usually refer to short-term aims that will help attain one or more goals, if met successfully. When developing organizational goals, many managers apply criteria expressed in the acronym **SMART**:

SMART objectives Are specific, measurable, achievable, realistic, and time-bound

Specific: Goals are clear. Vague statements have been eliminated. Clear goals have a much greater chance of being accomplished than vague ones.

Measurable: The goals can be assessed. Results can be quantified or in some way observed.

Achievable: You are able to figure out ways you can make the goals come true. You have, or can obtain, the necessary resources.

Realistic: They are "doable" (there is a "will").

Time-bound: They should be grounded within a time frame. A sense of urgency cannot be created if there is no time frame. "Someday" does not motivate others to do the tasks necessary to achieve the goal.

The terms *vision* and *mission* are used for describing the strategic direction of an organization. **Organizational vision** describes an organization's dreams and aspirations. It is a picture of where the organization wants to go and how it will get there. The vision statement reflects the organization's future.

An **organization's mission**, in contrast to its vision, is oriented toward the present. The mission is the purpose of the organization, the reason why it exists. The organization's mission is the basis for strategic goals and plans, which are usually developed at the highest levels of the organization. Walmart's mission, for instance, is to help people save money so they can live better.

A mission statement may evolve over time as the organization adjusts its purpose to changing customer needs and other external and internal variables. For example, in 2004, Facebook, the largest social networking Internet site in the world, stated its mission as, "The facebook is an online directory that **connects people through social networks at colleges**." In 2006, the site had modified its name to just "Facebook" and stated the following as its mission: "Facebook is **a social utility that connects you with the people around you.**" By 2019, its mission read, "Facebook **gives people the power** to build community and **bring the world closer together**. The evolution of the Facebook mission traces the change in the concept of Facebook from a directory to a social utility to a tool for social and political change. The mission was adapted to changes in its user base as different types of people—not just college students—found Facebook useful for their own communication.

> *Mission statement*
> *Walmart's mission is to help people save money so they can live better.*

Developing Strategies and Making Plans of Action

The planning process starts by asking and answering these questions:

- Where are we now?
- Where do we want to go?
- How are we going to get there?
- By whom are the objectives of the organization to be implemented?
- When do we start the process?

The first two questions, "Where are we now?" and "Where do we want to go?" can be answered by completing a **SWOT analysis**, which identifies the organization's strengths, weaknesses, opportunities, and the threats that it faces. Strengths and weaknesses are internal to the firm and can be easily assessed and corrected. Opportunities and threats are external to the company and less controllable, thus less easy to anticipate with accuracy. A thorough and realistic SWOT analysis helps a company build on its strengths, minimize its weaknesses, take advantage of opportunities, and compensate for threats. Basic questions to be answered by the SWOT analysis are shown in table 5.1.

Strengths and weaknesses include:

- Patents and copyrights/lack of patent and copyright protection
- Strong/weak brand recognition
- Good/poor location
- Access/lack of access to distribution networks

- Access/lack of access to natural resources
- High/low employee morale

Opportunities and threats include:

- Unmet customer needs in the marketplace/shifting customer preferences for the firm's products or services
- New technologies/availability of substitutes for the company's products or services
- Relaxed regulations, laws, or policies/new or harsher regulations, laws, or policies
- Lifting of trade barriers/increased trade barriers

Table 5.1   SWOT analysis matrix

	Strengths	**Weaknesses**
Organizational (internal)	<ul><li>What does our company do best?</li><li>What advantages do we have?</li><li>Why will customers purchase our product or service over another?</li><li>What resources do we have access to that might be unique?</li></ul>	<ul><li>What are others (customers, suppliers, competitors, for example) likely to see as our weaknesses?</li><li>In what aspects of our business do we have fewer or no resources to draw on?</li><li>Does our management team lack skills, knowledge, or abilities?</li></ul>
	Opportunities	**Threats**
Environmental (external)	<ul><li>What opportunities are open to us? For example, is there a need that is not being filled, or filled well? Has a competitor gone out of business? Have we received funds that we can use to start a business? Has a franchise become available?</li><li>What trends could we take advantage of?</li><li>Which strengths do we have that we could use to create opportunities?</li></ul>	<ul><li>What current and future events, forces, situations could threaten the success of our company?</li><li>What do our competitors do that could threaten or limit our success?</li><li>What other external factors could threaten or limit our company's success?</li><li>What weaknesses do we have that could expose our business to threats from the environment?</li></ul>

Types of Plans

Organizations develop and implement four types of plans: strategic, tactical, operational, and contingency (see figure 5.2). Top managers are responsible for **strategic planning**, which is the process of setting broad long-range goals and making decisions about resource allocations, company priorities, and steps needed to meet those goals. Middle managers formulate tactical plans, which are short-range plans concerned with implementing specific aspects of a company's strategic plans. Operational plans are made at the supervisory management level, and they set short-term targets for daily, weekly, or monthly performance. Figure 5.3 shows examples of a company's goals at the strategic, tactical, and operational levels.

A fourth type, **contingency planning**, can be done at any level. Contingency is another word for a situation that was not planned for. A contingency plan, also known as a backup plan, identifies in advance important aspects of a business or its market that might change, and suggests ways in which a company will respond to these changes, should they occur.

Crisis management could be considered a special type of contingency planning. An emergency plan describes the methods that an organization will use in dealing with emergencies. For example, many universities now publish on the Internet a detailed plan for coping with a disaster such as a tornado or earthquake or with an epidemic such as the avian flu. Their plans describe how the immediate crisis will be dealt with as well as how the consequences will be managed, for example, for interruptions in financial aid, and regarding the completion of coursework for a grade.

> **Strategic planning**
> *Setting broad long-range goals, identifying company priorities, and allocating resources to achieve the goals.*

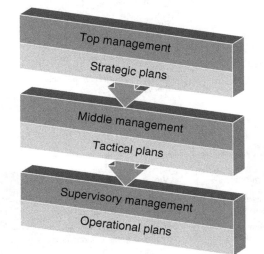

Figure 5.2 Organizational planning

Organizing

Organizing is the process of creating a structure that enables people to work together effectively toward the organization's goals.

> **Organizing** *Process of creating a structure that enables people to work together to achieve the organization's goals.*

Identifying and Grouping Tasks

Managers must determine all of the tasks and activities involved in producing their firm's product or service. They must then group these tasks into logical units of work and arrange the work in a structure that will allow for coordination and control of work flow.

Assigning Authority, Responsibilities, and Resources

After identifying and grouping tasks, managers then identify the job or positions that are needed in order to accomplish the tasks. The resources, such as budgets, materials, space, and equipment needed to accomplish the tasks, are allocated to the work units. The next step is to set the authority relationships, or reporting lines. In Chapter 6 the design of the organizational structure will be discussed more fully. At this point, it is sufficient to understand that in a mature organization there are usually three levels of management. Top management – the highest level – includes titles like chief executive officer (CEO), chief operating officer (COO), chief financial officer (CFO). Examples of middle management titles are plant

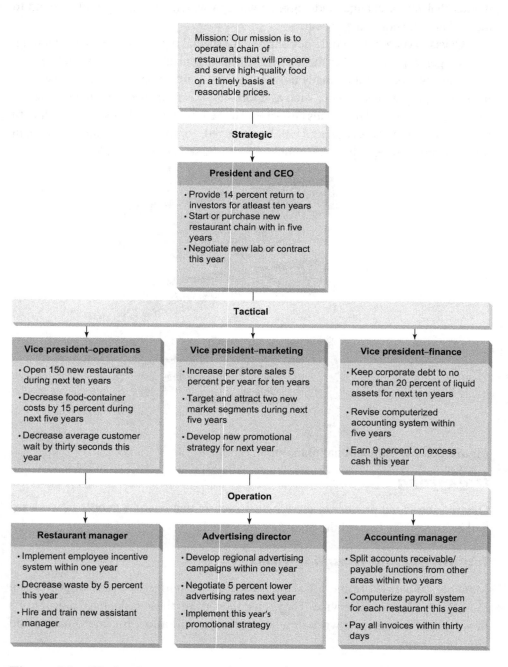

Figure 5.3 Kinds of organizational goals for a regional fast-food chain

Source: From Griffin *Management*, 9E. Copyright © 2008 South-Western, a part of Cengage Learning, Inc. Reproduced by permission. www.cengage.com/permissions

manager, division chief, branch manager. Supervisory, or first-line management, titles include supervisor, department heads, or section leaders.

Leading

Organizations need strong, effective leadership (**leading**) at all levels in order to meet goals and remain competitive. Leadership involves (a) motivating and guiding; (b) clarifying and explaining; (c) giving feedback; and (d) decision-making.

It is clear that leaders must have strong communication skills in order to successfully influence others to achieve the objectives of the organization. Leaders also show group members, often by setting an example, how they can reach their goals. Managers are responsible for directing employees on a daily basis as the employees carry out the plans and work within the structure created by management.

Leadership Styles

Each individual who is placed in a leadership role usually exhibits a consistent pattern of behavior when engaged in the activities of leading. This pattern of behavior is known as **leadership style**. One's leadership style can have a significant impact on organizational performance. Three different general patterns of behavior have been found to accurately describe most leaders. The three styles, as shown in figure 5.4, are really positions on a continuum that has as its two endpoints **task-** and **achievement-oriented**. Task-oriented means that the leader's primary focus is on getting employees to accomplish routine tasks. Achievement-oriented means that the leader's focus is on setting challenging goals, which may often involve employees in accomplishing many complex tasks without direct supervision.

Leadership styles
Leadership styles range from task-oriented to achievement-oriented.

The **autocratic leader** is task-oriented, making decisions without consulting employees. The autocratic leader tells employees what to do and is unconcerned with employee attitudes toward decisions. The autocratic leadership style is exhibited by military officers and sometimes by production-line supervisors. In the middle of the continuum of leadership styles is the **democratic leadership** style, also known as **participative leadership**. The democratic leader involves employees in decisions, delegates decisions to subordinates, and asks employees for suggestions. Democratic leaders will make the final decision after hearing all perspectives. At the furthest end of the continuum is the **free-rein**, also called *laissez-faire*, style of leadership, in which employees have complete authority and control to accomplish organizational goals.

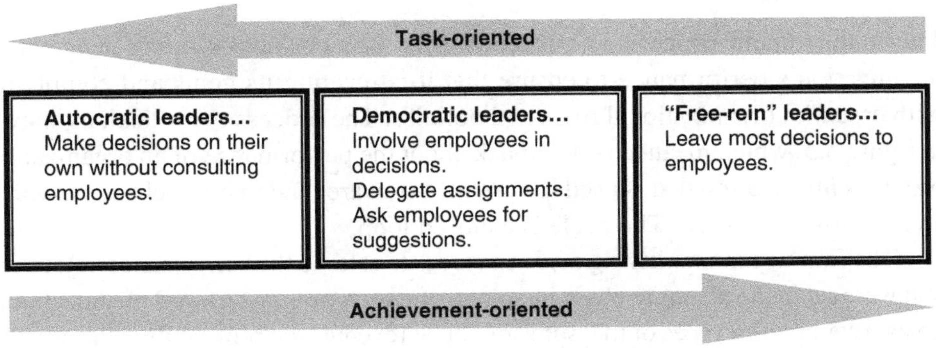

Figure 5.4 Leadership continuum

The effective leader chooses the style of leadership that best complements the skill level of the employees, the nature of the tasks that are to be done, and their need for achievement.

The **autocratic leadership** style, or directive approach, is most successful in leading employees who are less skilled, confined to performing routine tasks and jobs, and less interested in achievement. They seek direction and guidance, want to know exactly what is expected of them, and how they will be evaluated. An advantage of the autocratic leadership style is that it offers control and an efficient way to accomplish goals. For this reason it may be the best choice for a new business, leading a company through challenging times or a crisis, or for bringing uncooperative units into line. Highly skilled achievement-oriented employees, however, respond very negatively to an autocratic leadership style.

The **democratic leadership** style works well with highly skilled and experienced workers. The democratic leadership style enhances teamwork and collaboration. It is a good style to adopt when implementing operational changes or when there are problems to resolve within the organization or group. A disadvantage of the democratic leadership style is that it can take longer for decisions to be made.

Free-rein leadership is called for when employees will be expected to solve unique and complex problems, for example, as in the case of scientists. When an employee is highly skilled and possesses specialized expertise, the leader should step back and let the employee lead. In general, this type of employee has a high need for achievement and possesses an internal motivational drive. The key to success with this leadership style is to select employees who share the values of the organization. The organizational values and norms will guide them toward accomplishing its goals.

Servant leadership is a leadership style that has been widely adopted in the 21st century. The underlying philosophy is that the leader's main goal is to serve the employees. The leader shares power and strives to create an environment in which every employee will achieve his or her potential. The organizational outcome is the employees' increased commitment to and engagement in the company's success. Marriott International Hotels, Starbucks, and Nordstroms have embraced servant leadership.

Controlling

Controlling Continuous monitoring of performance directed at achieving goals while complying with rules and policies.

The management process of **controlling** is the continuous monitoring of an organization's performance to ensure that it is meeting its goals and complying with essential organizational rules and policies. The process is cyclical, as shown in figure 5.5, which means that feedback about the performance of an organization provides information that is used to correct, to reward, and to make changes, which are, in turn, monitored. The cycle is a closed loop.

The first step in monitoring performance is to refer to the performance objectives that were set in the planning phase in order to measure progress toward organizational goals. Examples of types of measures might be revenue and profitability, the amount of time that should be spent in assembling a product, or maximum customer service wait times. The nature of the standards will depend on the business function being monitored and the level of management controlling the activity. **Benchmarking** is a common way of setting standards. By looking at practices in use by other companies and industries, a firm can develop a reasonable set of standards of its own. Over time, the company may adjust its benchmarks based on its own performance criteria. Quality is another standard that can be used in monitoring performance. The **International Organization for Standardization (ISO)** publishes a set of highly reliable quality standards that can be used in monitoring both product and service quality.

Whatever standard is used, in order to be useful it should be specific, attainable, and measurable. For example, a standard such as, "Customers will not wait in line longer than 3 minutes at the express check-out during the hours of 4–6 pm" is specific, attainable, and measurable.

The next step in monitoring performance is to collect and organize data so that performance can be measured. Data can be collected in a variety of ways, and multiple data collection methods should be used in order to gain a complete picture of the performance being studied. Direct observation, as when a manager walks through a factory or a retail store, is one simple method that provides qualitative details that can help explain production or sales figures shown in reports. Closely related to direct observation are video and audio recordings of performance. The most common method of collecting data is by entering data into a computer system, then organizing it into weekly, monthly, or annual reports.

Managers then compare actual performance with standards and goals, look for patterns and deviations, and decide which patterns and deviations are critical and which ones can be ignored. After evaluating performance results, the manager must determine the causes of both lack of performance and excellent performance so that appropriate correction and rewards can be put in place. Some typical causes of inadequate organizational performance are poor planning, lack of training, insufficient coordination, ineffective supervision and communication, lack of resources, and poor implementation of plans. When the manager takes action, the manager is both completing and starting the cyclical process of controlling.

Benchmarking Way of setting standards by looking at practices in use by other companies and industries to develop a reasonable set of standards of its own.

International Organization for Standardization (ISO) publishes a set of highly reliable quality standards that can be used in monitoring both product and service quality.

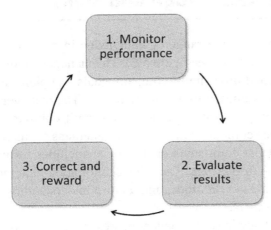

Figure 5.5   Management process of controlling

Levels of Management

Three distinct levels of management were mentioned earlier in this chapter in connection with organizational planning: first-level managers (also known as supervisory management), middle managers, and top management. Each level carries with it a unique set of challenges, yet managers at any level engage in all of the processes of management just described, and must possess the same set of essential management skills.

First-level managers are responsible for the work of non-managerial employees. They oversee the performance of the tasks fundamental to the production and delivery of the firm's products and services. Supervisors are in constant communication with their subordinates and therefore are the first to know about problems and conflicts. It is up to the supervisor to act as the interface between management and the rest of the employees. The supervisor is the manager who is most directly responsible for managing resources, such as supplies and machinery. Examples of titles that indicate first-level management positions are foreman, shift boss, sergeant, section head, office manager, account manager, ward nurse.

Middle managers are buffers between top managers and supervisors. They prepare information for top managers to use in decision-making and they communicate decisions to supervisors. In fact, middle managers spend 90% of their time on oral communication. Middle managers coordinate the work of supervisors, and they identify problems and develop innovative courses of action. Typical middle manager titles include: manager, "director of," department head, division head, dean, district manager, regional manager, plant manager, army officer (from lieutenant to colonel), administrator (public official).

Top managers may also be called **executives**. They decide the strategic direction of the organization and how it will achieve its goals. They oversee the overall planning of the organization. A top manager has the authority to buy another company or expand the business. Executive titles include chairperson of the board, corporate director, president, corporate vice president, corporate treasurer, CEO, chief financial officer, army general, secretary of state.

Managerial Knowledge and Skills

A manager requires a wide range of knowledge in order to successfully plan, organize, control, and lead (see figure 5.6). The manager should be well versed in company policies and procedures, company goals and plans, and the company's culture—that is, its values, norms, and traditions. The manager needs knowledge external to the company too, in order to interpret company goals in a larger context and enhance communication of goals and plans to subordinates and peers. Knowledge about the company's environment includes information about the type of industry the firm is part of and the technology of that industry, familiarity with key personalities in the trade, and a close understanding of the company's suppliers and customers.

In addition to knowledge, managers possess three types of managerial skills. **Technical skills** are the abilities to perform specialized tasks. These skills are developed through a combination of education and experience. Technical skills are

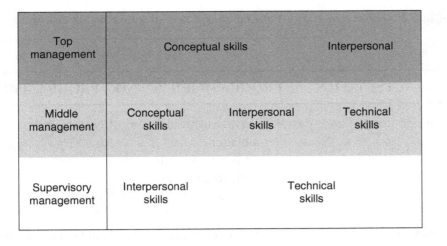

Top management	Conceptual skills		Interpersonal
Middle management	Conceptual skills	Interpersonal skills	Technical skills
Supervisory management	Interpersonal skills	Technical skills	

Figure 5.6 Importance of types of management skills to different levels of management

especially important for first-line managers because they spend most of their time with the day-to-day operations of the production system. Having **interpersonal skills** means being able to understand, communicate, and motivate people inside and outside the organization. These skills enable the manager to work with suppliers, customers, investors, and others who are not part of the organization. Put simply, good interpersonal skills allow a manager to successfully get along with everybody. As mentioned earlier, managers spend most of their time communicating with subordinates, peers, and higher level managers, so it is easy to see why interpersonal skills are so important to managing effectively, and to a manager's chances of being promoted.

    Conceptual skills allow a manager to see an overall view of a situation or an organization. Having conceptual skills means that a manager understands how the organization interacts with its environment and how the various parts of the organization interact with each other. This understanding allows a manager to understand the impact that change in one part of the organization or its environment will have on another part of either system, sometimes known as the "butterfly effect." When Jack Welch re-engineered General Electric in the 1980s he was displaying conceptual skills. He shut plants, pared payrolls, and eliminated non-performing products. Conceptual skills are considered a priority for top-level management because of their contact with the world outside the company.

Conceptual skills
Understanding how the organization interacts with its environment and how parts of the organization interact with each other.

Managerial Decision-Making

Another set of skills that all managers must possess in order to be effective is **decision-making skills**. Decision-making is a human activity that managers do in the face of the choices they must evaluate in order to select the one that gives a high-quality outcome. In general, there are two types of decision-making: **programmed** and **non-programmed**.

    Programmed decision-making works best in dealing with structured problems. Structured problems are easily defined, common, and routine. The structured problem

Table 5.2 Comparison of programmed and non-programmed decisions

	DECISIONS	
CHARACTERISTICS	**PROGRAMMED**	**NON-PROGRAMMED**
Nature of problem	• Well-structured situation, predictable, well-defined decision criteria	• Ill-structured
Frequency	• Frequent, routine, repetitive	• Unique, nonroutine
Information	• Readily available, complete and well-defined	• Not available, very ambiguous and incomplete
Time frame to solve problem	• Short period of time to come to a decision	• Requires long period of time because the challenge faced is new • No "cut and dried" solution"
Solution based on	• Habit or established policies, rules, and procedures the firm relies on	• Subjective judgment, intuition, and creativity (may use scientific solutions)
Decision-maker	• Lower-level managers (usually alone)	• Upper-level managers (usually in groups) • May involve strategic planning
Decision-making technique	• Computerized solutions, capital budgeting, management science	• Intuition, judgment, creativity

can be solved with pre-programmed decisions, for example, an algorithm that is based on the application of rules and yes-no responses at programmed decision points. Pre-programmed decision-making is common at the supervisory level of management.

Non-programmed decisions must be used to address unstructured problems, which involve complex, unique problems or opportunities with important consequences for the organization. Moving up the hierarchy of management levels, managers must consider external variables not under their control, so that non-programmed decisions become prevalent. Non-programmed decisions are handled using techniques that depend on judgment, intuition, and creativity. See table 5.2 for a comparison of these two types of decision-making.

Although few unstructured problems allow a manager to strictly adhere to a **rational decision-making** model, it is nevertheless extremely useful to use the model to guide the process. The rational decision-making process (see figure 5.7) starts with the *recognition of a problem or an opportunity*. For example, while reviewing a monthly report, a regional sales manager notices a 15% decrease in the total sales made by one of the sales representatives. The decrease is a *stimulus* that indicates that a decision is called for. The next step is to *generate alternatives*. The alternatives should be linked to the cause of the stimulus, and several creative alternatives should be developed. Alternatives in this case might be to wait and see what happens next month, schedule a day to ride along with the sales representative, recommend delayed payment of a bonus that the sales representative had earned for a prior month.

Rational decision-making model Six-step process that guides managers confronting structured and unstructured problems.

An important concept related to the rational decision-making model is that of **bounded rationality**, which is the idea that rationality is limited by the information available to the decision-maker, his or her cognitive capacity, and the time they have to make the decision. These variables affect the quality of a decision. For example, you may have thoroughly researched the purchase of an expensive appliance, but when confronted with a limited-time sale price on a satisfactory similar item, you buy the sale item. Your decision was constrained by time. This is also known as "**satisficing**," meaning that the decision is not completely logical but will suffice.

Once developed, the *alternatives must be evaluated* for feasibility, appropriateness, and effectiveness. The manager should take all situational factors into consideration. In this case, the sales representative has been doing fairly well over the past year as shown by the fact that she has a bonus check coming. This month's poor performance could be a one-time occurrence due to uncontrollable variables. On the other hand, if the poor performance is repeated next month, the manager is no closer to solving the problem, and worse, the sales representative will have received her bonus check, a reward, at a time when her performance does not merit it. The alternative of withholding the bonus check would signal the manager's dissatisfaction, but it might also demoralize the sales representative at a time when she needs encouragement. The manager decides to do a ride-along with the sales representative. The manager believes that this will provide an opportunity to obtain information that will explain the poor performance, and to communicate expectations and encouragement to the sales representative.

Next in the decision-making process is the *implementation* of the decision. The manager must cancel a planned business trip. The last step is to *follow up and evaluate the results* of the decision. By spending a day with the sales representative, the manager was immediately able to identify and correct gaps in her knowledge of the customers' needs and give her advice about how to present her proposals in meetings. Next month's sales by this representative recovered and slightly exceeded sales goals.

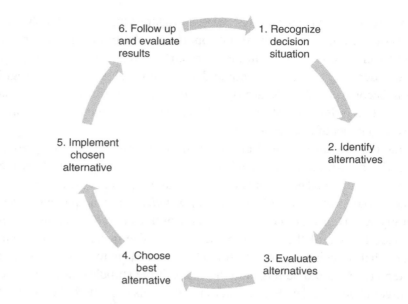

Figure 5.7 Steps in the rational decision-making process

Another Perspective on Managerial Knowledge and Skills

Henry Mintzberg
Canadian academic who categorized 10 managerial roles into interpersonal, informational, and decisional categories.

In 1973, Canadian academic Henry Mintzberg published a thesis based on his study of actual managers at work. Instead of studying teamwork and organizational structure as others had, he observed five CEOs of public and private organizations. In his analysis of his observations Mintzberg identified 10 *managerial roles* in three categories (see table 5.3).

Table 5.3 Mintzberg's managerial roles

Interpersonal (Focus on relationships)	Informational (Focus on communication)	Decisional (Focus on unit strategy)
• Figurehead • Leader • Liaison	• Monitor • Disseminator • Spokesperson	• Entrepreneur • Disturbance Handler • Resource Allocator • Negotiator

Interpersonal Roles

The manager as *figurehead* represents the management in performing symbolic or ceremonial duties, for example, providing introductory remarks at the opening of a company training conference. The manager as *leader* is responsible for creating an environment that will motivate the staff. When playing the role of *liaison*, the manager is responsible for dealing with people both inside and outside the organization.

Informational Roles

Playing the informational role of *monitor*, which means gathering internal and external information pertaining to the organization, is similar to developing managerial knowledge in order to become more effective. As *disseminator*, the manager transmits information to subordinates within the organization, while as *spokesperson*, the manager transmits information to people inside and outside the organization.

Decisional Roles

It is in decisional roles that the manager has the most visible impact. As *entrepreneur*, the manager initiates change. When the manager responds to situations that are beyond his or her control, the *disturbance handler* role is being played, which is a role closely related to that of *negotiator*, where the manager participates in a process of give and take until a satisfactory compromise is reached. Last, as *resource allocator*, the manager decides how and to whom the organization's resources will be distributed.

Mintzberg's work dispelled the myth that managers are careful, reflective planners and replaced it with an image of managers dealing minute to minute with constant interruptions, improvising as they go. His study of managers showed that managerial success does not depend on personal characteristics, but on how skillfully the manager adopts and plays the managerial roles appropriate to the situation at hand.

APPLY YOUR KNOWLEDGE

Leadership, Spirituality, and the Workplace

For Chip Conley, founder and former CEO of Joie de Vivre Hospitality for 23 years, integrating spirituality with business was a fundamental assumption. Upon receiving his MBA from Stanford University, he enrolled in the Esalen Institute, a retreat center for humanistic education. He says, "The most neglected fact in business is that we're all human. If we use this as a guide, each interaction—regardless of the relationship or situation—becomes an empathetic exchange based on respect for self and for others." By focusing on employees' sense of meaning and customers' emotional connection to the company, Joie de Vivre's customer loyalty skyrocketed and employee turnover dropped to one-third of the industry average between 2000 and 2005.

Conley was an early proponent of the "spirituality movement" that has transformed the definition of effective leadership over the past twenty years. Study after study shows that spiritual values such as integrity, honesty, and humility are the defining elements of effective leaders. Their spirituality guides them to inspire and motivate their employees, create a positive ethical climate, increase trust, promote positive work relationships, and achieve organizational goals. Drawing on spiritual beliefs helps give employees a sense of purpose and connection to each other and to the company. When leaders encourage spiritualty, employees feel that they can bring their "whole selves" to work, which increases their on-the-job energy and creativity.

Pacemaker inventor Earl Bakken's profoundly spiritual values still resonate throughout Medtronic, the company that he cofounded in 1960, now the largest medical technology company in the world. He believed that God gave him his gift for invention and that God wanted him to use it to improve the human condition. Portions of the Medtronic Mission that Bakken wrote are

"to contribute to human welfare by application of biomedical engineering in the research, design, manufacture, and sale of instruments or appliances that alleviate pain, restore health, and extend life," and *"to recognize the personal worth of all employees by providing an employment framework that allows personal satisfaction in work accomplished, security, advancement opportunity, and means to share in the company's success."*

Source: © Medtronic Reprinted by permission.

Bakken led by example, always showing empathy, humility, and compassion for others.

His spiritual leadership lives on through the mission he crafted and by nourishing employees' spiritual well-being. Twenty years ago, at about the same time that the workplace spirituality movement took hold, Medtronic opened a meditation center (now named after Mr. Bakken, who died in 2018) available to all employees at its headquarters in Minneapolis. It has organized Christian and Muslim Employee Resource Groups to focus on professional development and community building at a grassroots level. Employees regularly meet with customers whose lives have been changed by Medtronic devices, enhancing the employees' sense of purpose in their work.

In his groundbreaking book, *A Spiritual Audit of Corporate America*, Professor Ian Mitroff claimed "spirituality is the new competitive advantage." Practices associated with spirituality help attract top talent, raise employee morale, reduce turnover, retain customers, and enhance public perception of the company's brand image. It's a "virtuous cycle," according to former Medtronic CEO Bill George. "Motivated, satisfied employees produce satisfied customers, which produce good financial results, which benefit the shareholders."

Knowledge Application Questions

1. Explain how spiritual values might support any of the major leadership styles described in this chapter.

2. What is your personal definition of spirituality?

3. Have you ever had a strong spiritual experience at work, or have you had a supervisor who exhibited spirituality? If so, describe your experience.

Sources

Conley, C. 2010. "Measuring What Makes Life Worthwhile." Vide0. Accessed October 30, 2019. https://www.ted.com/talks/chip_conley_measuring_what_ makes_life_worthwhile?language=en.

Crotti, N. 2018, December 24. "Medtronic Founder Earl Bakken Knew How to Inspire His Employees." Accessed October 30, 2019. https://www.medicaldesignandoutsourcing. com/medtronic-founder-earl-bakken-knew-how-to-inspire-his-employees/.

McLaughlin, C. 2009. "Spirituality and Ethics in Business." Accessed October 30, 2019. http://www.visionarylead.org/spirituality-in-business.html.

Medtronic Mission Statement n.d. Accessed October 30, 2019. https://www.medtronic .com/us-en/about/mission.html.

Mitroff, I. and E. A. Denton. 1999. "A Study of Spirituality in the Workplace." Accessed October 30, 2019. http://strandtheory.org/images/Spirituality_in_the_workplace-Mitroff_Denton.pdf.

Zurer, R. 2018, June 30. "Top conscious business leaders 2018." Accessed October 30, 2019. https://consciouscompanymedia.com/personal-development/ top-conscious-business-leaders-2018/.

QUIZ YOURSELF

Without looking back at the chapter, choose the best answer to each of the questions below. Answers are in the back of the textbook before the Index. Review the chapter to find out why you missed any questions.

1. An organizational vision describes the company's dreams and aspirations. The company mission explains the purpose of the organization. Which one of the following statements is a vision statement and which is a mission statement?

   Statement 1: A hunger-free America
   Statement 2: To feed America's hungry via a nationwide network of food banks while organizing people to end hunger

   a. Statement 1 is a mission, while Statement 2 is a vision.
   b. Statement 1 is a vision, while Statement 2 is a mission.
   c. Both are vision statements.
   d. Both are mission statements.
   e. These statements are neither vision nor mission statements.

2. The Budget Director and the CEO of We Care, Inc. are meeting to discuss how to allocate next year's funding to the nonprofit's various projects. These two people are doing what type of planning?
   a. Contingency
   b. Tactical
   c. Financial
   d. Strategic
   e. Project

3. Dr. Singh Patel is chair of the Department of Biology at a university. He supervises ten full-time faculty members, all of whom have PhDs. The best leadership style for Dr. Patel to adopt is
   a. conceptual.
   b. autocratic.
   c. "free rein."
   d. technical.
   e. democratic.

4. Petra is formulating goals for a new pet care business of which she will be the owner and the only employee. An example of a SMART goal would be to
   a. break even.
   b. make $500,000 in the first year.
   c. acquire twenty-five repeat customers in the first twelve months of operation.
   d. open a second location.
   e. None of the choices listed is a SMART goal.

5. George Carlin, president of MNO Cleaning Company, wants to increase the productivity of the janitors that work for him. He has told his employees that he will give a bonus of $100 to anyone who finishes 100 percent of their assigned tasks during the night shift for four weeks in a row. George is a/an _____ leader.
   a. achievement-oriented
   b. task-oriented
   c. participative
   d. democratic
   e. laissez-faire

6. Benchmarking is a way to set performance standards in the management process known as _____.
   a. planning
   b. satisficing
   c. controlling
   d. supervising
   e. rational decision-making

7. The primary management skills that a line supervisor needs are
   a. conceptual, interpersonal, technical.
   b. conceptual and interpersonal.
   c. conceptual and technical.
   d. interpersonal and technical.
   e. technical only.

8. Juan was an executive with an aid organization helping to restore infrastructure in Puerto Rico after Hurricane Maria. All of the sewer lines in a mountainous section of the island were damaged. The roads on which trucks bearing new sewer tiles would travel were partially washed out. In order to get the sewers working again Juan most likely used all of the following, EXCEPT
   a. programmed decision-making.
   b. creativity.
   c. non-programmed decision-making.
   d. rational decision-making.
   e. satisficing.

9. Mintzberg's study of managers in action showed that they do not follow carefully laid plans but
   a. act like generals leading armies in combat.
   b. give free rein to their employees.
   c. skillfully improvise according to the situation at hand.
   d. use programmed decision-making.
   e. strictly apply company policies.

10. Dean Jager is in charge of the volunteer staff at the Booth Western Art Museum. He makes the work assignments, determines work schedules, and makes sure the museum uses all of its volunteer staff efficiently. Jager is a _____ manager.
    a. functional
    b. coordination
    c. supervisory
    d. top
    e. strategic

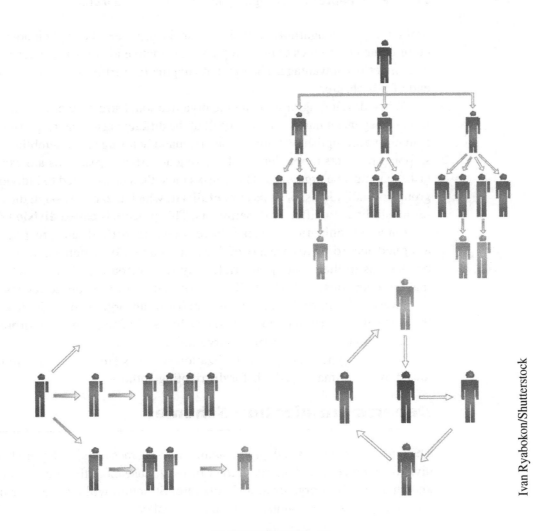

Ivan Ryabokon/Shutterstock

CHAPTER 6

Designing the Business Organization

Nature and Purpose of the Organizational Structure

We can say that an **organization** consists of at least two people working together to achieve a common set of goals or objectives. As you learned in the previous chapter about management, organizing is the process by which managers establish working relationships among employees to achieve goals. Organizational structure is the formal arrangement of jobs within an organization. The type of **organizational structure** chosen depends on a host of variables, which will be discussed in this chapter. A company's organizational structure should allow it to quickly and effectively respond to challenges and to take advantage of new opportunities, as pointed out by Roberto Goizueta, former chairman and CEO of Coca-Cola. He said, "There is no permanent organization chart for the world …. It is of supreme importance to be ready at all times to take advantage of new opportunities."

A well-designed structure helps reduce conflicts between individuals and between groups; can improve communication, collaboration, and decision-making; and can lower operating costs, contributing to profitability. A thoughtfully crafted structure incorporates the implicit organizational culture that contributes to the company's distinctive identity and helps to produce its competitive advantage. The topic of **corporate culture** will be discussed at the end of this chapter.

When developing or revising the organizational structure of a business, high-level management must first identify all of the different tasks and responsibilities the firm must accomplish. Billing customers, manufacturing and assembling products, shipping products to retailers, and creating advertising materials are examples of tasks that must be organized. Those tasks must then be assigned to individuals and groups of individuals, or **departmentalized**, which means to assign the tasks and responsibilities to different departments. This process is called **division of labor**.

Once organizational tasks have been identified and responsibilities assigned according to a variety of departmentalization schemes, decisions must be made as to the most appropriate way to distribute authority. Who will be making decisions, and who will be accountable for the consequences of those decisions? The **distribution of authority** in an organization is described as the vertical dimension that establishes a hierarchy, or **chain of command**, that will coordinate the efforts of the organization.

The main types of departmentalization schemes are explained here first, followed by the primary methods for distributing authority.

Departmentalization Schemes

The most commonly used departmentalization schemes in use today are functional, divisional, process, and matrix. Larger firms will use more than one structure, also known as a hybrid organizational structure. Structure will evolve over time as a company grows or encounters competitive challenges.

Functional Structure

Functional structure Organization design that is common in small firms that produce a limited number of products or services.

Departmentalization by function organizes tasks and responsibilities according to employee functions. A **functional structure** is usually the first "structure" that organizations adopt as they grow larger than what one or two owners can manage by themselves. This method sets up separate departments for functional areas such as finance, marketing, and production (see Figure 6.1). The functional approach is common in small firms that produce a limited number of products.

There are evident advantages and disadvantages to the functional structure. The functional structure best supports one or two products or services. Because

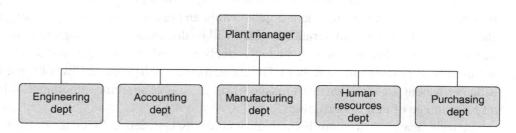

Figure 6.1 Example of a functional structure

each department is highly specialized around closely related tasks, employees are able to learn from others doing similar jobs. Managers can easily monitor and evaluate workers within the functional department. A functional structure, on the other hand, may lead to managers' preoccupation with their own departments at the cost of losing sight of company goals. Coordination among functions does not flow horizontally and must generally come from an upper level. The departmental focus and difficulties in cross-functional coordination often cause the company that is departmentalized by function to respond too slowly to environmental changes.

Divisional Structures

Divisional structures organize basic business functions around products, markets, or locations. This type of structure is more common in larger firms. Each division contains all of the functions and resources needed to support a product line, a customer base, or a geographic location.

Divisional structure Basic business functions are organized around products, markets, or locations.

Product Structure

Organizing by product or product line is common in larger firms that produce a wide variety of products. For example, General Motors' divisions include Chevrolet, Buick, GMC, and Cadillac. H.J. Heinz is organized around the major product categories of canned soups, frozen vegetables, frozen meals, and baked goods. A hospital organizes its services around inpatient and outpatient care, and each of the diagnostic services it may provide. This approach organizes tasks and responsibilities according to the type of product being made or the service being provided.

Product structure Basic business functions are organized around products or product categories.

In the **product structure**, functions such as production, finance, and marketing are performed for each product category separately (see Figure 6.2). This structure allows a large company to focus in depth on each of its products

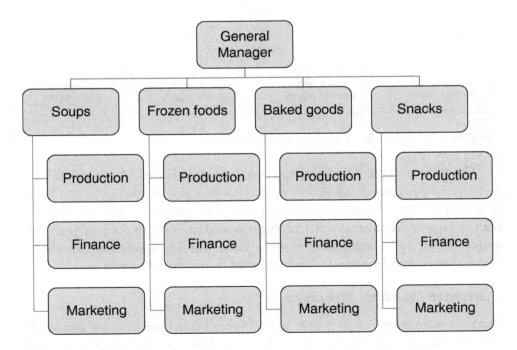

Figure 6.2 Example of a product structure

rather than spreading its attention and resources thinly across all of its offerings. As with the functional structure, the opportunity to specialize in a product leads to the development of expertise in the product and the industry of which it is part. Specialization also helps better meet the needs of customers. Decision-making is decentralized, allowing for the flexibility among product managers to respond to a fast-changing environment. Hallmark Cards, makers of greeting cards, decided to adopt the product structure when the company realized that it took two years to bring a new card to the marketplace.

A major disadvantage of the product structure is that it eliminates any savings realized from sharing support functions across all products. It is expensive to set up and operate. There can be a tendency for managers and their employees to become more loyal to their product than to the organization as a whole. It can also be difficult to integrate and standardize across all product lines.

Geographic Structure

Geographic structure Basic business functions are organized around the locations of the customers.

A company may choose to organize according to the location of its customers (see Figure 6.3). This approach to divisional structure may be desirable if the firm has customers in different regions who buy a variety of the firm's products. The **geographic structure** allows strategies and decisions to be tailored to circumstances specific to the location served. Pfizer Pharmaceuticals markets its products in over 100 countries. It organizes sales responsibilities by geographic location so that representatives are close to the customers they serve, and they can customize their service to the political, cultural, and legal environment of the region. The geographic regional structure helps Pfizer cut travel costs and maintain its competitive advantage.

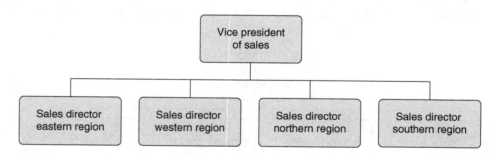

Figure 6.3 Example of a geographic structure

The disadvantages of the geographic structure are the difficulty in maintaining a consistent company image across varied locations and difficulties in accurately determining what to include as part of a region. For example, a region that includes both vast unpopulated areas and densely populated cities might not exhibit enough uniformity for a geographic structure to be successful. The benefits and drawbacks of this type of structure are similar to those of the product structure.

Customer (Market) Structure

Departmentalization by customer is another type of divisional structure that organizes the company into departments to deal with different types of customers (see Figure 6.4). A computer software company, for example, may have one division to deal with educational buyers, another to deal with households that buy software for entertainment or household use, and an another to deal with business customers. The benefits and drawbacks of the **customer (market) structure** are similar to those of the product and the geographic structures.

Customer or market structure A divisional structure that organizes around different types of customers.

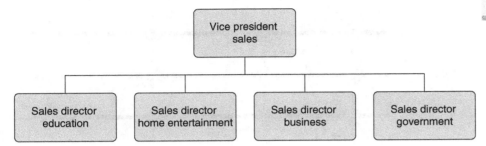

Figure 6.4   Example of a customer (market) structure

Process Structure

The **process structure** organizes tasks and responsibilities according to the production processes used to create a good or service (see Figure 6.5). The advantages of this type of structure are that there is no duplication of activities and it helps management to establish efficient performance control. A disadvantage is that specialists are needed for each process activity. Training must be provided for each activity, which may require extra time and resources. The benefits and drawbacks of this type of structure are similar to those of the other divisional structures.

Process structure Organizing around the processes used to create a product or service.

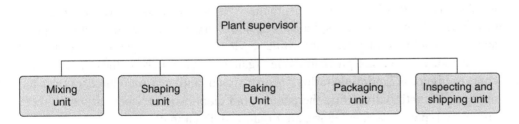

Figure 6.5   Example of a process structure

Matrix Organization

The **matrix structure**, also called the **project management** structure, uses cross-functional teams to integrate functional expertise with a divisional focus. It works best in a small or medium sized firm with multiple products or projects. The matrix brings together employees from various parts of the firm to focus on a specific project (see Figure 6.6).

Matrix structure Uses cross-functional teams to integrate functional expertise with a project focus.

This structure helps the company take advantage of the unique skills and knowledge of employees working in different departments across the company. Employees involved often work only part time in the matrix and spend the rest of their time performing their normally assigned tasks. The success of this organization strategy depends heavily on the ability of the project managers to balance their functional responsibilities with those of the special project. The matrix structure achieves both focus and cross-functional coordination. Employees learn new skills from project team members and can experience a sense of renewal that they carry back to their usual job function.

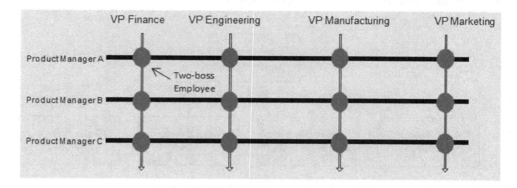

Figure 6.6 Example of a matrix structure

The most significant disadvantage is the potential for conflict between the two bosses: the functional manager and the product/project manager. The matrix structure violates the principle of **unity of command**, which states that an employee should have only one supervisor to whom he or she reports. Strong interpersonal skills are required of everyone, with management taking a proactive stance toward balancing functional and divisional interests.

Hybrid Organizational Structures

In actual practice, many companies combine different structuring schemes in order to take advantage of their strengths, realize cost savings, and to better serve their customers. For example, a hospital may decide to organize its administrative support activities in a functional structure, while services that require specific expertise and utilize highly specialized procedures are organized divisionally. In the organizational chart in Figure 6.7, administration, informational, and environmental services are organized functionally, while therapeutic and diagnostic services, of which there are many types in each category, are organized divisionally.

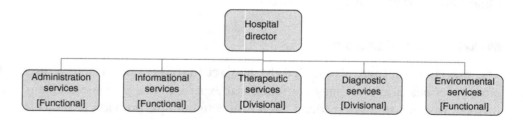

Figure 6.7 Example of a hybrid structure for a hospital

Distributing Authority in the Organization

Chain of command refers to the continuous line of authority that extends from upper levels of an organization to the lowest levels of the organization and clarifies who reports to whom. Traditional management theory argues for **unity of command**, which refers to the concept that a person should have one boss and should report only to that person.

The fundamental question to answer in organization design is whether decision-making will be directed from top management or delegated to lower levels. In other words, will authority be centralized or decentralized?

Centralization of Decision-Making

When authority is **centralized**, top managers make all the decisions and lower level employees carry them out. For example, fast food chains like McDonald's, Burger King, and Pizza Hut centralize authority as a way to maintain standardization so that the customer's experience is the same regardless of the location of the restaurant. These restaurants must follow precise steps in buying products, making and packaging burgers, and training their employees. Table 6.1 shows the advantages and disadvantages of centralizing authority.

Centralized authority
Top managers make all the decisions and lower level employees carry them out.

Table 6.1 Advantages and Disadvantages of Centralization

Centralization	
Advantages	**Disadvantages**
• Centralization can facilitate coordination. • It can help ensure that decisions are consistent with organizational objectives. • It can avoid duplication of activities by various subunits within the organization. • It can give top-level managers the means to bring about needed major organizational changes.	• It limits the firm's ability to respond quickly and effectively to changes in the environment because decisions cannot be made without top-level manager's permission. Financial losses for the firm could result. • Lower level employees might not take their work seriously, resulting in poor performance. • Middle-level managers might not work efficiently because they have less authority. • Top management takes credit for performance resulting in demoralized employees.

Decentralization of Decision-Making

When authority is **decentralized**, management shares decision-making with lower level employees. Decisions to decentralize often follow experiences with centralization. Table 6.2 shows the advantages and disadvantages of decentralization of authority.

When faced with the task of designing an organization how does top management decide whether to centralize or decentralize decision-making? In general, a large

Decentralized authority
Management shares decision-making with lower level employees.

company with just a few locations, doing business in a stable external environment, will choose centralized authority. If lower level managers are inexperienced or hesitant to take responsibility for decisions, upper management will want to retain authority. If most decisions have significant, far-reaching consequences or if the company is facing a crisis, centralizing authority would ensure that strategies are carried out effectively. Conversely, decentralized authority would make sense for a company that is geographically dispersed, operating in a dynamic or uncertain environment, and having a corporate culture that values and respects initiative, involvement, and flexibility. Effective decentralized decision-making requires experienced managers who communicate well.

Table 6.2 Advantages and Disadvantages of Decentralization

Decentralization	
Advantages	**Disadvantages**
• It facilitates management development. • It facilitates evaluation of employees for promotion. • It allows for greater creativity and innovation. • It increases higher order need fulfillment. • It facilitates implementation of decisions. • It frees upper management for more important tasks.	• It increases costs because more managers and a large staff are required, along with higher training costs. • It entails greater consumption of time initially. • It results in upper levels losing some control; hence their status is diminished. • It may lead to overlapping and duplication of effort.

Organization design experts Brafman and Beckstrom compared the decentralized organization to a starfish and the centralized organization to a spider in their book *The Starfish and the Spider*. Once a typical "spider," the U.S. military initiated the Starfish Program to decentralize its operations in order to confront the kinds of networked and decentralized threats it encountered during eight years of warfare in Iraq.

Determining the Span of Control

Span of control A wide span of control indicates a "flat" organization; a narrow span indicates a "tall" organization.

Related to the concept of distribution of authority is the concept of **span of control**, also known as *span of management*. Span of control refers to the number of subordinates who report to a supervisor (see Figure 6.8).

A *narrow span of control* means that a manager supervises few employees. A narrow span of control is usually associated with a **tall organization** and with centralized authority. A *wide span of control* means that a manager supervises a greater number of employees. A wide span of control is usually associated with a **flat organization** and with decentralized authority. The selection of a span of control balances the consequences of too little and too much supervision.

The conventional wisdom about an ideal span of control is seven subordinates per manager. However, when the nature of the work is highly standardized or routine, a broader span of control may be implemented, ranging from 15 to 40 workers. A wide span of control may also be adopted when decision-making is highly decentralized and the employees have the skill and experience to make good decisions without referring to a higher level.

Wide Span of Control

The wide span of control requires the formulation of clear policies that will guide employees' decision-making. Employees must be carefully selected for their ability and their judgment in carrying out their work without close supervision. When delegating authority, there is always a danger that the supervisor will lose control. Managers with a wide span of control must be exceptional in every aspect of their job.

The flat organizational structure of decentralized organizations with relatively few layers of management and wide spans of control has an impact on the level of employee involvement. Because employees have more responsibility, they can feel valued and motivated. Employees in a flat organization are more likely to be involved in decision-making processes. Fewer levels of management mean that communication is more efficient than in tall organizations. The flat organization has its disadvantages. Employees may need more training because they have a wider variety of responsibilities. The broad scope of their jobs may cause increased stress among employees. With fewer hierarchical levels, employees in the flat organization have fewer opportunities for promotion to management posts.

Narrow Span of Control

A narrow span of control means that supervisors can supervise work closely and communicate quickly with their subordinates. However, supervisors may tend to become too involved in subordinates' work, which can demoralize employees.

It is easier for managers to supervise staff in a tall organization, and employees are more likely to know their immediate boss quite well. There are more opportunities

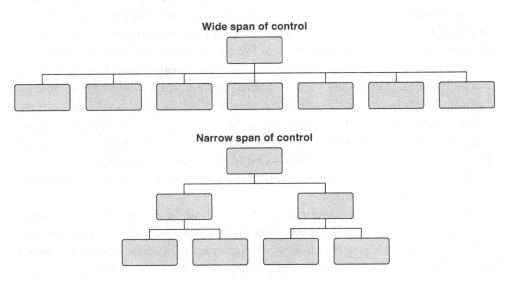

Figure 6.8   Wide span of control (flat) vs. narrow span of control (tall)

for promotion because there are more levels in the hierarchical ladder. It does take longer to communicate decisions and to disseminate information in the tall organization, however. Employees at the lower levels may not have the opportunity to suggest ideas or take initiatives.

Changing the Organizational Structure

If companies are to survive in today's highly dynamic business environment, it is likely that no business will keep the same structure year after year. A business may be growing in size or it may have to reduce its operations, either of which situation will require a structural change. If the firm is growing, then new departments may have to be created and more people hired. Reducing the size of the organization in order to cut costs is called **downsizing**. The goal in downsizing is to eliminate positions without reducing output.

Downsizing Reducing the size of an organization to cut costs.

One result of this restructuring strategy is that decision-making becomes decentralized as employees who used to report to managers whose positions have been eliminated are assigned additional responsibilities. With the addition of a broader range of duties outside their area of specialization, these employees may also find themselves viewed as "generalists" and thus redundant, or interchangeable, with other employees in the company. If a company must go through a second round of downsizing, redundant employees become a target for termination.

The Informal Organization

The organizational chart describes a publicly recognized description of tasks and responsibilities, but most firms also develop an **informal organization** that is never diagrammed. One type of informal organization is the communications network among a firm's employees, also known as the **grapevine**. This network develops as relationships among employees evolve over time. The astute manager will acknowledge and cultivate the informal organization because it is a powerful influence on employee behaviors and attitudes. The informal network fosters cooperation among people in various parts of the organization in ways that the formal structure cannot. Tasks can sometimes be accomplished more quickly and easily through the informal organization than through formal organization. The friendships that develop within the informal structure can improve worker morale and make the work environment more enjoyable. Informal communication among employees at different levels is yet another advantage because information is allowed to travel informally up and down throughout the organization. It has also been noted that a company's informal network can be a tool to stimulate and support improvisation and innovation. The grapevine should be treated with respect, however, for it is frequently used to spread incorrect or negative information about the firm and may perpetuate unfounded rumors.

Intrapreneurship The process of encouraging employees to come up with creative ideas as if they were running their own business.

Another type of organizational structure that can be either informal or formal is the **intrapreneurship program**, sometimes known as corporate entrepreneurship. Intrapreneurship is the process of encouraging specific employees within an organization to come up with and implement creative ideas, acting much as if they were entrepreneurs who were running their own businesses. Firms encourage intrapreneurship to foster creativity and innovative behavior. In order to successfully implement intrapreneurial behavior, firms must treat the ideas of employees seriously and find ways to reward employees who come up with successful innovations.

The now classic story of the invention of Post-it notes illustrates an effective intrapreneurship program. 3M scientist Spencer Silver had invented a repositionable adhesive in 1968, but it was not until his coworker Art Frey complained about losing his place in his hymnbook that anyone could think of a use for Silver's invention. 3M has a "Bootlegging Policy," which allows employees to spend up to 15 percent of their time working on creative ideas. The Post-it note product was finally launched in 1980. Annual sales top US$100 million.

Corporate Culture, the "Character of an Organization"

Corporate culture
Goffee and Jones
identified networked,
fragmented, communal,
and mercenary corporate
cultures.

Corporate culture is the composition of the traditions, ceremonies, values, and norms shared by the members of the organization. Table 6.3 describes the purpose of some common organizational rites. It reflects the organization's views: "The way things are done around here." Corporate culture has a powerful influence on a company's performance over time. The physical setting, advertising, dress code, employee loyalty, ethics, and preference for team or for individual work all express the culture of a company. It is part of the organization's identity, which differentiates it from others.

Table 6.3 Organizational rites

Rite of:	Example	Purpose or Consequences
passage	Basic training	Facilitates transition into new roles
integration	Office Christmas party	Encourages and reinforces common values that bind members together
enhancement	Company ceremonies where accomplishments are publicly recognized	Motivates commitment to values and encourages proper behavior through a system of rewards
degradation	Removal of high status manager, e.g., impeachment of President Richard Nixon	Reduces power and identity; reaffirms proper behavior

In actual practice, you will usually find more than one corporate culture existing within an organization. For example, the sales division might exhibit quite a different culture from that of the human resources unit. Researchers Rob Goffee and Gareth Jones identified four types of corporate cultures in their 1998 book *Character of a Corporation.*

- **Networked:** focus is on sociability, the company as a family, a sense of belonging to the company (not just working for it); strong identification with the company and its product or service; tolerance of ambiguity; loyalty is encouraged; atmosphere is easygoing and informal; negative politics are actively discouraged. Typical of small businesses.
- **Fragmented:** the company is an organization of individualists; a high degree of autonomy is allowed and encouraged; analysis is prized over intuition; individual productivity is rewarded; there is equality among employees; permits flexibility. Typical of universities and law firms.
- **Communal:** there is a sense of community but very goal oriented; leaders are seen as visionaries; followers are passionate and enjoy working in teams; employees are willing to make sacrifices for the greater good. Typical of high technology firms.
- **Mercenary:** goal- and task- oriented culture; employees thrive on competition; relationships are formed in order to achieve goals; little tolerance for ambiguity. Typical of sales organizations.

A corporate culture that synchronizes with a company's mission and formal structure will positively affect its performance. For example, a communal culture supports a structure based on teams. This synergy of culture and structure is likely to produce innovation. It is no surprise that high-technology firms often nurture a communal culture and work in close-knit teams.

Corporate culture is an invisible yet powerful factor in leading and organizing people to achieve company goals, yet companies contemplating a merger or acquisition often overlook it. On the other hand, the failure of a merger to produce the desired performance is frequently wrongly blamed on "culture clash" when actually other factors are the cause of the problem. Nevertheless, experts agree that it is important to analyze organizational culture when merging.

Several approaches can be taken. The most common approach is **assimilation**, in which the acquired company embraces the acquiring firm's culture. If the acquired firm is not willing to adopt the culture of the acquiring firm, and the acquiring entity imposes its culture, and conflict usually follows. This approach is likely to result in low employee morale and sets in motion a process of **deculturation**.

The two firms may elect to integrate cultures to create a new composite culture, or merging companies may remain separate, keeping their own cultures. For example, conglomerate Berkshire Hathaway's companies such as GEICO, Fruit of the Loom, and Benjamin Moore & Co retain distinct identities and cultures. No matter what approach to blending is taken, experts agree that communication and employee empowerment are the keys to success and that the process usually takes longer time than expected.

APPLY YOUR KNOWLEDGE

"Agile" Management Accelerates Response to Change

The World Wide Web and mobile technologies have disrupted every industry—from banking to retailing to medical care. Corporate executives are finding that the traditional chain-of-command hierarchy hampers efforts to invent new responses to fast-moving change in the dynamic global marketplace.

To survive and prosper, firms all over the world have adopted "agile" structures, a concept borrowed from the world of hi-tech where 90 percent of organizations use "agile" practices. In an agile company, work is organized by project and executed by cross-functional, self-organizing teams that set objectives, track their own progress, and make adjustments based on frequent peer feedback. Managers and executives act as coaches or advisors to the teams. They are responsible for coordinating the teams, removing constraints, and providing resources such as funding.

Global banking group ING, based in the Netherlands, realized in 2014 that 40 percent of all of its retail customer transactions were being done via its mobile app. Customers had discovered that they could do almost all of their banking on the train ride home from work. With Facebook and Netflix setting the standard for user experience, ING knew it had to become more customer-focused.

Using agile management advice from tech firms they admired, ING leadership reorganized its Dutch retail operations into tribes, squads, and chapters in 2015. They created thirteen tribes of up to 150 people, each dedicated to a type of banking service such as private banking or securities. A tribe lead, with input from the tribe, establishes cross-functional squads of up to nine people that work on new products to address a specific customer need. Squads might disband at the end of a project lasting from two weeks to 18 months. The members are free to join other squads, or stay together, ready to work on new customer needs. The chapters coordinate people in the same area of expertise—employees who are distributed across the company among the cross-functional squads. The chapter lead shares best practices, provides professional development, and does performance reviews.

CEO Ralph Hamers says that customer satisfaction and employee engagement have improved and ING has speeded up the delivery of new customer products. His next goal is to simplify the customer experience in all of ING's 13 retail markets by introducing the "agile" organization.

Knowledge Application Questions

International technology giant Bosch realized that its centralized hierarchical structure was no longer effective in managing its operations in over 60 countries. Initial attempts at transforming Bosch into an "agile" company failed because they were centrally organized and managed in a traditional way, with a goal, target completion date, and mandated progress reports. Employees were skeptical about the proposed transformation.

1. Which corporate culture described in Chapter 6 is it likely that Bosch had before its transformation? Why do you think so?

2. What cultural changes must a company make in order to implement the "agile" approach successfully?

3. What methods do you think would be effective in promoting cultural change in a large company transitioning to an "agile" structure?

Sources

Barton, D., D. Carey, and R. Charan. 2018, March-April. "One bank's agile team experiment: How ING revamped its retail operation." *Harvard Business Review*: 59-61.

Rigby, D. K., J. Sutherland and A. Noble. 2018, May-June. "Agile at scale." *Harvard Business Review*: 88-96.

QUIZ YOURSELF

Without looking back at the chapter, choose the best answer to each of the questions below. Answers are in the back of the textbook before the Index. Review the chapter to find out why you missed any questions.

1. The U.S. Army has a/an _____ organizational structure, with many organizational layers.
   a. tall
   b. short
   c. flat
   d. broad
   e. elliptical

2. One of the advantages of a wide span of control is
   a. a high degree of control.
   b. a lack of synchronization.
   c. an absence of managerial support.
   d. that employees need more training.
   e. better organizational communication.

3. Most firms use a combination of different types of organizational structures in order to
   a. enhance service to customers.
   b. save money by being more efficient.
   c. improve interorganizational communication.
   d. match supervisory control to tasks being performed.
   e. All of the above.

4. The CEO of Nutrix, a new pharmaceutical company, has given Lance the responsibility of developing a new product. The CEO told him that he can organize his team any way he wishes. Lance chose the vice president of marketing, the company's brightest engineer, and the associate vice president of manufacturing. This is an example of a
   a. divisional structure.
   b. functional structure.
   c. product structure.
   d. matrix structure.
   e. process structure.

5. The advantages of a product structure include all of the following, EXCEPT
   a. faster response to changes in the marketplace.
   b. opportunity to specialize, leading to enhanced product expertise.
   c. that customer needs are met by product experts.
   d. that functions are duplicated.
   e. the ability to focus resources on specific products or services.

6. In the matrix structure, employees have two bosses, thus breaking which rule about distributing authority in an organization?
   a. Span of control
   b. Decentralized authority
   c. Unity of command
   d. Hybrid control
   e. Autonomous supervision

7. ABC corporation manufactures parts for mobile phones and has factories and customers throughout the world. The company hires only experienced managers. This company would most likely adopt which of the following as its organizational design?
   a. Decentralized authority, a wide span of control
   b. Centralized authority, a narrow span of control
   c. Communal authority, networked control
   d. Centralized authority, a wide span of control
   e. None of the above

8. Cathy is a newly promoted middle manager at PamCo. She is having lunch with Jack, her old friend who is working on PamCo's factory floor. Jack tells Cathy that his coworkers make frequent mistakes that are slowing production. Cathy decides to offer additional training to these workers. This is an example of using
   a. unity of command.
   b. decentralized authority.
   c. matrix control.
   d. the process structure.
   e. the informal organization.

9. Google encourages engineers to spend 20 percent of their work time on projects that interest them. This is an example of
   a. intrapreneurship.
   b. flextime.
   c. an employee benefit.
   d. exploitation.
   e. an organizational rite.

10. Which type of culture would be best suited to a retail clothing store located on Main Street in Kendallville, Indiana?
    a. Mercenary
    b. Networked
    c. Fragmented
    d. "laissez-faire"
    e. None of the above

CHAPTER 7

Operations Management Basics

Operations management is the set of activities that creates value in the form of **goods and services** by transforming inputs into outputs. The goal of operations management is to make the **production management process** as efficient as possible while effectively fulfilling customer needs. The five elements of the production management process are shown in figure 7.1.

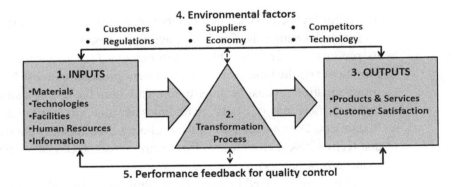

Figure 7.1 The production management process

Operations management
The set of activities that creates value in the form of goods and services by transforming inputs into outputs.

Regardless of the industry in which an organization operates, this process, with its inputs, processes, and outputs, is evident in virtually every formal organization in existence. The example of an automobile manufacturer is shown in table 7.1.

To understand how well the production management process is working, **production managers** must monitor it by taking measurements at every phase. They compare system **performance feedback** to previously established standards to see if adjustments are needed in order to maximize efficiency and control quality. For example, system feedback can indicate that machine settings should be changed, or that the production layout should be streamlined, or that the quality of incoming raw materials must be checked more closely. The production manager monitors the efficiency ratio—Output/Input—to make sure that it stays as close to 100% as possible.

Operations managers look at **environmental factors** that have an impact on the production process. **Customer feedback** data, for example, on buying patterns

Table 7.1 Production management process in automobile manufacturing

Inputs	Processing	Outputs
Tires	Assembling	
Engine	Testing	Finished automobiles in various configurations
Upholstery	Cleaning	
Chassis	Painting	
Computer chips	Inspecting	
Body	Painting	

and order levels, or types and number of complaints and returns, help managers understand whether the firm's production process is delivering value to buyers of its products or services. Other environmental factors have a significant impact, too. New **regulations** may mean that new procedures must be inserted into the transformation process in order to remain within the law. If a **supplier** goes out of business, there may be a delay in finding a new one, slowing the delivery of products to retailers. The general state of the economy, product innovations by **competitors**, and **technological change** are other environmental factors that affect the production management process.

Managers involved in **operations planning** (also called production planning) consider the competitive environment and the company's strategic goals in an effort to identify the production methods that will work best. The overall business plan guides operations planning, as do qualitative and quantitative forecasts. In developing the operations plan, managers make decisions regarding product design, quality management, process and capacity design, location, layout design, human resources nd job design, supply chain management, inventory planning, quality management, scheduling, and maintenance. **Business analytics** (to be discussed later) provides a logical, data-driven and verifiable basis to underpin decisions made in the listed subareas. Important considerations under some of these subareas are discussed next.

Similarities between Service Providers and Manufacturers

Services Cannot be inventoried because the customer must participate in their production.

It could be said that the similarities between **service providers** and manufacturers are greater than the differences. Like manufacturers, service providers must deal with customers, suppliers, scheduling, and staffing issues. Both must make effective use of technology in order to create value for customers. Each will have to deal with capacity, location, and layout issues. Rapid response to stakeholder needs, high productivity, and high quality are important to both. Both must effectively forecast demand. The similarities and differences between products and services are highlighted in Table 7.2.

Table 7.2   Differences between goods and services

Services	Goods
• Intangible	• Tangible
• Product cannot be inventoried	• Product can be inventoried
• Heterogeneous—inconsistent product definition	• Homogeneous—consistent product
• Short response time	• Longer response time
• Labor intensive	• Capital intensive
• Produced and consumed at same time	• Production separate from consumption
• High production interaction with consumer	• Low production interaction with consumer

Capacity Planning

The amount of a product that an organization can produce under normal working conditions is its **capacity**. A firm's capacity depends on the number of people it employs and the number and size of its facilities. Some examples of capacity and how it is measured are shown in table 7.3.

Table 7.3 Capacity planning

Type of Business	Input Measures of Capacity	Output Measures of Capacity
Computer manufacturer	Labor hours	Computers per shift
Nursing home	Available beds	Residents per year
Coffee house	Labor hours	Cups served per day
Shopping center	Floor space in square footage	Revenue per square foot

Location planning
Access to the factors of production is important in location planning.

Location Planning: Where Do We Make It?

Selecting the location of a facility is a critical decision that cannot be reversed easily, so considerable care and thought should go into the final choice. The cost of renting or buying a building varies considerably by region or country and thus directly affects the company's profitability. Access to human and physical resources and transportation are also key criteria affecting cost of production and flexibility. In particular, retailers and service providers must objectively weigh the merits of a location based on its convenience to potential customers.

Factors Affecting the Site Decision

Cost of Space

The cost of purchasing or leasing buildings or office space can vary significantly among regions. In the past 20 years, many U.S. companies have moved from the north to the south because space is less expensive there. In general, space in suburban and rural areas tends to be less expensive than in the city.

Cost of Labor

The cost of human resources also varies considerably among locations, in the same patterns as the cost of space.

Tax Incentives

Many state and local governments offer tax credits, suspend taxes for a specified fixed period of time, and offer other incentives to attract firms to their regions.

Source of Demand

Some firms want to locate as close as possible to their customers in order to reduce the cost of transporting the product and provide greater convenience to customers. This is particularly important in many service industries.

Access to Transportation

Whether a company operates locally or intends to sell its products nationally, access to good transportation facilities, like interstate highways, railroads, and major airports will be important.

Supply of Labor

If a company requires highly skilled workers or workers with specialized skills, it will want to locate near an abundant supply of this type of labor.

Selecting a Foreign Production Site

Locating in a foreign country involves research and balancing trade-offs. Labor in developing countries is relatively cheap, for example, but workers may be poorly trained and not as productive as workers in developed nations. Cheap space is available in Mexico, for example, but the cost of space is very high in Japan. The strength of the market for consumer goods is another factor to consider. Careful research of local culture and the character of various neighborhoods, cities, and regions should be done in advance of visiting foreign locations and making the final choice.

Layout Planning

Layout planning
The arrangement of production tasks determines how quickly the firm can respond to customer needs.

Layout determines whether firms can respond quickly and efficiently to customer requests for additional or different products or find themselves unable to match competitors' speed and convenience. The firm has to decide on how large the facility should be and how it should be arranged. Several alternative layouts exist.

In a **process layout**, equipment, supplies, and people are grouped according to function. This type of layout is the most effective in producing **make-to-order** products or services customized to the needs of each customer, such as in the spa layout shown in figure 7.2a. Each spa customer will desire a different combination of services, or just one service.

Tasks are arranged in the sequence that they are performed in a **product layout** (figure 7.2b). This is especially efficient for large-volume **make-to-stock** operations that mass-produce products quickly, often using an assembly line.

When the product is very large and difficult to move while it is being produced, a **fixed-position layout** is used (figure 7.2c). The fixed-position layout is used for manufacturing airplanes, ships, bridges, stadiums, and houses. The product stays in one place during its construction. Rather than move the product past workers in an assembly line, workers go to the product.

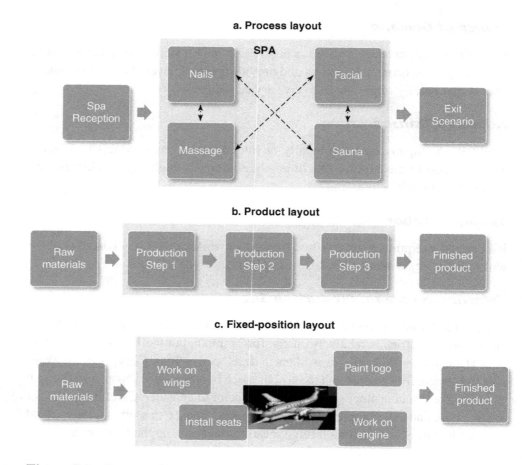

Figure 7.2 Layout planning

Use of Computers in Manufacturing

Computer-integrated Manufacturing (CIM) CIM speeds response to customer needs and lowers operating costs.

Computer-integrated manufacturing (CIM) is the use of computers to control the entire production process by allowing individual production processes to communicate with and regulate each other. For example, automation, just-in-time inventory control (JIT), flexible manufacturing, and CAD/CAM can all be integrated into one self-regulating production system. Using CIM helps companies increase productivity and quality while reducing costs.

Elements of computer-integrated manufacturing include:

Computer-aided design (CAD) is a computerized process for designing new products, modifying existing ones, or simulating conditions that may affect designs. An example is Turbo CAD Pro.

Computer-aided manufacturing (CAM) is a computerized process for planning and programming production processes and equipment. An example is Mastercam CAM/CAD software, founded in 1983.

Flexible manufacturing system (FMS) combines the efficiency of mass production with the ability to customize products. Advances in computer technology have made it possible for manufacturers to quickly reconfigure their production layouts to produce different products. The same assembly line can be used to produce a variety of products and the company can adjust its production in response to changes in demand. Automated materials-handling and transfer machines connect groups of production machines that perform operations on a part. A computer system coordinates and controls the actions of the types of machines in the FMS.

Automation is the automatic operation of a system, process, or machine.

Robotics is the use of programmable machines to perform a variety of tasks by manipulating materials and tools. According to the International Federation of Robotics there will be 3 million industrial robots in use worldwide by 2020.

Operations Control

Once the plant design and layout have been determined, production managers engage in operations control, which consists of **purchasing materials, inventory control, scheduling**, and **quality control**.

Purchasing Materials

When *purchasing materials*, the production manager must first select a supplier. Over time, the supplier will become a key contributor to the success of the company, so production managers evaluate suppliers based on a number of criteria: price, quality, speed, reliability, servicing, and the availability of credit. If the production manager is using an e-procurement system for ordering, another consideration in the selection of a supplier will be whether that company can respond to an order placed via the Internet. In the selection process, production managers must weigh the costs and benefits of **outsourcing**, which is the act of purchasing component parts from suppliers rather than producing the components internally. The production manager will also try to negotiate **volume discounts** and flexible payment terms, for example, be able to wait 60 days to make a payment for supplies.

Inventory Control

Inventory control is the process of managing inventory at a level that minimizes costs, requires the firm to control the costs of raw materials inventories, work-in-process inventories, finished goods inventories, and repair and maintenance inventories. In essence, the firm must establish beforehand how much inventory of each item it should have and when it should reorder. Firms must control two different types of costs when dealing with materials inventories – carrying costs and ordering costs.

Carrying costs are the costs of storing, insuring, and financing inventories. **Ordering costs** are the expenses connected with placing orders for more inventory. One way to reduce ordering costs is to place large orders so that fewer orders are made, but placing large orders results in increased inventory, which will drive up the carrying costs. A technique for reducing carrying costs that has become popular in recent years is **JIT (just-in-time) inventory control**. Production managers place frequent small orders for just the amount of supplies immediately needed. JIT does reduce inventories, but it results in high ordering costs and the risk that there will not be enough supplies to feed production. Another inventory control technique is **materials requirements**

Materials Requirements Planning (MRP)
Inventory control technique that helps managers determine when and how much to order from suppliers.

planning (MRP), a computerized technique that helps managers determine when to place orders to suppliers and how much of each material to order. MRP helps production managers ensure that the materials are available when needed.

Production managers must also control the inventory of finished products that a firm produces. This inventory includes **work-in-process**, partially completed products, and an inventory of **finished goods**. Managers monitor the work-in-process inventory in order to control costs and make sure that shortages in supplies do not arise, which could shut down production. Supply and demand for the company's products may cause the inventory of finished goods to increase too much. When this happens, the firm may want to produce other things, or it may try to increase demand for the product. The skill of the production manager in controlling inventory prevents excessive inventories, which can reduce the value of the company when inventory must be sold at lower prices.

Scheduling

A **production schedule** sets a time frame for completing tasks, showing how much time will be allotted, when output is due, and how much volume is expected. The schedule communicates expectations to workers of what they must accomplish and how much time they have to complete their tasks. Using the production schedule managers are able to predict how much will be produced in each time period. Firms that do not meet their production schedule will not be able to accommodate their customers' needs in a timely manner. Technology is having an impact on production scheduling. Some firms allow customers to place orders over the Internet, and these orders can be filled more quickly.

PERT Scheduling technique that helps managers find the critical path, the series of project tasks that will take the longest time to complete.

Complex **special projects** require their own **scheduling techniques**. The **program evaluation and review technique (PERT)** enables managers to schedule tasks so as to minimize project completion time (see figure 7.3). To use this technique, the manager represents the sequence and relationship of project tasks on a chart using nodes and arcs to represent these tasks and relationships. Then

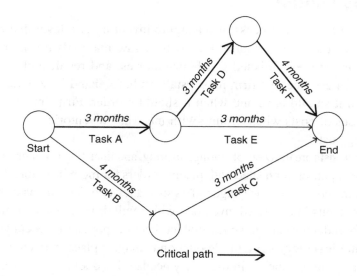

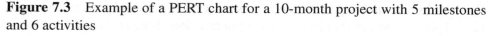

Figure 7.3 Example of a PERT chart for a 10-month project with 5 milestones and 6 activities

the manager locates the **critical path**, which is a series of related tasks that takes the longest to complete. For example, in figure 7.3 the critical path runs along lines A, D, and F and totals 10 months. By completing the tasks on the critical path on time, the manager can prevent delay of the entire project. Activities not on the critical path, shown by lines B, C, and E, may have more flexibility in their time frame for completion.

For simple projects, a **Gantt chart** (sometimes also referred to as a bar chart) can be used. It is a visual aid consisting of a horizontal bar chart that illustrates a schedule of tasks associated with a project (see figure 7.4). It shows not only the sequence of tasks to be performed, but also the amount of time for each task. Project management is able to monitor the progress of the tasks from start to finish. The chart is named after Henry Laurence Gantt, an engineer and social scientist to whom its invention is attributed.

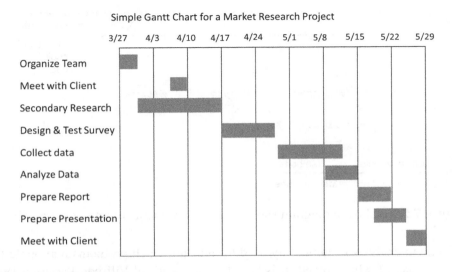

Simple Gantt Chart for a Market Research Project

Figure 7.4 Gantt chart

Quality Control

What is **quality**? One definition found in the literature states that "the quality of a product or service is a customer's perception of the degree to which the product or service meets his or her expectations." The International Organization for Standardization (ISO) defines quality as the totality of characteristics of an entity that bears on its ability to satisfy stated or implied needs.

Examples of quality factors:

- Automobiles: control of road noise, reliability, safety, appearance, audio and wireless systems
- Food: taste, smell, presentation, texture, freshness, organically grown
- Clothing: fit, materials, comfort, style
- Furniture: safety, durability, ease of assembly

Quality control means identifying and correcting product deficiencies to ensure that operations produce products that meet specific quality standards. A host of useful tools has been designed for quality improvement, inspired by both imagination and need. Statistical analysis of production data, satisfaction surveys of customers, "fishbone diagrams" (see figure 7.5), benchmarking, competitive product analysis—a process by which a company analyzes a competitor's products to identify desirable improvements—and Pareto analysis are some of the tools companies use to measure, monitor, improve and maintain the quality of their products and their operations.

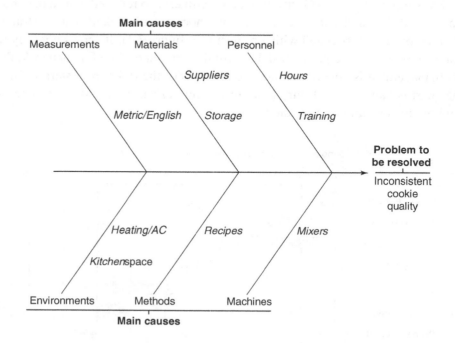

Figure 7.5 Fishbone diagram showing causes of inconsistent cookie quality

Vilfredo Pareto 19th-century economist who originated a technique to identify problems whose solutions would yield the greatest payoff.

Pareto analysis is commonly used to indicate which problems may yield the greatest payoff when solved. It is based on the work of Vilfredo Pareto, a 19th-century economist. The modern empirical interpretation of this holds that 80% of an organization's problems are a result of only 20% of the causes, often referred to as the "80/20 rule." Focusing on and solving that 20% yields the greatest benefit. The firm can thereafter turn its attention to the "lesser" causes. ABC analysis is an extension of this principle where charts are used to visually break down a problem into the relative contributions of its various components.

Total Quality Management (TQM) Refers to the act of continuously monitoring and improving the quality of products and services.

Managing for Quality

Total quality management (TQM) means planning, organizing, monitoring, and controlling every aspect of putting high-quality products in the hands of consumers. The guiding objective of TQM is to do the right things and to do them right the first time and every time. In other words, quality should be built into a product from the start, not "inspected in" at the end of the production process. TQM involves consideration of the interests of all stakeholders, including customers, suppliers, and employees.

When implementing TQM, the term commonly used to refer to the act of monitoring and improving the quality of products, firms may assess quality through various techniques such as:

- Using computer technology to detect defective parts and to determine if component parts meet quality standards;
- Using **quality control circles** made up of employees who assess the quality of a product and offer suggestions for improvement;
- **Sampling,** which means selecting some products at random and testing them to determine if they meet the firm's quality standards; and
- Monitoring **customer complaints** by collecting and analyzing customer feedback.

To implement quality control, a firm will set its own standards and develop its own techniques, but there are also international quality standards that it can use to measure the quality of its goods or services. The International Organization for Standardization (ISO) is a nongovernmental organization based in Switzerland that publishes international standards for an enormous variety of goods and services. Its goal is to benefit humanity by guiding organizations toward the production of goods and services that work well and safely. The standards and the organization are called ISO because it means "equal" in Greek. Thus the name of the organization will be the same throughout the world in all languages.

International Organization for Standardization (ISO) Non-governmental organization that publishes international standards for goods and services.

- The **ISO 9000** family of standards provides requirements for setting up and running quality management systems. ISO 9000 outlines a path by which an entire organization, public or private, may become certified as meeting minimum quality-management requirements set by ISO.
- The **ISO 14000** family of standards addresses the requirements and guidelines for meeting minimum levels of environmental management. These standards help companies manage and control the environmental impact of their activities, such as the use of resources and production of pollution.

Quality Experts

Contributions from many notable luminaries make up what we know today as TQM. The concept of TQM originated in the work of Frederick Taylor whose book, *Principles of Scientific Management*, gave rise to time-motion studies in the early 20th century. Statistician W. Edwards Deming, who taught quality control techniques to the U.S. War Department during World War II, is considered the "father" of TQM, though he never used the term himself. After the war, Deming taught statistical process control techniques to the Japanese during the reconstruction of the nation's automobile industry. Soon the Japanese were producing excellent vehicles and making inroads into the U.S. market. Deming's "14 Points for Management" (see figure 7.6), the key principles underlying TQM, are still followed today.

W. Edwards Deming Father of TQM though he never used the term himself.

Other quality control experts include Joseph Juran, who wrote the *Quality Control Handbook*, which redefined quality from the customer's point of view, and Philip Crosby, who introduced the concept of *zero defects*. Other renowned figures include Kaoru Ishikawa, who developed the concept of quality circles and pioneered the use of fishbone diagrams, Genichi Taguchi, who developed methods for optimizing the process of engineering experimentation, Amand Feigenbaum, who developed the concept of total quality control, and Walter Shewhart, who is credited with the creation of statistical process control (SPC) charts.

---

1. Make a commitment to constant improvement in order to stay in business, attain competitive advantage, and provide jobs.
2. Adopt a philosophy of leadership for change.
3. Build quality into the product in the first place. Don't wait for inspection to ensure quality.
4. Build long-term relationships with suppliers as a way of minimizing total costs. Don't award business based only on low price.
5. Adopt a philosophy of continuous improvement for constantly improving quality and productivity and decreasing costs.
6. Institute training on the job.
7. The aim of supervision should be to help people and machines and gadgets to do a better job.
8. Drive out fear, so that everyone may work effectively for the company.
9. Foster collaboration and coordination among departments.
10. Most of the causes of low quality and low productivity belong to the system and thus lie beyond the power of the work force to correct.
11. Replace production quotas and management by objective (e.g., numerical goals) with leadership.
12. Remove barriers that rob employees at all levels of their pride of workmanship.
13. Institute a vigorous program of education and self-improvement.
14. Transformation is everybody's job.

Figure 7.6 Deming's 14 points for management

Adapted from *Out of the Crisis* by W. Edwards Deming published in 1986 by MIT Press.

The highest honor for performance excellence (i.e. quality) in the U.S. is embodied in the Malcolm Baldrige Quality Award which was started in honor of Howard Malcolm Baldrige, Jr. who was secretary of commerce under President Ronald Reagan. He was widely recognized as an excellent manager and a proponent of quality management. He helped write the Quality Improvement Act of 1987. The now-coveted **Baldrige Award** recognizes companies producing world-class quality goods and services (see Table 7.4 for a list of 2016 winners). To win a Baldrige Award a company must:

- Exhibit senior executive leadership
- Obtain and analyze information about the quality of its products or services
- Engage in strategic quality planning
- Actively develop its human resources
- Effectively manage the entire quality process
- Show how it measures operational results
- Exhibit a customer focus

Table 7.4   Winners of the 2018 Malcolm Baldrige Award

Integrated Project Management Company, Inc., Burr Ridge, Illinois (small business)
Donor Alliance, Denver, Colorado (nonprofit)
Memorial Hospital and Health Care Center, Jasper, Indiana (health care)
Alamo Colleges District, San Antonio, Texas (education)
Tri County Tech, Bartlesville, Oklahoma (education)

Source: The National Institute of Standards and Technology (NST), an agency of the U.S. Department of Commerce.

Supply Chain Management (SCM)

A **supply chain** for any product is the integrated flow of information, materials, and money that starts with raw material suppliers and continues through the various stages of the production management process until the product reaches the end user. Materials flow from suppliers (and there may be more than one tier of suppliers) downstream to a manufacturer whose processes transform them into products that are shipped to consumers. Material and product flows are generally unidirectional (generally in the downstream direction). **Reverse logistics** occasionally happens when products or materials are returned due to any number of reasons (usually unacceptable quality). Information flows are usually bidirectional (both up and down the supply chain) and monetary flows are unidirectional (upstream), as seen in Figure 7.7.

Supply chain Flow of information, materials and money through the stages of the production management process until the product reaches the end user.

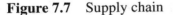

Suppliers   Manufacturer   Intermediaries   Consumers

Materials/Products flow

Information flow

Funds

Figure 7.7   Supply chain

For example, the supply chain for an automobile manufacturer would include the following elements: suppliers of steel and plastic, suppliers of robotic devices, auto part manufacturers, auto dealers, consumers who purchase cars, who create revenue for the manufacturer, and who provide feedback used in adjusting products to create satisfaction.

Supply chain management is the integration and management of all the activities involving procuring materials and services, transforming them into intermediate and final products, and delivering them to the end customers. The concept of supply chain management reflects the position that cooperation among producers, suppliers, distributors, retailers, intermediaries, and customers can reduce the time it takes to fill a customer's order, lower costs, improve quality, and increase profits for all members of the supply chain while creating satisfied customers.

Walmart is a pioneer in supply chain management, partnering with big suppliers such as Procter & Gamble. Using bar code and electronic data interchange (EDI) technologies, Walmart communicates stocking needs directly to suppliers who quickly respond by restocking the retailer's shelves with just the items that customers want.

Given that it encompasses the most costly set of activities in the organization, operations and supply chain management are integral to the success of the organization. They frequently represent the one area in the organization's operations where significant cost savings can be made.

Most organizations, especially those operating in the global arena, must carefully design and structure their supply chains to effectively respond to sudden changes in materials availability, currency rates, shipping channels, and political risks.

Supply Chain Management in a Global Environment

Thanks to technological advances on many fronts and the elimination of trade barriers between countries, today, more than ever before, we live in an interconnected global environment. Firms can source their materials and sell their products on the global market. Similarly, consumers can purchase goods or services from firms located anywhere in the world. It is common knowledge that the majority of businesses (more than two-thirds—both large and small) operate in global markets.

Offshoring and outsourcing are typical features of the globalization of business. **Offshoring** means sourcing or getting work done overseas. Over the last two decades, a lot of American companies have shifted significant amounts of their manufacturing to China. **Outsourcing** means contracting with an external firm (third party) to manufacture a good or deliver a service that initially was done internally. Besides the obvious benefits of globalization, there are significant downsides to outsourcing and offshoring, including loss of domestic jobs, the outside source's lack of in-house knowledge of critical business operations, and the loss of direct control over the production process.

Business Analytics

Advancements in information technology over the past several decades have made it possible for firms to collect, store, and quickly process large volumes of data about their business environment (both internal and external) and operational performance. Various terms have been coined to describe these capabilities namely **data mining**, **big data**, **business intelligence**, **business analytics**, etc. Collectively, they describe the set of tools and techniques (some of which have been in existence for many decades) for reporting, analyzing, modeling, forecasting, predicting, or cogently presenting a firm's past performance, prevailing conditions, or courses of action and alternatives based on available data. They are aimed at providing a logical basis to inform decision-making in the various operational processes of the firm. Successful supply chain performance is unattainable without effective use of the capabilities encapsulated in business analytics. This topic is revisited in the next chapter on information systems.

Business analytics Set of techniques for using information technology to report, analyze, model, forecast, predict, and present data for use in decision-making.

APPLY YOUR KNOWLEDGE

Quality Control Cost Cutting at Boeing: A Disaster in the Making?

Boeing, the Seattle-based airplane manufacturer, started streamlining its quality assurance program in 2016. Change accelerated when Ernesto Beltran, a quality assurance expert with thirty-two years of experience in the auto industry, became Boeing's vice president of total quality the next year. Boeing's goal was to speed production—it takes forty days to produce a 747—while cutting down on errors.

The company's Quality Assurance Transformation Plan called for reducing the number of inspections required before a plane takes flight, which would result in cutting the number of quality inspectors needed. In January 2019, Boeing announced 1,000 inspectors were to be reassigned to other positions by 2020. The International Association of Machinists was not happy about the move, and neither was the Federal Aviation Administration (FAA), which was investigating a quality control failure at the end of 2018. The crash of a Boeing 737 Max in Ethiopia in March 2019 intensified scrutiny of the company's quality transformation program.

Boeing had always used "a second set of eyes" to inspect and sign off on every step of the manufacturing process, with defects carefully documented. The new system was based on the auto industry model of building things right the first time. Key elements of the new quality-streamlining program included the following:

- Eliminating inspections of processes that have very few defects, called "stable" processes
- Use of "smart" tools that eliminate trial and error, are more accurate, and immediately document to a central database the identity of the worker and whether standards have been met
- Employee self-inspection of stable processes not related to airplane safety
- Sampling for inspection instead of inspecting all processes
- Redesigning parts so that workers make fewer errors when installing them
- Making assembly simpler by changing the sequence of processes

In December 2018, the "Bond and Ground" process failed an internal quality audit. This category of work insures that there is a grounded electrical pathway along the length of the plane. The audit of 1,200 jobs out of 60,000 found that 93 percent were done correctly, falling short of the 95 percent benchmark. The failure required a return to inspection of 100 percent of this type of work until 10 consecutive airplanes met the standard. The FAA began a mandatory, on-site investigation.

The machinists union wanted Boeing to provide evidence to support its claim that certain processes produce very low defect rates. Local union president Jon Holden suggested that Boeing "prove by a specific, definitive, and consistent standard that there are extremely low defects" before stopping inspections and re-assigning workers.

Workers at the Boeing Dreamliner plant in North Carolina claimed that letting mechanics self-inspect to accelerate production—no matter how "smart" their tools were—had led to falsified documentation and mistakes. One worker reported to the Charleston, South Carolina, *Post and Courier* that planes left the plant with cut tires, fluids that had not been serviced, untested gears, and partially functional hydraulic systems. Production time had been cut in half, but fully 90 percent of the work that went into building a plane was no longer being inspected by a second set of eyes. When mechanics did find their own mistakes, workers said that they feared disciplinary action if they reported them. "It's quantity over quality," workers said.

Knowledge Application Questions

1. "Lean manufacturing," which originated in Japan and became the "Toyota Way," focuses on eliminating waste. Waste is defined as anything that does not create value for the customer. Boeing has decided that it is wasteful to inspect processes that have a very low error rate. What suggestions do you have for Boeing to make its manufacturing more efficient without sacrificing quality?

2. Karl Albrecht, founder of the Aldi grocery chain, said, "You seldom improve quality by cutting costs, but you can often cut costs by improving quality." What did Albrecht mean? Give examples to support your explanation.

3. In your opinion, are the Boeing inspectors more concerned about losing their jobs than helping the company meet quality standards efficiently? Explain your answer after reading one of the source articles listed here.

Sources

Gates, D. 2019, January 20. "Boeing overhauls quality controls: More high-tech tracking but fewer inspectors." *Seattle Times*. Accessed October 30, 2019. https://www .seattletimes.com/business/boeing-aerospace/boeing-overhauls-its-quality-controls-more-high-tech-tracking-but-fewer-inspectors/.

Gates, D. 2019, February 1. "Shortcoming in Boeing quality-control audit draws scrutiny from inspectors, FAA." *Seattle Times*. Accessed October 30, 2019. https://www.seattletimes.com/business/boeing-aerospace/boeings-move-toward-fewer-inspectors-questioned-following-quality-control-audit/.

Woodward, C. 2019, May 6. "Amid scrutiny over 737 Max, Boeing to replace 900 inspectors. And union is not happy." *USA Today*. Accessed October 30, 2019. https://www.usatoday.com/story/news/nation/2019/05/05/boeing-737-max-alert-issue-not-safety-threat-statement-says/1112643001/.

Wren, D., and G. Smith. 2019, May 6. *Boeing SC lets mechanics inspect their own work, leading to repeated mistakes, workers say*. Accessed October 30, 2019. https://www .postandcourier.com/business/boeing-sc-lets-mechanics-inspect-their-own-work-leading-to/article_5ccc89ce-6cea-11e9-af3c-bfe34127eb85.html.

QUIZ YOURSELF

Without looking back at the chapter, choose the best answer to each of the questions below. Answers are in the back of the textbook before the Index. Review the chapter to find out why you missed any questions.

1. All of the following are activities involved in the operations management function of Purdue Fort Wayne EXCEPT
   a. accounting services.
   b. maintenance of facilities and grounds.
   c. marketing and communication.
   d. admissions.
   e. fundraising.

2. Operations management at Parkview Hospital and at General Motors could be considered the same because both organizations
   a. produce products that cannot be inventoried.
   b. are labor-intensive.
   c. must make effective use of technology.
   d. must engage in capacity planning.
   e. Both options c and d are correct.

3. Tata, an Indian auto maker, wants to choose a site in the United States to build a new factory. In making this decision, Tata should consider locations
   a. where there is little demand for small cars.
   b. situated on or near major interstate roads.
   c. in Chicago or New York where real estate is more expensive.
   d. where the average hourly wage is $15 per hour or less.
   e. Both options b and d are correct.

4. The difference between a product layout and a fixed position layout is that
   a. in a product layout the workers go to the product, and in a fixed position layout, workers and equipment are grouped according to function.
   b. in a process layout, workers are grouped according to function, and in a fixed position layout, workers stay in one place.
   c. in a product layout, tasks take place in the order that they are performed, and in a fixed position layout, workers and equipment are grouped according to function.
   d. in a product layout, tasks take place in the order that they are performed, and in a fixed position layout, workers go to the product.
   e. None of the above.

5. Starting in 1981 Deere & Company's extensive use of computers and robots enabled the company to run numerous small assembly lines simultaneously for different products and turn a profit even with low levels of output. Deere & Company was probably using
   a. PERT scheduling.
   b. cheap labor.
   c. process layouts.
   d. flexible manufacturing systems.
   e. All of the above.

6. Ordering techniques such as JIT and MRP help reduce
   a. ordering costs.
   b. customized orders.
   c. carrying costs.
   d. processing costs.
   e. work-in-process.

7. In the supply chain, _____ flows both downstream and upstream.
   a. money
   b. materials
   c. information
   d. labor
   e. products

8. The set of tools and techniques for reporting, analyzing, modeling, and predicting a firm's performance is known as
   a. business analytics.
   b. blockchain.
   c. data mining.
   d. quality control.
   e. Pareto analytics.

9. _____ is used to determine if the firm is producing a product that meets or exceeds the desired product characteristics.
   a. The critical path
   b. Quality control
   c. The program evaluation and review technique (PERT)
   d. Hoteling
   e. None of the above

10. Jamal's company now employs twenty-five people. He is thinking of hiring the Paychex company to handle his payroll, benefits, and hiring functions. This is an example of
    a. offshoring.
    b. outsourcing.
    c. onboarding.
    d. off-ramping.
    e. restructuring.

mama_mia/Shutterstock

CHAPTER 8

Information Systems and E-Business Basics

In the 20th century, the term **information systems** brought to mind vast rooms filled with computers owned by large multimillion-dollar companies. Today, the computational power of several mainframe computers resides on your desk or in your laptop computer. Wireless technologies have made it possible to place the benefits of network computing in the hands of a cell phone owner. Because of these advances in technology, there is practically no aspect of life today that is not touched by information systems. Business owners, managers, and employees must understand how information systems work, and most importantly, how to use information technology to create value for customers and profit for their companies.

What Is Information?

"You can give people responsibility and authority, but without information they are helpless. Knowledge is the ultimate power tool." Bill Gates, former CEO of Microsoft in his 1999 book *Business at The Speed of Thought: Using a Digital Nervous System.*

Data, information, knowledge. These terms are often used interchangeably, but they should not be. It is important to understand the differences between data, information, and knowledge in order to understand how information systems work. **Data** are raw facts, figures, texts, activities, and transactions that are recorded and stored in a database (see figure 8.1). For example, a department store will keep records of your address, the items that you buy, when you bought them, and the total amount of your purchases, among other pieces of data about your shopping. These pieces of data only become information, however, when they have been organized in a meaningful way. The data collected from your store visits will be accumulated along with data from other customers' visits for a time period, and reported in categories such as "item number," "units sold," "monthly sales total," and so on. The report organizes the data, transforming it into **information**, from which **knowledge** is derived by reading and analyzing the report for a specific purpose. Since we operate today in a global, wants-driven economy, it is essential to know the competition and to know what customers want. As Bill Gates observed, knowledge is power in business because it helps you make the right decisions. Never has the axiom "what you don't know may put you out of business" been truer.

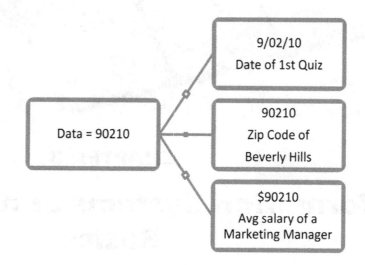

Figure 8.1 Data organized into information

Useful Information and Knowledge

Information Useful information is complete, accurate, relevant, up-to-date, and available.

On the other hand, never before have individuals and companies had such unprecedented access to data and information, due largely to the advent of sophisticated, high-performance supercomputers, the **Internet**, and the proliferation of wireless mobile devices. Anyone, anywhere, and at any time may publish information that almost anyone in the world may use. Knowing what is useful and what is credible information has replaced access to information as the major challenge for business people in using information systems.

Determining which information will provide useful knowledge rests on whether the information meets certain criteria.

1. Useful information is *complete*. It describes all aspects of a situation from a variety of perspectives. Obtaining all of the data and information relevant to a business decision involves examining all internal and external

variables. For example, a product research and development team that failed to examine the findings of other scientists would not have complete information about the research pertinent to the team's project. Poor sales reports alone do not provide a thorough understanding of the situation of a failing store.

2. Useful information is *accurate*. Basing important decisions on inaccurate or unreliable information can be disastrous. The greater the precision and absence of error, the more confident managers can be in basing their decisions on the information. Among measures that ensure the accuracy and reliability of internal company information include cases where all types of data needed are collected, errors are detected at the point of data entry and in the assembling of reports, and only those authorized are permitted to enter or change data.

    The credibility of external sources of information must be thoroughly checked. The practice of "crowdsourcing" (a play on the term "outsourcing") information, in which volunteer experts answer an open call to provide solutions to a problem, underscores the need for managers to carefully evaluate information found on the Internet.

3. Another challenge posed by the enormous amount of information available to us is determining which information is *relevant*. Out of concern for capturing all of the data that might be needed, companies often collect unneeded data. Having to sift through data unrelated to a decision or a problem wastes time and causes "information overload."

4. Last, useful information is *up-to-date and available* when it is most needed. For example, investors can find up-to-date stock quotes on the NYS Euronext website.

The successful management of any organization in this modern era requires evidence-based decision-making. This invariably means using results from analyses of quantitative data to underpin decisions made by management.

Quantitative analysis, however, is only successful if the underlying data measures performance metrics or functions that are aligned with the firm's envisioned outcomes. Thus, a critical first step before any quantitative methodology (such as demand forecasting, quality control, or optimization) is applied, is selecting the measures or numerical data to collect, monitor and evaluate. This raises issues of which data measures (and by extension, organizational objectives) should be pursued and when, because some performance measures react counter cyclically to each other. For example, server utilization and queue length are fundamentally conflicted with one another. Thus, choosing one or the other of these measures as an objective for improvement leads to opposing results in the other.

The significance of the following categorical statements cannot be overstated:

*   Much of management (especially at the operational or supervisory levels) frequently concerns quantitative analysis and usage of data, but that analysis is useful only if the underlying data represents the objectives of the organization.

- An important step in managerial analysis and problem solving is choosing which data measures to collect and analyze.
- "Measurements" are critical factors that must be chosen very carefully because much of managerial analyses ultimately is about choosing and evaluating measurements.
- Data must be tangible, visible, and "measurable." They cannot be vague desires, feelings, or opinions.
- Data measurements should be defined in such a way that there is mutual agreement; that all users of said data agree on how the data are collected and what the data mean.
- The firm must install appropriate information systems to collect the necessary data to inform and underpin required decision-making at each level in the organizational structure.

What is an Information System?

A system is a set of parts or components that work together to accomplish a goal. An organization is an example of a system, just as your laptop and its software is a system. An information system is a set of interrelated elements that collect, manipulate, and disseminate data and information while providing a feedback mechanism in order to meet an objective.

The information system is made up of both "hard" and "soft" components. Among the hard components are desktop and laptop computers along with mobile devices connected via an internal network or the Internet. Soft components include software such as operating systems and application programs; the data, defined as the facts and figures entered into the system; procedures, which are the rules for achieving optimal ad secure operations; and trained personnel, that is, the knowledge workers.

Cloud computing Using information systems hosted on the Internet rather than located on-site.

Many companies have implemented "**cloud computing**," which simply means that they use information systems not physically located on-site. A third party provides data storage and access via the Internet to software applications that employees of the client company may use to access and manipulate that data. The result is reduced labor costs and access to a far greater variety of software than a company might have the budget for.

Major Applications of Information Systems

Information systems collect and store the firm's key data and produce the information that managers need for analysis, control, and decision-making (see figure 8.2). A different type of information system supports each of these business activities. Each type of system is described in this section.

Transaction processing systems (TPS) focus on data and information about routine, day-to-day operations such as preparing a payroll, billing customers, and warehouse operations. The data collected via the TPS support the information systems used by middle managers and executives above them. Because the TPS forms the foundation for all of the other systems, it is vital that transaction data be complete, accurate, and up-to-date. An airline reservation system is an example of a TPS. It keeps records of flight schedules, passenger reservations and seat assignments, aircraft loading, flight inventory, ticket purchases, and fare tariffs. Today the reservation systems of multiple airlines are linked via computer networks and are available directly to consumers via the Internet. The airline reservation systems most used today are SABRE, Abacus, Worldspan, Galileo, and Patheo.

The **management information system (MIS)** is closely linked to and fed by the TPS. It provides decision-making support for routine, structured decisions made at the operational and tactical level. An MIS generates summary and exception reports such as monthly production summaries, travel expense reports, and the difference between expected sales and actual sales of a particular product. Examples of tactical decisions that are supported by an MIS would be a decision to run a sale on a particular product, or a decision to make changes in the types of products and services that a company offers.

Knowledge management systems (KMS) are used to store information about business processes, customers, inventory, and products, so that every employee has access to the same information. The KMS is usually custom designed to meet user needs. The KMS facilitates the process of knowledge management, which is the gathering, organizing, and sharing of organizational knowledge. The aims of knowledge management are to improve productivity, foster innovation, and gain competitive advantage.

Knowledge workers are responsible for finding or developing new knowledge for the organization and integrating it with existing knowledge. They analyze and filter the information from the TPS to make it useful for decision-makers. Examples of knowledge workers include institutional research analysts, marketing analysts, and financial analysts who use the knowledge stored in the KMS to make recommendations about changing business processes. Knowledge workers act as advisors and assistants to both top and middle management.

Data mining helps knowledge workers to find hidden patterns and relationships in large databases, called **data warehouses,** to predict future behavior. By creating mathematical models based on patterns and relationships, managers can predict consumer behavior such as "If an airline ticket is purchased, then a car will be rented at the same time in 50% of the cases." Data mining helps pinpoint reasons for customer loyalty, analyze the impact of pricing, and forecast sales. Within the data warehouse are subsets of data called **data marts.** Each functional area of a business—human resources, marketing, finance, operations—has its own data mart in which data are organized for querying and analysis.

Data mining Process of analyzing large databases to find hidden patterns in order to create useful information.

The **decision support system (DSS)** is an information system application that provides its users with decision-oriented information whenever a decision-making situation arises. It is generally an interactive system that helps decision-makers in the solution of semistructured and unstructured problems (see chapter 5). For example, a decision support system may be used to run hypothetical scenarios of the consequences of cutting certain items from an annual budget or of opening a new plant. The interactive nature of the DSS allows managers to consider many alternative solutions, increasing their chances of making an informed decision.

Data mart Subset of a firm's data warehouse pertaining to a functional area.

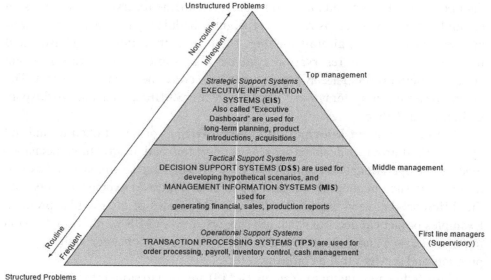

Figure 8.2 Applications of information systems

An **executive information system (EIS)** is a special type of DSS designed to support decision-making at the top level of an organization. An EIS may help a CEO to develop an accurate picture of overall operations and a summary of what competitors are doing. These systems are usually easy to operate and present information graphically in charts and graphs so that it can be easily grasped.

Expert systems (ES) and **artificial intelligence (AI)** systems are advanced systems that support decision-making of a technical nature at various levels in an organization. They specialize in analyzing the needs and problems of a particular industry and suggest best practices to resolve the problems. Expert systems are able to reason through information from TPS and KMS in much the same way humans do—that is, they recognize patterns, problems, or issues in that information. Artificial intelligence helps to suggest solutions to problems based on expertise and knowledge built into the system. AI systems have been used to help explore for oil, schedule employee work shifts, and diagnose illnesses.

Working with "big data"

As alluded to earlier, the corporate world is awash with data. It has been estimated that the quantity of data stored on corporate computers doubles every six months. Walmart, the retail giant, handles more than 1 million customer transactions every hour, feeding databases estimated at 2.5 petabytes – the equivalent of 167 times the books in the U.S. Library of Congress, and still growing. This quantity is growing every second as cash registers continue ringing, web browsers continue leaving those trails of cookie crumbs, and radio frequency (RFID) devices continue updating inventory records, among others. These huge accumulations of data are frequently referred to as **big data**. **Business intelligence** and **business analytics** are encompassing terms used to describe activities that combine aspects of data reporting, exploration, ad hoc querying, and explanatory and predictive modeling (i.e. data-mining) to underpin managerial decision-making and actions.

In 2004, Walmart crunched its sales data and noticed that before a hurricane struck, there was a run on flashlights and batteries (which was not surprising) but

Big data *Extremely large data sets that can be mined for patterns, trends, and associations.*

also Pop-Tarts – a sugary American breakfast snack. While this was surprising, on reflection it is clearly evident that the snack would be a handy thing to eat in a blackout. Such "crunching" of sales and other data has moved into the mainstream as the price of computing and storage has fallen and software systems have become cheaper and better. An increasing number of firms (even small businesses) are collecting more data than ever before and using data-mining techniques to get a "complete picture of their operations" that allows them to operate more efficiently, pick out trends and improve their forecasting.

Cloud computing and **open-source software** are technological trends that are helping to make big data possible. By using the internet as a platform for the collection, storage and processing of data, cloud computing allows firms to avoid buying expensive equipment. Instead, they lease computing power as and when they need it. Free open-source software such as Hadoop allows ordinary desktop computers to analyze large data sets across clusters of computers. Hadoop does this by parceling out processing tasks to numerous computers at the same time. When hundreds of computers are used, the processing time is reduced to miniscule fractions of what it would have been otherwise.

System Security

Companies need to protect the vital, proprietary knowledge contained in their databases from Internet users and competitors, while being able to network their computers to take advantage of the efficiencies of the Internet. Individuals, too, must be aware of threats to the security of their own machines, which if breached can lead to harm of others' computers as well.

The solution to managing the interface between a company's internal network, which is sometimes called a **local area network (LAN)** or an **intranet**, and the Internet is a firewall. A **firewall** is software or hardware that blocks outside users from accessing an intranet without a valid password. It protects a computer system from **hackers** who try to access private systems for malicious or illegal reasons. Sometimes, however, a company will want to give outsiders access to its internal data. For example, Walmart allows suppliers such as Procter and Gamble or Kraft to access the Walmart MIS to determine inventory levels and product availability. Allowing suppliers to have this information means that Walmart avoids stocking too many items, a cost savings it passes along to the customer. FedEx decreases the number of customers phoning service centers when it allows them to log on to a FedEx website to check on the status of a package. In these situations companies will set up an **extranet**, which can be viewed as part of a company's Intranet that is extended to users outside the company.

Intranet A company's internal network, sometimes called a local area network.

Computer viruses, worms, and Trojan horses are the most common forms of security threats to network security and to that of individual computer users. A **virus** is a self-replicating program that loads itself onto a computer without the user's knowledge. A **worm** is a small piece of software that exploits a security hole in a network to replicate itself. A **Trojan horse** is a program that claims to do one thing, but in reality does something else, usually something malicious.

Spyware is not illegal but it allows an individual or a company to gather user information through the user's Internet connection without his or her knowledge, usually for advertising purposes. **Spam**, or unsolicited ("junk") email, may also carry viruses, worms, and Trojan horses. **Identity theft**, which also happens without the victim's knowledge, is illegal and easily perpetrated on the Internet. In schemes called "**phishing**" or "spoofing," individuals are tricked into giving out personal information when they are contacted by what seems to be a trusted source, or when they are directed to a website that looks exactly like that of their bank or credit card company.

Companies and individuals both can protect their system's security by installing antivirus protection such as Norton Antivirus software and making sure that updates of virus definitions are scheduled regularly and automatically. It is wise not to open spam email, nor to respond to email from a bank or credit card company. It is best to contact financial services in person or by phone.

E-Business

E-business is the trade that takes place between individuals and companies using information technology and the Internet. This trade takes a variety of forms, explained below and summarized in table 8.1.

> **Business-to-business (B2B)** commerce takes place between companies by linking the value chains of different companies. For example, an automobile company may go to the website of a tire manufacturer or distributor to buy tires for its automobiles. The B2B website acts as an intermediary in this transaction.
>
> **Business-to-consumer (B2C)** trade takes place between a business and its individual customers using IT and the Internet. Amazon.com is a general merchandiser that sells consumer products via the Internet.
>
> **Consumer-to-consumer (C2C)** transactions occur between a customer selling goods to another customer, as individuals do on e-bay.com.
>
> **Peer-to-peer (P2P)** transactions take place among customers without the intervention of a market maker as in C2C. Gnutella is a software application that allows users to exchange music files.
>
> **Government-to-business (G2B)** transactions occur between governments and businesses in which a government sells to or provides services to businesses or a business sells products and services to a government. Examples of G2B are tax collection, government procurement, and auctions.
>
> **Government-to-government (G2G)** category of e-commerce involves transactions within and between government agencies.
>
> **Government-to-employees (G2E)** category describes activities between units of government and their employees.
>
> **Government-to-citizens (G2C)** group denotes the government's use of the Internet to provide citizens with access to information and to facilitate transactions, such as renewing a driver's license or paying taxes online.

Websites in the B2C category must be able to compete in a global marketplace, utilizing multiple languages and currencies. The Web Globalization Report Card found that the average number of languages supported by 150 global websites was 31. Internet giant Amazon.com did not make the list of the Top 25 Global Websites for 2019. (See table 8.2)

Extranet Part of a company's intranet that has been set up to share with users outside the company

Phishing Scheme in which the Internet user is tricked into giving out personal information when contacted by what appears to be a trusted company.

Peer-to-Peer (P2P) E-business transactions that take place among customers without the intervention of a market-maker.

Table 8.1   Types of E-business

DEMAND (selling to....)	SUPPLY (business originating from . . .)		
	Business	**Consumer**	**Government**
Business	B2B	C2B	G2B
Consumer	B2C	C2C	G2C
Government	B2G	C2G	G2G

Table 8.2   Top 25 Global Websites 2019

Rank	Website
1	Wikipedia
2	Google
3	NIVEA
4	Microsoft
5	IKEA
6	Adobe
7	Philips
8	Cisco Systems
9	Hotels.com
10	Facebook
11	Siemens
12	Intel
13	Uber
14	Nestlé
15	Nikon
16	Volvo Cars
17	Deloitte
18	Hitachi
19	Canon
20	Booking.com
21	GoDaddy
22	Emirates
23	Church of Jesus Christ of Latter-day Saints
24	Toyota
25	Audi

Source: The 2019 Web Globalization Report Card, retrieved from
https://bytelevel.com/reportcard2019/#top25

APPLY YOUR KNOWLEDGE

Data Philanthropy: How "Big Data" Will Save the World

The Urban Institute, a nonprofit research group, defines data philanthropy as "the act of sharing private data assets to serve the public good." Researchers say that for-profit companies that collect mountains of data in the course of doing business are ideally suited to become data providers to universities, nonprofits, and government. Companies collect data more frequently and in more detail than public entities, complementing publicly available data. Providing this data to public researchers saves time and resources at the same time improving the quality of the database. Data philanthropy enhances the brand image of the donator, can result in new insights leading to innovation, helps mitigate corporate risk, and benefits the community at large.

The Nielsen Company, best known for its ratings of television channels, supplies data to advertisers, media owners, retailers, and consumer packaged goods manufacturers throughout the world. Since 2010, the company has shared the food pricing information that it gathers for retailers with Feeding America, a network of 200 food banks. Feeding America uses this data to create its annual *Map the Meal Gap* report to show the locations of the "food-insecure" households. (See the interactive map at https://map.feedingamerica.org/)

Nielsen assigned each UPC-coded food item in its database to one of the 26 food categories in the USDA Thrifty Food Plan (TFP) database (available https://www.fns.usda.gov/data-research). These categories were weighted within the TFP market basket based on pounds purchased per week by age and gender. A county price index was then calculated for each of the 3,142 counties in the United States to enable Feeding America to provide local estimates for meal cost, food budget shortfall, and meal gap.

Mobile phone datasets were among the first large datasets available, starting in the 1990s. Kenya-based Safari.com was among the first mobile phone companies to share its data for the public good. The Harvard School of Public Health (HSPH) mapped each of the 14,816,521 calls made on the network between June 2008 and June 2009. When a caller left home, the researchers calculated the duration and destination of the caller's journey, then mapped the information against malaria prevalence maps provided by the Kenya Medical Research Institute. Researchers were surprised to learn that most "imported" infections ended up in Nairobi, despite the fact that malaria mosquitoes do not thrive in an urban environment.

Data providers always anonymize and aggregate the data before sharing it with third parties, but frequently the provider uses only the simplest technique to anonymize so that it is possible, with little effort, to re-identify an individual. Companies must follow information privacy laws now in effect in over 80 countries. The legal principles most relevant to data philanthropy are that there must be a stated purpose for collecting the data and that the data cannot be disclosed to other organizations unless specifically authorized by law or the individual gives consent for the disclosure. One way to comply with these restrictions is for a company to prepare a dataset for public use, as Uber did with its Uber Movement data. Twitter users agree to make their data available when they set up their public accounts. If a data provider chooses this method, it must insure that the person's data cannot be linked with third party databases and relinked. As data philanthropy has become more popular, there is concern that best practices and laws to guide the sharing of sensitive personal data have not kept pace.

Knowledge Application Questions

1. Do the benefits of data philanthropy compensate for the risks involved in sharing people's detailed personal and behavioral information with third parties? Consider the ethical approaches and processes described in Chapter 3 of this textbook when justifying your answer.

2. Some innovative thinkers believe that you ought to be able to trade or sell your personal data (called "personal data trading") to pay for products and services. For example, you would receive a free automobile in exchange for the valuable data generated by digital accessories and controls. If you chose not to sell your data, you would pay full price, thus insuring your privacy. How practical is this idea? What are some of the short- and long-term consequences of enacting such a scheme?

3. Use Google or indeed.com to find job postings for "Data Scientist" positions. What degree is required? Identify three terms in the description that you do not understand and find out what they mean. For example, the terms machine learning, data mining, and predictive modeling frequently appear in advertisements for data scientists.

Sources

Decuyper, A. 2016. "On the research for big data uses for public good purposes." *Netcom* 30(3): 305-314.

Holley, P. 2018, June 26. "Privacy as a product: The argument for trading your personal data to get a discount on a car." [Blog post]. Accessed October 31, 2019. https://www.washingtonpost.com/news/innovations/wp/2018/06/26/privacy-as-a-product-the-argument-for-trading-your-personal-data-for-a-cheaper-car/?utm_term=.c97809c9e72b.

Information Privacy Law n.d. Accessed October 31, 2019. https://en.wikipedia.org/wiki/Information_privacy_law.

McKeever, B., S. Greene, G. MacDonald, P. Tatian, and D. Jones. 2018. "Data Philanthropy Unlocking the Power of Private Data for Public Good." Accessed October 31, 2019. https://www.urban.org/research/publication/data-philanthropy-unlocking-power-private-data-public-good.

Nielsen.com. 2015, September 15. "Nielsen and Feeding America collaborate to 'map the meal gap'." [Press release]. Accessed October 31, 2019. http://sites.nielsen.com/newscenter/nielsen-and-feeding-america-collaborate-to-map-the-meal-gap/.

QUIZ YOURSELF

Without looking back at the chapter, choose the best answer to each of the questions below. Answers are in the back of the textbook before the Index. Review the chapter to find out why you missed any questions.

1. How is data different from information?
   a. Data provides context, while information does not.
   b. Data is not organized, while information is.
   c. Information is not organized, while data is.
   d. Data is more meaningful than information.
   e. All of the above.

2. The New York Stock Exchange website shows stock prices as of the time that the site is accessed. The prices for the previous 12 months and press releases from all companies trading on the exchange are accessible from the website along with copies of annual reports. Which criteria for judging the usefulness of this information are being met?
   a. Interchangeability, attractiveness, and clarity
   b. Volume, crowdsourced, and dynamic
   c. Completeness, up-to-date, and available
   d. Low cost, transactional, single sourced
   e. None of the foregoing options

3. "Soft" components of an information system include
   a. keyboards and other input devices.
   b. data, procedures, and personnel.
   c. mobile devices and laptops.
   d. servers and routers.
   e. cables and cell towers.

4. Deena sells office products to small businesses. She uses an information system that tells her the dollar amount each customer has ordered in the past year, the date of her last sales call, and her total sales to date for her territory. This is an example of
   a. a transaction processing system.
   b. data storage.
   c. open-source software.
   d. cloud computing.
   e. a management information system.

5. Ali is the CEO of Instaventure LLC. He wants to launch an initial public offering of shares but is not sure when to do it. He will likely use what type of information system to support his thinking?
   a. A transaction processing system
   b. A management information system
   c. An expert system
   d. An executive information system
   e. A data mart

6. At Smithson Steel mill, delivery times, sales, profits, and customer service and loyalty have been boosted by a/an _____ that gives customers electronic access to the mill's inventories.
   a. distribution channel
   b. intranet
   c. handbook
   d. extranet
   e. None of the above

7. Some of the security threats that an organization must guard itself against include
   a. phishing.
   b. hackers.
   c. scammers.
   d. viruses and worms.
   e. all of the above.

8. Angela is an artist who sells her drawings via the Internet. Her biggest customers are other artists. This form of trade is called
   a. C2C.
   b. B2C.
   c. B2B.
   d. G2B.
   e. A2C.

9. The term _____, _____ refers to a broad range of tools and activities used to explore Big Data in order to make forecasting models that will inform decision-making.
   a. data warehouse
   b. information system
   c. business analytics
   d. expert system
   e. knowledge management

10. A _____ is software that blocks outside users from using an intranet without a password.
    a. smokescreen
    b. malware
    c. spoof
    d. Trojan horse
    e. firewall

CHAPTER 9

Managing Human Resources

This chapter focuses on the human side of business, frequently described by many business leaders as the most important and most valuable resource of any organization. Human beings are complex creatures. Their nature as individuals and their interactions as groups in production processes must be understood and properly managed if an organization is to be successful in the transformation of inputs into outputs in value-added manner.

Nature and Scope of Human Resources Management

Human resource management (HRM) is the set of organizational activities that is directed at attracting, developing, and maintaining an effective workforce. The management of human resources involves the following activities:

- Planning for staffing needs (HRP)
- Recruitment and selection
- Training and development
- Performance appraisal and feedback
- Compensation (pay and benefits)
- Labor relations

In a small firm, the owner is generally responsible for managing human resources. As the business grows and becomes organized into separate functional departments, the management of human resources will be carried out by specialists with input from line managers. If you examine the structure of human resources in large companies or organizations, you will find that each HRM activity may be directed by a separate unit (see figure 9.1).

Human Resource Planning (HRP)

The goal of **human resource planning (HRP)** is to make sure that the organization has the right employees with the right skills at the right place at the right time. Being overstaffed, particularly with full-time employees receiving benefits, can be costly and can lead to failure of the business, especially in difficult economic times. On the other hand, it can be equally costly to the future well-being of a firm if there are insufficient staff on hand to allow it to take advantage of a business opportunity such as expansion into a new geographic area or into the manufacture of a new product. Those responsible for human resource planning must be attentive to changes in the external business environment so that the firm is ready to respond and adapt to those changes.

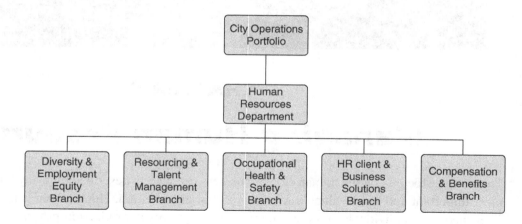

Figure 9.1 Human resources management function in a municipal organization

One of the activities involved in human resource planning is **forecasting staffing needs**. If a firm finds that it is overstaffed, a variety of actions may be taken. New hiring may be frozen until a future date, employees may be asked to work fewer hours, early retirement incentives may be offered, the firm may choose to temporarily or permanently lay off or discharge workers, or the firm may decide to simply become smaller, eliminating some of the products or services it offers. Obviously, if a shortage of workers exists, a firm will start recruiting new employees.

Another activity of human resource planning is **job analysis**, which is a process that determines the tasks that must be carried out by a worker in a particular position and the credentials a worker needs in order to adequately fulfill the responsibilities of the job. The position analyst writes a **job description** that states the tasks and responsibilities of the position and a **job specification** that states the credentials necessary to qualify for that specific position. Figure 9.2 shows an example of a job analysis.

MyCo *MyCompany, LLC*

Job Title:	Program Assistant	**Job Category:**	Administrative
Department/Group:	Training Department	**Job Code/ Req#:**	005
Location:	Fort Wayne, Indiana	**Travel Required:**	No
Level/Salary Range:	Grade 5 Administrative/Clerical	**Position Type:**	Full-time
HR Contact:	Linda Jones	**Date posted:**	April 14, 2017
Will Train Applicant(s):	Will train qualified applicant	**Posting Expires:**	May 15, 2017
External posting URL:	www.myco.com/jobs		

Applications Accepted By:

FAX OR E-MAIL:

(425) 555-0123 or L.Jones@myco.com

Subject Line:

Attention: Program Assistant, Training

MAIL:

Linda Jones, HR Manager

MyCo, LLC

PO Box 999

Fort Wayne, IN 46825

> *Job description* states the tasks and responsibilities of the position.

Job Functions and Requirements

ROLE AND RESPONSIBILITIES

Working under the direction of the Training Manager, the Program Assistant insures the smooth functioning of the MyCo training program by: is responsible for, creating and monitoring registration and attendance, collecting evaluation data, coordinating workshop facilitators, and publishing promotional materials pertaining to the company's training program.

- Scheduling locations and facilitators for training events
- creating and posting the company training catalog and workshop schedule
- creating and monitoring registration and attendance
- collecting evaluation data
- developing and distributing promotional materials pertaining to the company's traini[ng]

> *Job specification* states the credentials necessary to qualify for the position

QUALIFICATIONS AND EDUCATION REQUIREMENTS

Required experience: At least two years of full time experience working in an office.

Minimum required education: Associate degree (2 year college diploma)

PREFERRED SKILLS

Must be fluent in Microsoft Office and able pass MyCo competency test. Experience working with survey software desirable.

Reviewed By:	Martha Manners, Job Analyst	**Date:**	January 16, 2017
Approved By:	Linda Jones, HR Manager	**Date:**	February 13, 2017
Last Updated By:	Martha Manners, Job analyst	**Date/Time:**	January 16, 2017

Figure 9.2 Example of job analysis

Recruitment and Selection of Employees

The next activity in the management of human resources is recruiting and selection. Recruiting refers to the search for candidates that match the job description and specifications of a position. Recruiting involves publicizing the availability of a position and collecting the data necessary for screening the candidates. Selection must be done with care to make sure that the organization hires only the most appropriate candidates. Studies have linked poor recruitment and selection to higher rates of turnover, lower employee performance, less job satisfaction, diminished work motivation, and lawsuits. Refer to Figure 9.3 for an overview of the process.

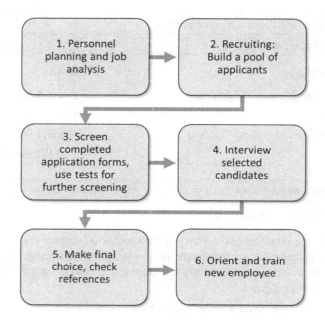

Figure 9.3 Recruitment and selection (staffing) process

Recruiting

Methods for Building Applicant Pools

Internal recruiting
Recruiting and hiring from within a firm can boost morale and improve productivity

The goal of recruiting is to build a pool of applicants from which the most qualified individual will be chosen. Firms frequently hire from within, called **internal recruiting**, because this method is less costly than seeking applicants from outside the firm. The job opening can be posted in the company newsletter, tacked to a bulletin board, or advertised on the company's intranet. One advantage of internal recruiting is an existing employee is already familiar with the firm and has a proven track record that can be evaluated. Internal recruiting can improve morale by giving current workers a chance to move to more attractive jobs and to receive promotions to positions with more responsibility and higher pay. A disadvantage of internal recruiting is that it limits the applicant pool and does not invite fresh viewpoints. Hiring from within the company may cause employees to believe that seniority will automatically lead to promotion. Furthermore, the company must fill the vacancy left by the internal hire, so the recruiting process begins anew.

A firm may choose **external recruiting** of applicants in addition to, or instead of, internal recruiting. Recruiting from outside the organization gives the firm access to a much broader pool of people and may allow the firm to find a greater number of qualified candidates. When a firm needs specialized expertise, fresh perspectives, or an experienced person to lead an endeavor new to the firm, external recruiting must be undertaken. However, the firm will have less information about how well an outside applicant will function within the organization and interact with other employees.

The external recruiting process usually takes longer than internal recruiting and is more expensive. In the past, recruiters had to buy space in the "Want Ad" section of the newspaper or in trade publications. Recruiters now use social media platforms such as LinkedIn and Facebook to find prospective candidates, reducing the time and expense of external recruiting and allowing even very small firms to build a large applicant pool. (See Apply your Knowledge at the end of this chapter.) Recruitment websites such as Glassdoor, Indeed.com, and Monster.com have also reduced the expense of external recruiting.

Other sources of applicants from outside the company are referrals from employees, employment agencies hired to find qualified applicants, also known as "head-hunters," and specialized online job boards, for example, HealthcareJobSite or Engineering.com.

The Benefits of Diversity

The benefits of **diversity** in the workforce and the preservation of equal opportunity for all prospective job candidates are two factors that today's recruiter must keep in mind at all times.

Companies that actively seek applicants from diverse ethnic, educational, and socioeconomic backgrounds enjoy enhanced corporate reputations and have reported higher retention rates, along with improved employee motivation, creativity, and innovation. Some examples of such companies are listed in Figure 9.4. Managers involved in recruiting should be careful not to discriminate based on factors not related to the candidate's ability to perform the job, such as age, race, gender, or religion, referred to as "protected characteristics." The recruiting process should take into consideration key federal laws prohibiting job discrimination. These laws include the following:

- **Title VII of the Civil Rights Act of 1964** (Title VII), which prohibits employment discrimination based on race, color, religion, sex, or national origin.
- **The Equal Pay Act of 1963 (EPA)**, which protects men and women who perform substantially equal work in the same establishment from sex-based wage discrimination.
- The **Age Discrimination in Employment Act of 1967 (ADEA)**, which protects individuals who are 40 years of age or older.
- **Title I and Title V of the Americans with Disabilities Act of 1990 (ADA)**, which prohibit employment discrimination against qualified individuals with disabilities in the private sector and in state and local governments.
- **Sections 501 and 505 of the Rehabilitation Act of 1973**, which prohibit discrimination against qualified individuals with disabilities who work in the federal government.
- The **Civil Rights Act of 1991**, which, among other things, provides monetary damages in cases of intentional employment discrimination.

Americans with Disabilities Act of 1990 (ADA) Federal law that prohibits employment discrimination against qualified individuals with disabilities.

1. AT&T	11. Cox Communications
2. Marriott International	12. BASF
3. ADP	13. Wells Fargo
4. Hilton	14. Target
5. Eli Lilly and Company	15. TIAA
6. Comcast NBC Universal	16. Neilsen
7. Accenture	17. Northrup Grumman
8. Mastercard	18. Toyota Motor North America
9. KPMG	19. TD Bank
10. Abbott	20. The Walt Disney Company

Figure 9.4 Top 20 companies for diversity

Source: The DiversityInc Top 50 Companies for Diversity, retrieved from https://www.diversityinc.com/the-2019-top-50-diversityinc/

Selecting the Best People for the Job

Screening Applicants

Once the firm has a sufficient number of applications, the process of identifying the most qualified among them begins. **Screening** starts with the completed application form, resume, and cover letter which provide the recruiter with information about the applicant's qualifications and experience. The recruiter compares the information in these documents to the job specification that was prepared in the job analysis (see Figure 9.2). The job specification acts as a filter that enables the recruiter to objectively assess the qualifications of each applicant and prepare a list of candidates. The recruiter may schedule short screening phone calls with qualified applicants. During the screening phone call, the recruiter will ask questions about any omissions in the application or resume, explain the job to the applicant, answer questions about the position and the organization, and learn whether the applicant can start on the date required or can relocate.

For some positions, recruiters may require additional screening via a job-related test. For example, the NFL uses the Wonderlic Basic Skills test, which measures basic math and verbal skills. Other types of tests include an audition or demonstration of selling skills, taking a personality test online or in writing, and a typing test. If the applicant obtains the desired score or performance level, he or she will advance to the interview stage.

The Society for Human Resource Management (SHRM) recommends that recruiters avoid using social media or Internet searches during the screening process. There is a risk that the recruiter will learn about the "protected characteristics" of the applicant and eliminate the individual from further consideration. Doing so is against the law. Once the applicant has advanced to the candidate list, SHRM encourages the recruiter to use the Internet find out more about the candidate's background. It is recommended that the recruiter keep records of all searches and of the decisions that were made based on the results.

Interviewing Selected Candidates

Interviews may be accomplished in person, on the phone, or via video conference. The interview yields valuable information about the applicant's interpersonal skills, knowledge, abilities, energy level, and potential compatibility in the workplace. Depending on the position and the organization, more than one interview may be conducted.

The interview process should be conducted in a consistent, systematic way in order to ensure fairness to all applicants, remove the influence of personal bias, and to be certain that the firm has all the data needed in order to make an informed hiring decision. The **structured interview** is the best way to maintain consistency and comparability in the process, especially if there is more than one interviewer assigned to meet with multiple candidates for a position. In the structured interview, the same questions are asked of each candidate in the same order.

Structured interview
Asking the same set of
standardized questions of
all job applicants

In some organizations, the human resources department will supply a list of questions that should be asked of all candidates, usually for entry-level positions or jobs that do not require specialized knowledge, skills, or abilities. For professional, technical, managerial, or other positions requiring knowledge and experience in a specific field, the manager or supervisor in charge of the recruitment and selection process will develop a set of questions relevant to the job analysis (see Figure 9.2). Each candidate will be asked the same questions regardless of who does the interview.

The impact of the aforementioned job discrimination laws can be observed in examples of questions that interviewers can and cannot ask (see Figure 9.5). A well-run human resources department will have a list of these and other questions to use or avoid so that managers and human resources staff are able to stay within the law. Examples of interview questions that help determine whether the candidate will be able to handle job duties include the following:

- How did you overcome difficulties in communicating with a coworker? (**Communication skills**)
- What's the best way to make decisions when working on a team project? (**Soft skills**)
- How would you handle an angry client who demanded to speak to your supervisor without discussing the problem with you? (**Situational**)
- How would you explain structured interviews to someone who is not a human resource professional? (**Behavioral**)

Before meeting a candidate, the interviewer should review the candidate's application form and resume, especially if the interviewer has not been involved in the screening process. Open the interview by putting the applicant at ease and provide a brief preview of the topics to be discussed to help the applicant feel more relaxed. Listening carefully to the candidate's answers is just as important as asking the same questions of each candidate. The interviewer should close the interview by telling the candidate what is going to happen next and write an evaluation of the candidate while the interview is still fresh. It is important to provide the candidate with a time by which a decision will be made and to communicate the final decision within that period.

In the unstructured interview, the order of the questions depends on the responses given by the interviewee, and the same open-ended questions may not be asked to every candidate. When conducted by a well-trained individual, an **unstructured interview** helps to gain a deeper understanding of the candidate's personality, temperament, and ability to think quickly in an unscripted situation, traits that a structured interview might not detect. An insight into these qualities is very important when hiring individuals for high-level positions because it helps employers distinguish among candidates who possess similar knowledge and experience.

Unfortunately, the use of an unstructured interview process more often reflects poor planning, not an intentional effort to acquire deeper knowledge of the attitudes, abilities, and qualifications of candidates. The unstructured interview is subjective, which compromises its accuracy and may invite legal challenges.

Unstructured interview
The candidate's responses to open-ended questions guide the direction of the interview.

Can't Ask	Can Ask
• What's your birthdate?/How old are you?	• Are you over 18?
• What are your child care arrangements?	• Would you be able to work a 9:00 a.m. to 6:00 p.m. schedule?
• How long has your family been in the U.S.?	• Are you eligible to work in the U.S.?
• Do you have any pre-existing health conditions?	• Can you perform the essential functions of the job, with or without reasonable accommodation?
• What religious holidays do you celebrate?	• Can you work on weekends?

Figure 9.5 Some inappropriate/appropriate interview questions

Source: Illegal or Inappropriate Interview Questions retrieved from http://www.gsworkplace .lbl.gov/DocumentArchive/BrownBagLunches/IllegalorInappropriateInterviewQuestions.pdf

Final Selection and Reference Checks

The hiring manager will contact references provided by the candidate and ask each reference a standard set of questions about past job performance, strengths and weaknesses, integrity, and work habits. A background check may be conducted. For certain positions, a physical exam may be required at this point. The final step in selection is for the hiring manager or committee, in some cases, to analyze all of the data that have been collected about each candidate and make a decision about which one to hire. The hiring manager or human resource department should contact the chosen candidate to offer the job to him or her. Some companies may require the offer to be made initially in writing.

Employee Training and Development

Firms provide training to develop a variety of skills needed by their employees. Training may take place on the job or off the job—that is, at the job site or at a time and place not during work hours. The use of technology has become pervasive in support of both on-the-job and off-the-job training.

A common form of on-the-job training is the new employee **orientation**, which takes place soon after hiring. Orientation formats vary widely, but the content almost always includes an introduction to the mission, values, policies, structure, and operations of the firm. An orientation may take place in a large group, or it could be conducted by a department head with one or two new employees. It is important for the firm to reveal itself to the new employee in a positive way in order to set a tone for the new employee's first days with the firm.

Much on-the-job training is accomplished through **"shadowing"** an experienced employee as that individual works through daily tasks and responsibilities. This type of training is easy to implement and works well when the job being learned is fairly simple and repetitive, such as clerking in a store or working on an assembly line. The trainee is more likely to remember how to do a task if it is done in the actual context of work. In other instances, the employee will simply start doing the job he or she was hired to do.

A new employee may be formally assigned a **mentor** or a **"coach"** who can provide advice and helpful feedback while the employee learns the job. In trades such as masonry and plumbing, new workers must serve a specified number of years as apprentices in order to achieve the rank of "journeyman." In both cases, a formal relationship between the learner and a more experienced colleague is defined along with standards that the learner must meet in order to be considered ready to function as a full-fledged member of a profession or team.

A technique commonly used in management training is **job rotation**. Trainees work in various functional departments of a firm, giving them a broad perspective on the organization and how their actions as managers will impact it. Job rotation can be used to cross-train line workers too, allowing more flexibility in their assignments and making their jobs more interesting.

Other on-the-job training methods include **vestibule training**, in which employees receive training in a space located near their work areas using equipment and materials similar to what they will encounter in their jobs. Another technique similar to vestibule training is **job simulation**, in which the actual conditions of the workplace, including situations that most commonly occur, are duplicated. Job simulation is used when the consequences of an error are grave, such as piloting an airplane or operating a space shuttle or army tank.

Vestibule training *Employees receive training in a space near their work areas using tools and materials similar to those that they will use in their jobs.*

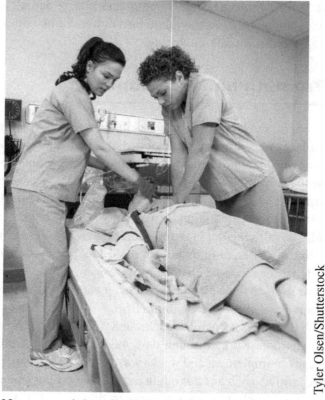

Tyler Olsen/Shutterstock

Nurses receiving simulation training

Off-the-job training refers to any training offered away from the work site. This type of training includes off-site classroom training, conferences, and seminars. Common strategies used in classroom training include case studies and role playing. Off-the-job training allows trainees to focus on the knowledge and skills they are learning, and sometimes helps them to form closer work relationships with each other. However, it is a very costly form of training and can disrupt the flow of work left behind at the office or at the plant.

A growing amount of formerly off-the-job training is now being offered as **online training**. Internet-based training programs offer employees the convenience of being able to complete training whenever and wherever they wish. Furthermore, the training can be repeated or accessed while on the job. Online training programs can be designed to be just as informative, interactive, and socially engaging as formal classroom training. Web-based videoconferencing personalizes online courses. Companies have realized millions of dollars in savings from reduced travel expenses and increased productivity when workers can be trained without leaving the job site. Because of the reduced design and delivery costs, companies may be able to afford to offer more training than they did in the past.

Online training
Internet-based training offers convenience and cost-savings, allowing employees to be trained without leaving the job site.

Evaluating Employee Performance

The practice of regularly evaluating employee performance serves several critical purposes. Most importantly, the supervisor provides feedback and direction to an employee that can help that person improve individual performance and the productivity of the organizational unit. Through the use of an evaluation instrument that rates performance against a set of criteria relevant to the employee's job, the supervisor can identify and communicate the employee's strengths and weaknesses. These ratings can help the employee and the supervisor to develop a training or development plan tailored to the employee's needs. **Performance evaluations** provide evidence necessary in determining whether an individual qualifies for a promotion and how raises and bonuses should be allocated.

Upward appraisals allow employees to evaluate their supervisors. These appraisals are most effective if they are anonymous. As with other types of appraisals, the evaluation should segment criteria in order to provide more precise and detailed feedback. Another recent trend in employee evaluation is **360-degree feedback**, which gathers feedback from co-workers, supervisors, team members, subordinates, and sometimes customers and other stakeholders.

Upward appraisals
Employees anonymously evaluate their supervisors.

madpixblue/Shutterstock

Best Practices in Performance Evaluation

Supervisors must take care to clearly communicate job responsibilities to newly hired employees. Changes to these responsibilities should be explained and documented. Setting down expectations in writing helps the employee to perform the job properly and provides a point of reference should there be disagreements in the future about what the employee is expected to do.

Employees need consistent and timely feedback, not only when their performance is deficient but even when they are doing well. To build a cooperative working relationship, supervisors should allow employees to respond to criticism and attempt to work with the employee to remedy problems. Supervisors should be consistent in their treatment of employees whether performance is deficient or excellent. Consistent acknowledgment of good work builds morale and motivates all employees by showing that good work will be publicly appreciated.

Supervisors must take particular care in formulating plans to address poor employee evaluations. The first step is to determine the cause of the performance problem by gathering data from the employee and reviewing documentation of the problem. In most cases there is no single cause but a complex set of factors that must be understood before proceeding. The reason for the performance problem will usually point to its solution. For example, lack of a job skill or poor training would point to additional on-the-job training and some coaching. The supervisor should work to enlist the cooperation of the employee and stress the importance of helping the unit achieve organizational goals.

The supervisor must specify deficiencies in the employee's evaluation and give the worker a chance to respond. If the employee is unwilling to improve, the supervisor may have to reassign, suspend, or fire the worker. Employers usually require supervisors to follow a set of procedures to ensure fair treatment of employees and to comply with laws governing employment.

Although following best practices in supervision to achieve maximum productivity from employees ought to be sufficient motivation to engage in them, firms are also mindful of penalties that may result from **wrongfully firing** workers. The Civil Rights Act of 1991 gave dismissed workers the right to a trial by jury and the right to receive punitive as well as compensatory damages such as back pay. Although lawsuits can be very costly, firms should not avoid firing an employee because of fears the employee will sue. Not firing someone who is clearly unwilling to perform to the standards that others are at undermines the morale of other employees. When the supervisor has followed the steps outlined by the employer and provided the employee with ample opportunity to correct problems, the court system has usually sided with the firm.

Wrongful firing The Civil Rights Act of 1991 gave dismissed workers the right to a trial by jury and the right to receive both punitive and compensatory damages.

Compensating Employees

Compensation refers to the payment employees receive in return for their labor. A company's compensation system is a major factor in recruiting and retaining skilled workers. The most common types of compensation are:

- Hourly wage
- Weekly or monthly salary
- Incentives
- Commission
- Lump-sum salary increase
- Profit sharing

Some people use the terms "wages" and "salary" interchangeably to express the same idea—what an employee is paid for work in a specific time period. **Salary**, however, specifically refers to an annual amount that is paid to an employee divided into monthly or bi-weekly payments. The employee is expected to work as many or as few hours as is needed to fulfill the duties and responsibilities of the position. **Wages** usually refer to the amount that the employee will receive for each hour of work. The U.S. minimum wage is currently $7.25 per hour. States set their own minimum wage rate at or above the federal minimum. For example, the minimum hourly wage in the state of Washington is $11.50.

Commission is a form of compensation commonly used in sales, or in any situation in which performance can easily be quantified. When a specified sales goal is met, the employee receives a commission. In some sales positions, commission is the only compensation. This is called working on "straight commission." The employee in this type of position is usually selling expensive items or services.

An **incentive** is compensation in addition to salary or wages that rewards extra effort and outstanding performance. Effective use of incentives can improve organizational performance too. One type of incentive is a **bonus,** a one-time payment made to an employee at the end of a time period for reducing costs or improving efficiency, for example. **Merit pay** increases the employee's base pay depending on how well the employee has met a performance standard. **Commission** may be considered an incentive when it is offered along with a salary. **Awards,** both with or without cash, are also incentives, and are most effective when paired with employee recognition programs.

The **lump-sum salary increase** is tied to merit. It is a way that employers can reward top performing employees, especially long-term employees who may be earning well above the market rate, without increasing their fixed costs. The lump-sum salary increase is a one-time payment made at the end of a designated time period such as the end of the fiscal year.

In **profit sharing** employers give employees stock in the company so that when the company is profitable a portion of the profits comes back to employees. Employees are motivated to perform well by having a vested interest in the success of the company.

A compensation package will often include **benefits** in addition to pay. A good benefits package can be instrumental in keeping morale high and in securing the loyalty of employees through good times and bad.

Required benefits
Pay benefits like workers' compensation, unemployment insurance, and Social Security are all required by federal law.

Employers are required by law to pay benefits like **workers' compensation, unemployment insurance,** and **Social Security.** Workers who are injured on the job or who develop a work-related illness receive medical treatment and cash payments to partially replace lost wages from workers' compensation insurance. Employers pay this insurance at a rate of $.75 to $2.74 per $100 of covered wages, depending on the state and industry. Employers in private industry, agriculture, and government are required under the Social Security Act of 1935 to pay into a state unemployment insurance program that will pay benefits to individuals who involuntarily become unemployed and are still able to work. The rate the employer pays is a percentage of the covered payroll set by unemployment insurance laws in each state, as low as about 3%. Employers must also pay 6.2% of an employee's earnings in Social Security taxes. The employee matches the employer's contribution. Self-employed individuals must pay 12.4% of their earnings.

Pay for time not worked
This most frequently offered benefit includes vacations, paid holidays, and sick leave.

Pay for time not worked is probably the most common benefit offered to employees, whether they are part-time or full-time. **Vacation time, paid holidays,** and **paid sick leave** are the ones most frequently offered. Various types of **insurance,** such as health, dental, and life are also fairly common. Employer-paid health insurance premiums can total 15% to 20% of an employee's pay. Employees usually pay a small percentage of the premium. The amount that the employee pays is steadily increasing as healthcare costs continue to climb, and companies seek to reduce costs in order to remain competitive. Other benefits include **pension or retirement programs, tuition reimbursement,** membership in a **credit union,** access to low-cost or on-site **childcare,** a company **cafeteria** or **fitness center,** and **flexible hours,** among other benefits designed to attract and retain qualified workers. Technology companies competing for top talents have been creative in assembling benefits packages that will appeal to innovators while at the same time shaping corporate culture. Examples of some unusual benefits include yoga, unlimited paid vacation, catered lunches, free ice cream, dog-friendly offices, working from home, and surfing lessons.

Labor Relations

Relationships between labor and management are frequently adversarial. Labor unions are often blamed for driving manufacturing out of the United States to seek cheap labor because companies must honor the high wages and benefits negotiated by unions in order to keep a skilled workforce. Balancing the needs of employees and the needs of the company is a goal of human resources management.

Labor unions grew rapidly in the 1930s when the Norris-LaGuardia Act made it more difficult for companies to prevent workers from joining together to protest working conditions, to lobby for higher pay and shorter working hours, and to achieve greater job security. The National Labor Relations Act of 1935 further increased the power of labor unions by requiring employers to bargain with unions in good faith and prohibited discrimination against workers who joined unions. The National Labor Relations Board (NLRB) was set up in order to certify unions.

Indeed, unions had grown so powerful by 1947 that it was necessary to pass an amendment to the National Labor Relations Act to prevent unions from forcing workers to join. Under the amendment, called the Taft-Hartley Act, states could pass "right to work" laws that outlawed "union shops." Twenty-eight states now have "right to work" laws. Two of these states, Indiana and Michigan, passed these laws in an attempt to lure back manufacturers seeking lower labor costs.

"Right to work" laws
State laws that forbid
requiring workers to join
a union as a condition of
employment.

Managing the relationship between a company and the labor unions that represent its workers is called **labor relations**. **Collective bargaining** is the process of negotiating a mutually beneficial contract between company management and labor. The process usually starts before the end of an existing contract, which usually lasts two or three years. Management and representatives of the union present each other with a list of demands and concessions. Negotiation teams establish the rules for the bargaining process and schedule meetings during which agreement is reached on such topics as pay raises or cuts, benefits, overtime rates, work schedules, production standards, and discipline, to name some of the most common topics. The contract is then presented to the union members who vote to ratify or reject it. After rejecting a contract a union may organize strikes, boycotts, and picketing to pressure management into accepting its demands.

A **strike** is the refusal of union members to work for the company until their demands are met. Strikes can be devastating to a company. In 1997 the United Postal Service lost more than US$600 million when 185,000 members of the UPS Teamsters (truck drivers) went on strike for the entire month of August. The union gained public support and achieved its goals of replacing part-time jobs with full-time positions, higher pay, and retention of its pension plan. More recently, 50,000 members of the United Auto Workers Union (UAW) went on strike in 2019 against three General Motors plants to demand compensation for the pay and benefits that they sacrificed when the company hit hard times several years earlier. Credit Suisse estimated that the strike cost GM $50 million per day.

Unions can also start boycotts of the company's products or services in which union members and sympathizers refuse to buy from the firm with which the union has a dispute. Union members may also decide to picket outside the employer's buildings, walking or standing in circles carrying signboards with slogans on them. Pickets may not prevent other workers from entering the building, but "crossing the picket line" is very intimidating.

Companies respond to union tactics by securing a court-ordered injunction that prevents picketing and sometimes strikes. Firms may even lock out union members, preventing them from working until an agreement is reached. The National Hockey League famously locked out its players for an entire season (2004 – 2005) when owners and the players' union could not reach an agreement on salary caps. In this case, the owners won, but lost revenue and fans.

Companies frequently engage in actions or adopt policies that will reduce employees' desire for unions, which employers believe encourage inefficiency and higher costs. Some of these tactics include promoting from within to increase employee satisfaction with their careers, avoiding layoffs, adopting a democratic leadership approach, maintaining good working conditions, and paying competitive wages.

APPLY YOUR KNOWLEDGE

Online Recruiting Trends and You

It is now easier than ever to apply for jobs using online job boards like Indeed. com and Monster.com, and social media like Facebook, Twitter, and LinkedIn. One consequence, though, is that companies are flooded with resumes. Almost all large and mid-sized companies use technology to screen the deluge of applicants. Applicant tracking systems (ATSs) eliminate up to 70 percent of resumes before a human being sets eyes on them. An ATS not only makes recruiting more efficient but helps manage communications with candidates and provides proof of compliance with Equal Employment Opportunity Commission (EEOC) rules.

If you have applied for a job at a company website using an online form, you have interacted with an ATS. Taleo, iCMIS, and Greenhouse are top ATS brand names. The software scans your application for keywords, then builds a profile that can be filtered and matched with a profile of the ideal or acceptable candidate. The drawback of this system is that it can wrongfully eliminate qualified candidates who have not carefully prepared their resumes and cover letters.

The Society for Human Resource Management (SHRM) reports that 43 percent of the organizations it surveyed are using social media to screen the prospective candidates who do make it through the application process. Searching Facebook, Twitter, Instagram, and LinkedIn, for example, gives the recruiter a robust description of the applicant's professional life, behavior in the community, hobbies, politics, and personal relationships. A picture of the applicant is usually available. The majority of companies completing the SHRM survey were reluctant to use social media for screening, though, because of doubts about the accuracy of this information, fear of invading the individual's privacy, and the risk of job discrimination. To avoid discrimination, SHRM has recommended that recruiters use social media only after conducting either a phone or in-person interview.

Recruiters are also becoming sophisticated in using social media to build talent pools, a technique called "social recruiting." Social media helps talent managers reach people who are not actively looking for a different job by making it easy to build relationships with these "passive candidates" before they start looking for a new position. Recruiting passive job candidates is the top reason companies give for using social media to find talent, according to a 2016 SHRM survey. LinkedIn, a social network for business and professionals, is rapidly becoming the online recruiting tool of choice, stealing business from online job sites like Monster.com and Indeed.com, according to stock analyst Craig Huber of Huber Research Partners.

Social networks greatly facilitate employee referrals, which 80 percent of organizations rank as their top source for quality candidates, according to the SHRM. A study by the Federal Reserve Bank of New York confirms what employers already know. It found that referred employees are 15 percent less likely to quit. The downside of "word-of-mouth" recruiting, though, is that people tend to refer others who are like them. If the company's workforce is not diverse, the EEOC says that this type of recruiting results in a homogeneous talent pool that might become a "barrier to equal employment opportunity," leading to violations of the Equal Employment Opportunity Act. SHRM's advice to employers is to avoid relying too much on one method of recruiting.

Knowledge Application Questions

Automated resume screening software has changed the rules for writing resumes. Social media has given jobseekers another tool to master. Use the Jobscan website to revise your resume and polish your "brand."

1. Find a description of a job that you want to apply for on Monster.com, Indeed.com, or at a company's website. Visit the Jobscan website at https://www.jobscan.co/ and use their software to receive an analysis of your resume from the perspective of an applicant tracking system. (The Basic subscription is free.) How did you do? Update your resume and save a copy for future use.

2. Create a free LinkedIn page if you do not already have one. Use Jobscan to analyze your LinkedIn presence. Did you achieve a score of 80 percent or more? If not, read "9 Things Recruiters Expect from Your LinkedIn Profile" on the Jobscan Blog at https://www.jobscan.co/blog/recruiters-expect-linkedin-profile/ and revise your page until you improve your score.

Sources

Schwartz, N. D. 2013. "In Hiring, a Friend in Need Is a Prospect, Indeed." Accessed October 31, 2019. https://www.nytimes.com/2013/01/28/business/employers-increasingly-rely-on-internal-referrals-in-hiring.html.

Shields, J. 2017, December 21. "What is an Applicant Tracking System?" [Blog post]. Accessed October 31, 2019. https://www.jobscan.co/blog/what-is-an-applicant-tracking-system/.

Shields, J. 2018, August 30. "8 Things You Need To Know About Applicant Tracking Systems." Accessed October 31, 2019. https://www.jobscan.co/blog/8-things-you-need-to-know-about-applicant-tracking-systems/.

Smith, A. 2015, January 6. "Social Media Recruiting Has Similar Risks as Word of Mouth." Accessed October 31, 2019. https://www.shrm.org/ResourcesAndTools/legal-and-compliance/employment-law/Pages/social-media-recruiting.aspx.

Using Social Media for Talent Acquisition. 2017, September 20. Accessed October 31, 2019. https://www.shrm.org/hr-today/trends-and-forecasting/research-and-surveys/pages/social-media-recruiting-screening-2015.aspx.

QUIZ YOURSELF

Without looking back at the chapter, choose the best answer to each of the questions below. Answers are in the back of the textbook before the Index. Review the chapter to find out why you missed any questions.

1. All of the following are components of the human resources function, EXCEPT
   a. recruitment and selection of employees.
   b. pay and benefits.
   c. total quality management.
   d. performance evaluation.
   e. training.

2. Human resource planning is critical to the success of an organization because it
   a. helps make sure that the company has the skill sets required to carry out its business strategy.
   b. helps the organization to control costs.
   c. ensures that legal requirements are met.
   d. frees top executives to focus on meeting the revenue goals of the organization.
   e. All of the above

3. The education and experience requirements for a position is called the
   a. job description.
   b. duties and responsibilities.
   c. job announcement.
   d. curriculum vitae.
   e. job specification.

4. Gina, a research assistant with Purdue University Fort Wayne, noticed a job posting on the bulletin board in the hallway. The posting says that the position will not be advertised to the public. This is an example of
   a. external recruiting.
   b. internal planning.
   c. the intranet.
   d. internal recruiting.
   e. intrapreneurship.

5. Challenges associated with diversity in the workplace include
   a. educating employees to accept and respect ethnic and cultural differences.
   b. preventing gender discrimination.
   c. accommodating physical and mental disabilities.
   d. obeying laws relevant to employment.
   e. all of the above.

6. Which of the following questions should NOT be asked in a job interview?
   a. Are you over 18?
   b. Do you need child care?
   c. Do you have a U.S. passport?
   d. Can you work on the weekends?
   e. Choices b and c

7. Why is it important to regularly evaluate employees?
   a. To ensure quality of service to customers
   b. To reward employees who are performing well
   c. To provide documentation of performance over time
   d. To jointly develop problem solutions or discover new ideas
   e. All of the above

8. John received a link to an online survey that asks him to evaluate his supervisor. This is an example of
   a. 360-degree feedback.
   b. lateral performance feedback.
   c. online training.
   d. upward appraisal.
   e. none of the above.

9. An incentive is different from salary and wages because
   a. only employees who exhibit outstanding performance will receive it.
   b. it is not part of the compensation package.
   c. it is given only at the end of a calendar year.
   d. salary and wages reward excellent performance.
   e. None of the above

10. The _____ prohibits job discrimination based on race, color, religion, sex, or national origin.
   a. Civil Rights Act of 1964
   b. Civil Rights Act of 1991
   c. Equal Pay Act of 1963
   d. National Labor Relations Board
   e. Taft–Hartley Act

Sarah2/Shutterstock

CHAPTER 10

Motivating Employees

What Is Motivation and Why Is It Important?

The word "motivation" comes from the Latin root *movere* meaning "to move." **Motivation** is defined as a process or set of processes that causes, sustains, regulates, and gives purpose to behavior. Motivation is what causes a person to start a project, expend energy and effort to complete it, and persist in the execution of the project over time. To return to the Latin origin of the word, motivation *moves* a person toward a goal. It is therefore not difficult to understand the importance of motivated employees to a productive workplace. Since motivated behaviors are voluntary choices controlled by the individual employee, supervisors need to understand what motivates an employee to reach peak performance.

It is not an easy task to increase employee motivation because employees respond in different ways to their jobs and their organization's practices. Supervisors want to influence the factors that motivate subordinates to perform at higher levels of productivity. Motivated employees can provide competitive advantage by offering suggestions on better ways to satisfy customers and feel compelled to go the extra mile for the organization when necessary. Loyal and committed workers are more likely to stay with a firm through difficult times.

Traditional Theories of Motivation

Extrinsic motivation
Motivation that comes
from receiving a reward
or a punishment from an
external source.

The study of motivation in the workplace focuses on the supervisor as well as on the employee. Motivation theories are important to supervisors attempting to be effective leaders. Underlying all the theories are the concepts of extrinsic and intrinsic motivation. **Extrinsic motivation** means motivation stemming from receiving a reward (for example, money, good grades, fringe benefits, or a good performance evaluation) or avoiding a penalty (for example, demotion or dismissal). **Intrinsic motivation** is choosing a behavior because of the enjoyment or sense of accomplishment the behavior brings. Intrinsic motivation comes from within the person. An intrinsically motivated student, for example, is eager to learn and will spend time to fully understand a subject. This student derives enjoyment and satisfaction from the act of studying itself, which is motivation to continue this activity.

Intrinsic motivation
Motivation that comes
from within a person

An analysis of the data generated by studies of the effects of factory lighting on productivity at the Hawthorne Works near Chicago between 1924 and 1932 showed that changes in lighting had no direct effect on productivity. The **Hawthorne effect** refers to the observation that employees perform better when they feel singled out for attention or if they feel that management is concerned about their welfare. The Hawthorne effect is an effective motivational theory that is easy to apply.

Maslow's "hierarchy
of needs" Influential
theory of motivation
that arranges workers'
needs into five levels of
importance.

Maslow's "hierarchy of needs" was one of the most influential motivational theories ever developed. Writing in the 1950s, Maslow proposed that workers have needs that they seek to fulfill in their jobs and that these needs are arranged in a hierarchy of importance. Maslow further proposed that once people have achieved their needs in a given category, they are motivated by the desire to satisfy the needs of the next higher level. Firms can motivate workers by helping them satisfy their needs.

Maslow's hierarchy is usually depicted as a pyramid (see figure 10.1). Maslow hypothesized that a person will first satisfy the needs at the bottom of the pyramid. Once these needs have been satisfied, the worker will be motivated to advance to the next level of needs. Once the first four levels of needs have been satisfied, their motivational power is neutralized. The fifth level, self-actualization, represents needs for growth, which by its very nature, can never be completely satisfied. The human desire for self-fulfillment is a durable, persistent motivator.

Though the research on which Maslow's theory is based has recently been invalidated, Maslow's ideas are widely used to motivate employees by fulfilling their needs.

- **Physiological needs**
  - Offering higher entry-level salaries than other companies in the same industry.
  - Permitting employees to set their own work hours.
  - Providing choice in the selection of office furniture and décor (ergonomics).
  - Providing generous meal breaks or a low-priced cafeteria on site.
- **Safety needs**
  - Provide training to employees in proper lifting techniques; inform employees of how to prevent back and eye strain.
  - Provide employees with ergonomically correct furniture.
  - Accommodate the needs of employees with permanent and temporary disabilities.

- **Social (belongingness) needs**
  - Sending memos to all employees introducing the new ones; employees sending individual welcoming messages.
  - Organizing social gatherings where employees engage in team activities.
  - Publishing an annual employee yearbook.
  - Providing discounted memberships at a nearby health club.
- **Esteem needs**
  - Regularly assessing and recognizing performance.
  - Creating a peer-to-peer recognition program and publishing kudos in a company newsletter.
  - Conferring annual performance awards at a company ceremony.
  - Publishing promotions and awards in the local newspaper.
- **Self-actualization**
  - Providing a leave of absence for pursuing personal and professional development.
  - Offering employees unlimited time off to perform volunteer work in the community.
  - Offering a variety of training opportunities.

Figure 10.1   Maslow's hierarchy of needs applied to the workplace

Theory X, Theory Y, and Theory Z

Douglas McGregor, a professor of management at MIT in the late 1950s, provided an explanation of how supervisors' perceptions of workers affect the way they attempt to motivate workers. In his book, *Human Side of Enterprise*, McGregor described two types of supervisors, which he categorized as Theory X or Theory Y supervisors.

Theory X supervisors believe most workers dislike work and will avoid it when possible. This type of supervisor will monitor workers closely, exercise tight control, and delegate very little authority.

Theory Y supervisors view employees more favorably, believing that they are willing to work and to accept responsibility. This type of supervisor will give workers more freedom to use their creativity and is more willing to delegate authority.

Theory Z Management approach that focuses on gaining employee loyalty by making the worker happy on and off the job.

Theory Z, developed by William Ouchi, refers to "Japanese-style" management, and gained much attention during the Asian economic boom of the 1980s. Theory Z management focuses on making the individual employee happy on and off the job, with the goal of gaining the employee's loyalty. Theory Z supervisors assume that workers want to form relationships with co-workers and with management. Theory Z emphasizes a long-term perspective in the development of a company's workforce. The outcomes of Theory Z are high productivity, high job satisfaction, and a stable work force. Workers have a high level of participation in decision-making.

Two-factor Theory of Motivation

Hygiene factors Work conditions that prevent employee dissatisfaction.

Frederick Herzberg, an American psychologist writing in the 1960s, proposed that job satisfaction depends on **motivating factors**, such as recognition in the workplace, as well as the presence of **hygiene factors**, such as work conditions. Hygiene factors do not enhance satisfaction, but they do prevent dissatisfaction. Herzberg's theory is known as the **two-factor theory**. Research suggests that his theory may explain only a limited set of workplace situations.

In Herzberg's theory, the hygiene factors or "dissatisfiers" work independently of the motivational factors. This means that an employee may be highly motivated but dissatisfied with the work environment. Furthermore, being satisfied with the work environment does not prompt high motivation.

No Dissatisfaction	HYGIENE FACTORS	Dissatisfaction
High Motivation and Few Dissatisfiers *Ideal situation* – Work is stimulating with many opportunities for advancement. Supervision, salaries, and working conditions are adequate.		**High Motivation and Many Dissatisfiers** Employees' jobs offer achievement, recognition, and advancement, but supervision, salaries, and working conditions are inadequate.
Low Motivation and Few Dissatisfiers Supervision, salaries, and working conditions are adequate, but the work is not stimulating and there are few opportunities for advancement and recognition. Work is a job, not a career.		**Low Motivation and Many Dissatisfiers** *The worst situation* – Poor supervision, unclear and/or unevenly applied company policies, poor physical working conditions, poor interpersonal communication with supervisors. Little to no recognition, achievement, or opportunities for advancement.

(Vertical axis: MOTIVATIONAL FACTORS — No Satisfaction to Satisfaction)

Figure 10.2 Motivational and hygiene factors in the workplace

Hygiene factors (see figure 10.2) include:

- Pay and benefits
- Friendly co-workers
- Good working conditions
- Job security
- Holidays and vacations

Motivational factors (see figure 10.2) include:

- Interesting, challenging work
- Working to one's full potential
- Meaningful work
- Access to information
- Involvement in decision-making
- Recognition for achievement
- Sense of importance

Reinforcement Theory

Behavioral psychologists E.L. Thorndike and B.F. Skinner developed the principles underlying **reinforcement theory**, which states that behavior is a function of consequences received as a result of past behaviors. **Punishment (negative reinforcement)** is used to change behavior by presenting people with unpleasant consequences if they exhibit undesired behaviors. Ignoring undesired behavior, however, is more effective than punishment, which may create additional dysfunctional behaviors. **Positive reinforcement** is providing a reward when employees exhibit desired behaviors. Positive reinforcement is preferred for its long-term effects on performance.

Contemporary Theories of Motivation

The theories of motivation developed in the first half of the 20th century still represent a firm foundation on which managers can build strategies to inspire superior performance from employees. More recent theorists, though, have put forward more complex models of employee behavior and motivation that may be applied more widely to a greater range of situations.

Equity Theory

Another useful contemporary theory of motivation, developed by behavioral psychologist John Stacey Adams, is **equity theory**, which is simply the perception of fairness in allotting the rewards offered for specified levels of performance. A fair situation is one in which people with similar inputs experience similar outcomes. For example, Bob, a factory foreman with five years of experience working the swing shift and meeting performance standards is paid the same amount as Ana, another foreman with the same experience and performance. Bob and Ana perceive that they are compensated in the same way for the same amount of work—that is, for equal input they each receive an equal outcome. They are likely to be satisfied,

Equity theory Perception of fairness in the rewards received by different people who have the same skills, experience, and performance.

and their work relationship is likely to be good. If the ratios of input to outcome for each worker are perceived as unequal, inequity exists and the employee feels under-rewarded, resulting in anger and resentment, or over-rewarded, resulting in a feeling of guilt. If the employee perceives inequity, she or he will act to try to compensate for lack of equity in behaviors that will have a negative impact on individual and unit performance. These behaviors include lower productivity, reduced work quality, absenteeism, and even voluntary resignation. Managers should take care to consider the effect that improving one employee's pay or working conditions may have on the motivation of other employees. Another example of the application of this theory is shown in figure 10.3.

	Inequitable relationship		Equitable relationship	
	Amina	*Bill*	*Amina*	*Bill*
Input	40 hours/ week	40 hours/ week	40 hours/ week	40 hours/ week
Outcome	$30,000	$25,000	$30,000	$30,000
Feelings	Guilty	Angry	Satisfied	Satisfied

Figure 10.3 Example of application of Equity Theory

One problem with applying equity theory in the workplace is that the comparisons employees make between themselves and other employees are rarely as simple as the example of Bob and Ana given here. Measuring employees' contributions in comparison to those of other workers whose positions and performance outcomes are different is complex and subjective. If the process of making decisions about work equity is not perceived as both just and fair, disagreements between employees and managers may arise.

Expectancy Theory

Expectancy theory, developed in 1964 by Victor Vroom, suggests that an employee's efforts are influenced by the expected outcomes of those efforts. Employees will be motivated to achieve goals if they are achievable and offer a reward, such as an opportunity for advancement or better compensation. Expectancy theory rests on the concept of **self-efficacy**, which is a person's confidence in his or her capacity to perform a specific task. For the expectancy model to work as a motivational strategy, the employee must first of all be convinced of his or her ability to perform a task, and second, believe that if enough effort is applied, the employee will succeed in doing the task to the desired level of performance. This part of the model is called "expectancy." However, according to the expectancy model, workers are only motivated if they think that performance will lead to a specified outcome. This aspect of the model is called "**instrumentality**." The third part of the model suggests that the specified outcomes must be desirable to employees, known as

Self-efficacy A person's confidence in his or her capacity to perform a specific task, the principle behind expectancy theory.

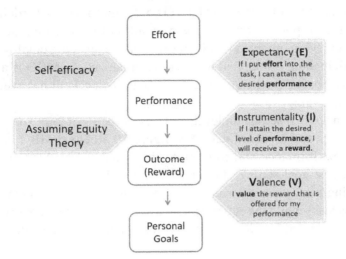

Figure 10.4   Expectancy theory from the employee's point of view

the "**valence**" or value of the outcome. Motivation is highest when expectancy, instrumentality, and valence levels are high (see figure 10.4). If just one of these levels is low, motivation will be low. If employees do not value the reward, that is, if the valence is zero, then there will be no motivation, regardless of the expectancy and instrumentality levels.

Expectancy theory provides the organization and its managers with a guide to ways in which they might enhance employee motivation. The organization should provide employees with education, training, time to learn and gain experience, and proper equipment so that their effort is optimized. Correct work behaviors should be demonstrated and performance measures carefully explained. At the same time managers should listen to employees' suggestions and should address problems that interfere with employee performance. To ensure that employees value the rewards offered, organizations should take care to identify employees' individual needs and adjust the rewards to match these needs.

Goal-setting Theory

Edwin Locke, an industrial psychologist, published his highly influential **goal-setting theory of motivation** in 1968. Goal-setting theory is based on the idea that an individual's intention to work toward a goal is, in itself, a primary source of motivation. Goals provide direction and describe what needs to be accomplished; they stimulate increased effort, persistence, and the quality of performance. Locke claimed that a specific and challenging goal is more motivating than an easy or vague goal. At the same time, a goal should be achievable and measurable. A key element of the theory is that prompt and frequent feedback about progress toward the goal will enhance performance. Locke's theory is frequently summarized in the acronym **SMART: specific, measurable, attainable, relevant, and time-bound** (see chapter 5 for a detailed discussion on this topic).

Management by Objectives

> ***Management by Objectives (MBO)***
> *Form of participative management based on goal-setting theory.*

Management by objectives (MBO) is a popular form of participative management that incorporates within it the principles of goal-setting theory. MBO aims both at achieving organizational objectives and enhancing employee commitment and participation. As applied to an entire organization, MBO is a system of collaborative goal setting, extending through all its levels. It has even been used for strategic planning.

When applied at the unit level, MBO is a process of joint goal-setting between a supervisor and a subordinate. See figure 10.5 below. MBO has been used to appraise performance and to motivate individuals. The MBO process involves three phases: goal setting, during which the subordinate actively participates in developing performance goals; action to achieve goals, in which the subordinate performs tasks while the supervisor coaches and provides support; and evaluating goal achievement, in which the subordinate actively participates in performance review.

	1 Set Goals	2 Perform tasks	3 Provide support	4 Evaluate results	5 Recycle process
Supervisor	✓		✓		
Subordinate		✓		✓	✓

Figure 10.5 MBO Process

Enhancing Job Satisfaction and Motivation

Herzberg identified the job itself as a motivational factor. Managers can use several strategies to design jobs in order to enhance job satisfaction and to improve motivation.

Job rotation allows employees to periodically rotate their assignments so that they can learn new skills and gain different perspectives of different job functions and operational units. Job rotation is also used to cross-train workers so that they are able to fill in for sick or vacationing colleagues or move into a different position if their original job is eliminated. Often businesses will emphasize **job specialization** (doing the same job all of the time) in hopes of reaching peak performance and higher productivity. The consequence of job specialization, though, is that workers experience boredom and dissatisfaction, and productivity suffers. Job rotation relieves the boredom associated with job specialization.

Job enlargement is a type of job redesign that seeks to relieve boredom by adding more tasks of a similar skill level, also known as "horizontal loading." A common example of job enlargement is modularizing work activities so that an employee performs several different tasks on one item. As you might imagine, after a period of time, even an enlarged job can become routine and boring. Another negative aspect of job enlargement is "job creep" in which the number of activities assigned to a position make the job unmanageable.

Herzberg believed that giving employees more responsibility to make decisions, more recognition for good performance, and making jobs more challenging were all motivators. These are all concepts behind the job redesign strategy known as

job enrichment, also called "vertical loading." Researchers Hackman and Oldham refined Herzberg's ideas while focusing on job design as the primary motivational factor. Their Job Characteristics Model states that if five key job characteristics are present, they will produce critical psychological states that lead to positive job outcomes. An often-cited downside to job enrichment is the reclassification of job titles, which can have far-reaching effects throughout an organization.

A broader approach to employee involvement is **worker empowerment**, which seeks to engage workers in decision-making and give them more authority. Empowered employees are often in a position to make more informed decisions concerning the tasks they perform than supervisors who are not directly involved. Although technically not the same thing, **participative management** is closely linked to worker empowerment. Empowerment actually gives workers the authority to make decisions about their jobs, while participative management simply means that managers seek more input from workers before making decisions. Both approaches transfer more responsibility to employees.

Worker empowerment Gives workers the authority to make and execute decisions about their jobs in contrast to simply providing input to supervisors.

A popular strategy for motivating employees is the **modified work schedule.** This strategy takes a variety of forms, depending on the nature of a business and the characteristics and needs of its employees. Almost all hospitals use the strategy of the **compressed work week,** when an employee will work longer daily hours but fewer days. The compressed work week will run on a four-days-on-three-days-off schedule. An employee with **flexible work hours (flextime)** will work specific weekly hours with varying arrival, departure, lunch and break times around certain core hours during which all employees must be present. Sometimes it may be possible for two or more employees to **job share**, splitting the hours and the pay of one full-time position. The Internet, paired with the proliferation of personal computers and mobile electronic devices, has made **telecommuting**, in which employees work from home or remote locations, a common way to work. A variation of telecommuting is "**hoteling**" or "**hot desking**," which occurs when employees, for example, sales representatives, will check into a space in the office for a few hours to complete work.

Modified work schedules help improve job hygiene factors, reducing dissatisfiers related to working conditions and time off. Employees are able to coordinate work around family members' schedules, reducing anxiety about balancing work and personal commitments. Employees experience a greater overall feeling of freedom and control. Disadvantages of modified work schedules may include the inability of employees to meet deadlines, difficulties in successfully coordinating work schedules with personal schedules, and the employer's perception that workers not at the workplace are not actually working.

Most of the advice for motivating employees focuses on *tailoring the strategy to individual needs* and *focusing on support for self-actualization.* Money should not be underestimated as a motivator, but motivation to work rarely comes only from money. Managers should recognize and respond to individual differences. Doing so involves getting to know employees personally and understanding their professional culture. Sales managers are motivated differently than engineers, for example. The power of well-defined, challenging, and attainable goals cannot be overstated. Helping people to attain their own career goals and providing opportunities for employees to learn and grow are other effective ways to motivate workers. Many companies provide funding and time off for employees to obtain academic degrees that will help them advance in their careers and in the company. Some companies send promising managers on one-year leaves to volunteer for a nonprofit undertaking. Lastly, rewards should be clearly linked to performance, and those rewards must be granted equitably across the organization.

Measuring Job Satisfaction

People voluntarily leave their jobs for a variety of reasons. The most frequently given reasons are: boredom and lack of challenge, limited potential for advancement, inadequate salary, lack of recognition, and dissatisfaction with various aspects of the work environment. Since recruiting, hiring, and training are costly activities, retaining existing employees is important to any company's profitability. Continuously monitoring employee **job satisfaction** is therefore an important managerial activity.

A manager can measure job satisfaction directly by observing and documenting the behavior of employees over a period of time. By interviewing workers about their level of satisfaction, the manager can add detail and insight in support of his or her observations. The use of questionnaires can help managers gauge satisfaction in a systematic way. Several relevant survey instruments are available: *Faces Scale* (Kunin, see figure 10.6), *Minnesota Satisfaction Questionnaire* (MSQ), and the *Job Descriptive Index* from Bowling Green State University. When employees do leave their jobs, managers can use exit interviews to identify factors that contributed to the decision to resign.

Figure 10.6 Scale based on the Kunin *Faces Scale*

APPLY YOUR KNOWLEDGE

Motivating Millennials: Truths and Myths

"Millennials," people born between 1981 and 1996, now make up half of the U.S. workforce, and by 2025 this age group will be 75 percent of it. If you think that the millennial worker is "an entitled recipient of hundreds of plastic participation trophies who cares less about paying his dues at work and more about perks like flex-time, beer carts, and nap rooms," nothing could be further from the truth, claims Harvard Business Review editor Sarah Green Carmichael.

In fact, research shows that as a group, Generation Y—as millennials are also known—seems intrinsically motivated to work too hard. For example, a survey of 5,000 employees conducted by the U.S. Travel Association found that millennial respondents could be labeled "work martyrs" because of their fear of being seen as slackers or undedicated to their jobs.

The larger truth, however, is that when it comes to motivation, millennial workers are like everyone else, just younger. Individual characteristics are far more useful in determining the most effective way to motivate an employee than a birth year. Most of the advice to supervisors of youthful workers sounds a lot like the advice given for motivating other age groups:

- provide positive reinforcement,
- deliver frequent and timely feedback,
- take time to get to know the employee,
- show care and concern, be fair and inclusive,
- provide opportunities for control of work processes and for learning,
- supply small, frequent rewards,
- ensure a good "fit" of skills and job assignment, and most of all,
- communicate openly and often.

The secret to motivating millennial workers is no secret at all.

Knowledge Application Questions

Complete the motivation inventory below. Compare your answers with a classmate who is different from you in age, ethnicity, or gender.

Put an X next to the **five (choose only 5)** job-related needs that are **most important** in motivating you at your job.

__Assurance of regular employment
__Feeling safe at work
__Feeling that my job is important
__High degree of autonomy on the job
__Opportunities to do work that's challenging
__Written job description so that I know what's expected

__Health insurance and other benefits
__Involvement in decisions affecting my work
__Being told that I am doing a good job
__Getting along with coworkers
__Good pay

Adapted from the book *222 Secrets of Hiring, Managing, and Retaining Great Employees in Healthcare Practices* by Robert Levoy, published by Jones and Bartlett Publishers, Sudbury, MA, in 2007.

Sources

Carmichael, S. G. 2016, August 17. "Millennials Are Actually Workaholics, According to Research." Harvard Business Review. Accessed November 11, 2019. https://hbr.org/2016/08/millennials-are-actually-workaholics-according-to-research

Macrae, I. 2017, May 24. "The great Millennials myth: The secret to motivating young people." HR Magazine. Accessed October 31, 2019. https://www.hrmagazine.co.uk/article-details/the-great-millennials-myth-the-secret-to-motivating-young-people.

U.S. Travel Association. 2016, August 17. "New survey: Millennial attitudes making America's vacation Problem Worse." Accessed October 31, 2019. https://www.ustravel.org/press/new-survey-millennial-attitudes-making-americas-vacation-problem-worse

Villa, D. 2018, March 30. "All You Need To Know To Motivate Millennials." [Blog post]. Accessed October 31, 2019. https://www.forbes.com/sites/forbesagencycouncil/2018/03/30/all-you-need-to-know-to-motivate-millennials/#2d5cc92f60ae.

QUIZ YOURSELF

Without looking back at the chapter, choose the best answer to each of the questions below. Answers are in the back of the textbook before the Index. Review the chapter to find out why you missed any questions.

1. In a survey of middle-level managers in service industries, a majority stated that employees have an inherent distrust of managers and will respond to instructions only if they perceive their treatment to be fair. This statement indicates the managers would be most successful using the _____ to motivate their employees.
   a. equity theory
   b. expectancy theory
   c. theory of objectivity
   d. theory of equality
   e. fair treatment theory

2. According to expectancy theory, the probability of an individual acting in a particular way depends on the strength of the individual's belief that
   a. the act will have a particular outcome and on whether the individual values that outcome.
   b. job responsibility is adequate.
   c. salary and fringe benefits matter.
   d. the job is challenging.
   e. supervisors treat their employees with equity.

3. The set of beliefs a person holds about his or her ability to succeed at a certain task or in a particular situation is called
   a. self-efficacy.
   b. self-motivation.
   c. self-confidence.
   d. self-esteem.
   e. self-awareness.

4. In Herzberg's theory, salary is an example of a/an
   a. job satisfier.
   b. self-actualizing factor.
   c. motivating factor.
   d. employee-controlled factor.
   e. hygiene factor.

5. Which of the following is designed to increase the job satisfaction of an employee?
   a. Job-related hygiene factors
   b. Across-the-board compensation
   c. Job enrichment
   d. Worker safety training
   e. Hawthorne studies

6. Increasing the number of different tasks an employee has to perform in a job is called
   a. empowerment.
   b. job enrichment.
   c. group cohesiveness.
   d. expectancy.
   e. job enlargement.

7. Julia Li is a low-level manager for a manufacturer of collectible plates and figurines. She is assigned to different departments every few months so that she can learn all aspects of her company's operations. Management is utilizing the concept of job _____ in training Li.
   a. enlargement
   b. rotation
   c. enrichment
   d. development
   e. satisfaction

8. The motivation theory that suggests that employees will be motivated if the degree of responsibility over the way their job is performed is increased is called:
   a. expectancy theory.
   b. Maslow's needs hierarchy.
   c. MBO.
   d. equity theory.
   e. job enrichment.

9. A theory that suggests that people are motivated by a desire to satisfy the next level of their unmet needs is the
   a. Herzberg theory of motivation.
   b. McGregor theory of motivation.
   c. product life cycle.
   d. Skinner's reinforcement.
   e. Maslow's hierarchy of needs theory.

10. Roberto believes that his employees are self-motivated and growth-oriented. He is a _____ manager.
    a. classical
    b. Theory Y
    c. Theory X
    d. Hierarchical
    e. None of the above

Tang Yan Song/Shutterstock

CHAPTER 11

Marketing Products and Services to Customers

What Is Marketing?

People associate the term **marketing** with selling and advertising goods and services. Marketing, however, encompasses much more than promoting a **product** and offering it for sale at a competitive price. Marketing is everything a business does to place **goods** or a **service** in the hands of potential users. It is a process by which a firm keeps its loyal customers and wins new ones.

To be able to reach the "ideal" customer for its product or service, a firm's marketing efforts are directed at finding out what customers need, and determining which products (goods and services) will best satisfy those *needs*. This effort is a constantly evolving process. By addressing the needs, marketers can translate them into *wants*. For instance, when you desire to satisfy your thirst, it is a need. When you feel like having a soda just because you like the taste, it is a want. Marketing can also forecast how much, when, and where the goods or service will be purchased.

U.S. marketing guru **Philip Kotler** offers this definition of marketing: "Marketing is a social and managerial process by which individuals and groups obtain what they want and need through creating, offering and exchanging products of value with others." He goes on to emphasize, "The most important thing is to forecast where customers are moving, and be in front of them." The **American Marketing Association** website defines marketing as ". . . the activity, set of institutions, and processes for creating, communicating, delivering, and exchanging offerings that have value for customers, clients, partners, and society at large." To sum up, marketing:

- Analyzes **customer needs**
- Deduces the types of products or service the ideal **customer wants**, and
  - **how much** he or she will buy,
  - **when** he or she will want to buy, and
  - **where** he or she will buy the product or service.

The aim of marketing is to create a **utility** that satisfies the needs of its ideal customers.

What Is Utility?

Utility *The quality or condition of being useful.*

Utility as defined by *The American Heritage Dictionary* is "the quality or condition of being useful." Utility is the power of a product to satisfy the needs and wants of its customers. Marketing is the impetus behind the intrinsic utility of a product. The four intrinsic utilities are:

- Form utility
- Time utility
- Place utility
- Possession (ownership) utility

Form utility is achieved when raw materials and components are converted into finished products or services. This is the only utility created by production rather than by marketing. For example, the process of pizza production turns the ingredients of flour, yeast, tomatoes, and cheese into your take-out pizza.

Marketing provides the other three utilities via intermediaries, as indicated in the examples below.

Time utility refers to the availability of a product for consumers at a convenient time. An example is when *The New York Times* delivers the paper early in the morning to your doorstep so that you may read it while having your breakfast.

Place utility refers to the availability of a product or service at a location where the consumer needs or wants it. For example, some department stores are making the shopping experience easier for their customers by offering an online store, as well as a physical ("brick-and-mortar") store location. This way the customers have easy access to the product.

Possession utility is achieved when the seller allows easy transfer of a product's ownership to the buyer. For example, cash, credit/debit cards, checks, layaway, customer credit, and leasing strategies can make goods and services more attractive to customers. For example, car dealerships offer lease and credit purchase options to ease the transfer of car ownership from the dealer to the customer.

What Is the Marketing Concept?

The marketing concept philosophy holds that the main focus of an organization's efforts should be its customers. This is called "customer orientation." Addressing the needs of the ideal customer and satisfying him or her better than competitors is the way an organization will be able to achieve its goals. The key activities or steps behind the marketing concept are:

1. Start by identifying the ideal customers, also called the **target market**.
2. Determine their needs.
3. Provide products that satisfy those needs through an integrated marketing effort.
4. The above three, if done effectively, will help the organization achieve its objectives.

Marketing concept The philosophy that the organization should focus its efforts on its customers' needs in order to prosper.

Customer Relationship Management

It is estimated that it can cost a company up to five times more to gain a new customer than to keep an existing one. For companies to sustain profitability over time, it is important for them to retain customers who will repeatedly buy their products. Modern marketing efforts therefore focus on establishing and maintaining a relationship with customers rather than focusing on single sales transactions. This approach is called **relationship marketing.** Common customer retention strategies include: **loyalty programs** that reward customers' repeated purchase of a product or service; product/service **bundling** that offers several complementary items at a single "package" price; and **cross promotions** that offer customers discounts on related products or services. A characteristic of relationship marketing is the use of a team of marketers and customer service providers to increase the number of contacts that the customer has with the company in order to strengthen the relationship. The advent of the Internet and social media has facilitated the growth of relationship marketing.

Customer relationship management (CRM), also referred to as customer service management, is an IT-based knowledge management system designed to support dealing with customers on a day-to-day basis and is instrumental to a firm's success in using relationship marketing. In her 2003 book, *Customer Relationship Management: Getting It Right*, customer service expert Judith Kincaid defines CRM as "the strategic use of information, process, technology, and people to manage the customer's relationship with your firm across the whole customer life cycle."

Customer relationship management A focus on establishing and maintaining a relationship with customers rather than on single sales transactions.

CRM views marketing as a process the aim of which is to piece together information about customers, marketing efforts, and trends. Marketing managers using CRM have access to a database of customer profiles to improve product differentiation, match customer needs, generate sales leads, and implement efficient and effective marketing campaigns. By maintaining a CRM database, marketing management is able to retain its loyal customers while attracting new ones.

Marketing Mix

The **marketing mix** is used to describe the combination of a set of variables, which if carefully selected and orchestrated, will contribute to the creation of utility for the ideal customer. The marketing mix is also known as "the four Ps." These controllable variables are **product, price, promotion**, and **place (distribution)**, as shown in figure 11.1 below. Firms use the elements of the marketing mix to build

Marketing mix Set of variables (4 Ps) that will create utility for the firm's ideal customer.

their marketing strategies as a part of the marketing plan. An appropriate marketing mix is essential to the success of a firm's marketing plan. A sloppily constructed marketing mix may also be a recipe for disaster. A successful formula addresses:

1. the right product
2. at the right price
3. in the right place
4. with the most appropriate promotion

Effective managers monitor external environmental forces and adjust the marketing mix frequently to be able to meet the needs of the target market.

The four Ps have been described as oriented toward sales and the firm's perspective, therefore describing only one side of the marketing concept. Experts like Philip Kotler have suggested that a more customer oriented "mix" might be called the **four Cs**, which takes into consideration the buyer's viewpoint:

1. Product is *Customer's needs and wants*
2. Price is *Cost to customer*
3. Place is *Convenience*
4. Promotion is *Communication with ideal customer*

> ***The 4 Cs*** *Set of customer-oriented variables that takes into consideration the customer's viewpoint*

The four Ps, however, remain a standard definition of the marketing mix because these variables are all under the firm's control.

Figure 11.1 The four Ps of the marketing mix

The four Ps apply equally to the **service marketing mix**, with some experts adding three or more additional Ps. Hospitality, travel, health care, professional services (for example, lawyers and financial advisors), personal services, and government are all part of the service sector of the economy. You will recall from chapter 7 that services differ from products in several important ways:

- A service is *intangible* in that it cannot be touched, smelled, or seen before the customer buys it;
- A service is performed and *cannot be separated* from its consumption—the customer and service provider must interact in order to perform or produce the service;
- A service *cannot be placed in inventory*; carrying costs are low or nonexistent because it is only the cost of paying the service employee and the cost of any necessary equipment;
- Service quality is often *inconsistent* because it is people-based and thus much more difficult to standardize than products.

Because of these differences, the service marketing mix includes three additional variables: **people**, **process**, and **physical evidence**.

- The *people* who perform the services are critical to providing the benefits that the company promises its customers. The firm must invest in its employees by training and rewarding them well in order to ensure high quality service. Service companies emphasize interpersonal skills and customer service in order to assure customer satisfaction.
- The *process* used to deliver the service to the customer must be defined in detail so that employees can follow the process quickly and with consistent quality.
- *Physical evidence* enhances the customer's experience and differentiates one company's service from another. For example, customers will prefer a restaurant with a nice ambience to one which supplies only good food and a place to eat it.

Gaining a Competitive Advantage

In order to successfully compete in the marketplace, a firm must create a **competitive advantage**. A competitive advantage is something that a firm can do or offer that others cannot. Firms gain competitive advantage by designing goods and services to better satisfy customer needs and deliver more value to them than other firms can. A firm offers consumers greater value by means of lower prices or by providing greater benefits and service that justify higher prices. Distinguishing a product from competitors' products in a manner that makes the product more desirable is called **product differentiation**. Differentiation attempts to make a product more attractive by contrasting its uniqueness and superiority with other competing products and by creating a perception that the added value the product is offering is not available in the marketplace.

Product differentiation
Distinguishing a product or service from a competitor's offering and creating a perception that the value provided to the customer is unavailable in the marketplace.

Differentiation can help a firm defend its pricing strategy. Once the target customers perceive the existence of a difference, the producer of the goods can have some influence over the price. That firm is said to be a "price maker" since its products have no substitutes as opposed to a "price taker" with many available substitutes for its products. For example, Starbucks coffee is distinguished from other coffee retailers because of the quality of its coffee. Although the price is high, Starbucks coffee has become very popular because the needs of the target customer, who valued excellent coffee, were better met by Starbucks than by other providers.

Identifying and Reaching Target Markets

A **target market** is the set of buyers sharing *common* needs or characteristics that the firm decides to serve/sell to. Common needs or traits used to describe a target market are the consumer's *gender, age*, and *income level*. In the case of business customers, the target market may be defined in terms of the industry the firm is part of, the size of the firm, its organizational structure, and its location in the distribution channel. Target markets can be broadly grouped as follows:

Consumer markets (Consumer [B2C] products, also called industrial goods), which represent all individuals or households who desire goods and services for personal consumption or use, and

Industrial markets (Business [B2B] products), which are comprised of individuals and organizations that desire goods and services in order to produce other goods and services, or to sell, rent, or supply the products to others. Some markets fall into both categories, for example, prescription drugs, which are marketed both to doctors and to end users.

The three-step approach that companies use to develop a marketing plan involves **segmenting**, **targeting**, and **positioning (STP)**.

Segmenting Markets

The process of **market segmentation** involves taking a large market made up of different kinds of customers and organizing it into distinct groups of customers who have something in common with each other. The sorting of potential customers into market segments, in which members share similar attributes, is guided by who the customers are and how they behave.

Demographic variables Gender, age, family life style, race, ethnic group, occupation, family size, household income.

Market segments are frequently described in terms of **demographic** and **geographic** variables. Examples of demographic variables include: gender, age, family life cycle, race or ethnic group, occupation, family size, religion, home ownership, income, and occupation. Geographic variables include country and region, as well as climate, population density, and rural/suburban/urban location.

Psychographic variables Characteristics of a target market described in terms of values, attitudes and lifestyles.

Customer behavior may be categorized according to **psychographic variables**, such as values, attitudes, and lifestyles **(VALS)**. Another form of **behavioral segmentation** is according to the anticipated benefits that the customer seeks from the use of a product or service, the usage rate of the product or service, and loyalty to the brand or to the store. See Table 11.1 for a summary of segmentation variables.

Market segmentation helps a firm make effective use of its resources. For example, the marketing mix can be customized for each segment. Using the same marketing "recipe" for everyone in the market might mean wasting money on billboards when many customers in an important market segment do not own or drive cars.

Table 11.1   Common segmentation variables

Main Dimension	Segmentation Variables	Typical Categories	Applied to a Target Market for a Beauty Apa
CUSTOMER CHARACTERISTICS			
Demographic	Gender	Male, female	Female
	Age	Under 6 yrs; 6 – 11 yrs; 12–17 yrs; 18 – 24 yrs; 25 – 34 yrs; 35 – 44 yrs; 45 – 54 yrs; 55 – 64 yrs; over 75 yrs	25 – 44 yrs
	Race	African-American; Asian; Hispanic, etc.	
	Life stage	Infant, youth, young adult, adult, senior	Adult
	Household size	1; 2; 3 – 4; 5 or more	Household size of 3 – 5 or more
	Home ownership	Own home; rent home	Own home
	Marital status	Never married; married; separated; divorced; widowed	Any marital status
	Annual income	<$15,000; $15,000 – $24,999; $25,000 – 34,999; $35,000 – 49,999; $50,000 – 74,999; $75,000 – 100,000	Household income of $75,000 – 100,000
	Education	Some High School or less; HS graduate; some college; college graduate, etc.	High school graduate or higher

(Continued)

Table 11.1 Common segmentation variables (*Continued*)

Main Dimension	Segmentation Variables	Typical Categories	Applied to a Target Market for a Beauty Apa
	Occupation	Managerial and professional specialty; technical; sales, administrative support, etc	Stay-at-home, professional, administrative
Geographic	Region, city size	Northeast, Midwest, South, West; Under 10,000; 250 – 499,999, 1 million or more	Northeastern city between 250 – 499,999 in population
	Metropolitan	Metropolitan	
	Density	Density Urban, suburban, rural	Suburban
Psychographic	Personality	Gregarious; compulsive, introverted, ambitious	Gregarious
	VALS	Actualizers, fullfilleds, achievers, experiencers, strivers, makers, strugglers,	Strivers and experiencers
	Claritas categories	Over 40 segments such as "Settled in," "white picket fence"	"Kids & Cul desacs"
BEHAVIORAL SEGMENTATION			
Distribution type	In-store Direct	Department; specialty; outlet store; convenience; hypermarket; catalog	In-store
Benefits sought	Product features Needs	Situation specific; general quality; service; price/value; financing; warranty	Confidence in appearance; relaxation; parental responsibilities fulfilled

Main Dimension	Segmentation Variables	Typical Categories	Applied to a Target Market for a Beauty Apa
Usage	Usage rate	Light user; medium user; heavy user	Bi-monthly usage rate
	User status	Nonuser; ex-user; prospect; first-time user; regular user	Ex-spa patron, new and regular user
Awareness and intentions	Product knowledge	Unaware; aware; informed; interested; intending to buy, purchaser; rejection	Potential customers are aware, interested, and intending to buy
Behavior	Involvement	Minimum effort; comparison; special effort	Potential for high involvement

Targeting the Best Customers

For market segmentation to be effective, the segments must be readily identifiable as distinct groups, the members of which share particular characteristics and who will respond to appeals different from those made to other segments. **Targeting** involves deciding which segments will be the most profitable. The segment or segments should be large enough to generate sufficient revenue to cover operating costs and still make a profit. Ideally, your chosen segment(s) should be growing and not already populated by numerous competitors. Targeted segments should be accessible so that promotions can easily reach members of the segment and so that the firm is able to serve the customers. Limits to accessibility may include geographic location, political and legal barriers, availability of technology, or cultural barriers such as language.

Finally, the firm should be realistic about its ability to execute the strategy. A great marketing strategy is useless if the firm does not have the resources to act upon it. For example, Procter & Gamble has targeted eight distinct segments for its laundry detergent products based on specific needs such as "whitening," "softening," and "stain removal," to name a few. A smaller company with fewer resources might choose to serve only one or two of these market segments.

Positioning

Positioning is the place the product occupies in consumers' minds relative to competing products. Positioning expert Walter Landor expressed the importance of positioning this way: "Products are created in the factory, but brands are created in the mind." For example, Toyota Yaris and Honda Fit are positioned as "economical"

Positioning The place a product or service occupies in the customer's mind compared with other products or services in the same category.

automobiles, while Mercedes and Cadillac are positioned as "luxurious." Other examples include Yuengling, a "full-bodied" beer; Olive Garden, a restaurant "popular with women"; and Purex, an "economical" laundry detergent.

A firm may decide to **reposition** a product when it has reached the maturity stage of the product life cycle (PLC) and is not enjoying previous sales levels. Market research may have revealed that the product occupies a different place in consumers' minds. A competing brand may now occupy the position that the firm's product once held.

Morton, the salt company, started to experience competition from different types of salt, such as kosher salt, flake salt, sea salt, and Himalayan pink salt, among others. The company realized that it was no longer enough to rely on the positioning of its product as a simple cooking ingredient. In 2017, the company repositioned its brand as an "emotional lifestyle choice." Denise Lauer, director of Morton's brand strategy, stated that the repositioning was inspired by the iconic Morton Salt Girl "who plays an essential role in everyday life ... [and] now helps us stride with greater purpose."

Market Coverage Strategies

Once the segments have been identified, a firm must decide whether to make products for one, several, or all of these segments, and how to tailor a marketing mix to each market segment. Figure 11.2 compares the three market coverage strategies.

Undifferentiated marketing, also called **mass marketing**, aims at reaching the entire unsegmented market. This type of market coverage dismisses the three-step STP approach of segmenting, targeting, and positioning in order to maximize sales to offset the cost of distribution. The focus is on marketing a particular type of product using a single strategy for the entire market. This marketing mix typically consists of a single product (or, in the case of retailers, a homogeneous set of products), one price, one promotional program, and one distribution system. Firms that adopt mass marketing assume that all customers in the market have similar needs and that these needs can be reasonably satisfied with a **single marketing mix**. The classic example of this strategy is Henry Ford's Model T automobile, sold in one style only and in one color—black. Examples of other mass marketed products are detergents, newspapers, and soft drinks.

Differentiated marketing (multisegment marketing) employs a different marketing strategy for each segment. This approach achieves increased penetration into each segment with the expectation of higher sales. For example, Samsung offers less elaborate models of cell phones to a price conscious segment of the market while offering more elaborate models to a segment that is not sensitive to price. This is, however, a fairly costly approach. If the segments have enough buying potential, and the product is successful, the resulting sales increases can more than offset the increased costs of offering multiple marketing mixes.

Concentrated marketing, also called **niche marketing**, targets a small market that could be conceived of as a market segment in itself. Small firms use niche marketing as a way to make effective use of limited resources because it takes less effort to seek a large share of a narrowly defined market. The main advantage of market concentration is specialization, as it allows the firm to focus all its resources toward understanding and serving a single segment. However, by focusing so much

Niche marketing Aims to take a large share of a small market segment.

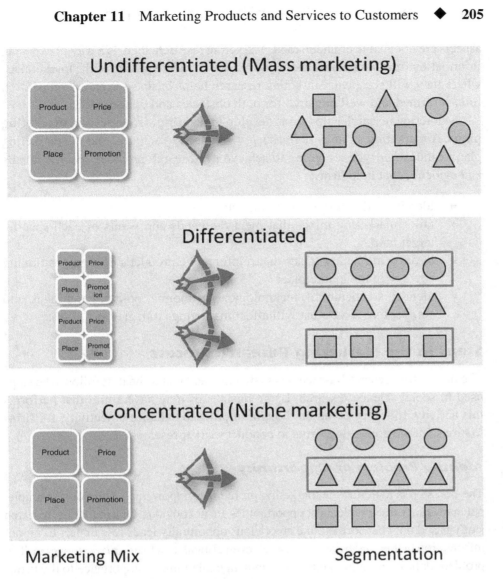

Figure 11.2 Three market coverage strategies

on one distinct market, the firm makes itself vulnerable to changes in its market segment, such as economic downturns, demographic shifts, and changes in trends or fads. Examples of niche marketers include Lefty's San Francisco which caters to left-handed people, UNTUCKIT Men's Shirts which sells shirts that can be worn untucked, and Square, a credit card reader software application that allows business people to use tablets or mobile phones to process credit cards. Niche marketers Mercedes Benz and Rolex concentrate their efforts on high-income customers.

The Importance of Marketing Research

By now it is probably obvious that marketing is a complex process that a firm can only partially control. The unpredictable external business environment and often fickle **consumer behavior** are intervening factors that can derail even the best laid marketing strategies and plans. A wise approach to marketing is based on the view that marketing problems and opportunities are like icebergs—the most dangerous aspects are not visible or understood. Marketing research, then, is a way of exposing information from which businesses can build a complete picture of the marketplace where they will compete. Marketing research helps businesses enter competition fully informed and well prepared for both obstacles and opportunities.

Marketing research helps firms develop **marketing strategies** and **marketing plans**. A marketing strategy defines *what* you need to achieve, and the marketing plan explains *how* you are going to achieve it. Research provides specific details and evidence that help firms:

- identify and describe target markets.
- tailor marketing mixes that meet the needs and wants of each specific target market.
- develop marketing mixes that reinforce the product's desired positioning strategy in the marketplace.
- identify sociocultural, technological, economic, political and legal, and competitive forces that will affect marketing strategies and plans.

Steps in the Marketing Research Process

Marketing research methods Surveys, observation, controlled experiments, focus groups, and test screening are all common marketing research methods.

The **marketing research process** is systematic and methodical. It follows the steps used in social science research. Large businesses may have a unit that performs this activity. It is very common though, in order to enhance objectivity, for firms to hire separate consulting firms to conduct market research.

Identify Problem or Opportunity

The first step is to define the marketing problem or opportunity. This sounds simple, but many times true problems or opportunities are not obvious. Or a marketing research study based on what seemed like an obvious opportunity leads researchers to ignore information that would have been useful, even critical, to a firm's marketing plan. The problem definition might include a statement explaining its importance to the firm.

Choose Methods

Research methods are chosen next. In general, market researchers use a variety of methods in order to gain a complete understanding of the problem. **Surveys** are most common because they are easy to conduct and fairly inexpensive when compared to other methods. Almost any U.S. consumer, including children, has completed a marketing survey of some type, whether with paper and pencil in a restaurant or retail store or online. Sometimes surveys are conducted in person, too, with the questions guiding a brief interview.

Observation of human behavior is another method frequently used. **Observation** may be conducted directly, for example, in stores by paid staff, or indirectly, by recording behavior on video, or by tracking it digitally online. For example, consumers' buying behaviors at an online retailer will be saved so that the next time the shopper enters the store, choices tailored to his or her buying habits will be presented. This type of observational data will also be analyzed by market researchers.

Another research method is to set up an **experiment**, either in a controlled environment or in the actual marketplace. Members of the target market are invited to use or shop for products or services under conditions set by the researchers, who then systematically note the results. Fewer firms choose to use experiments over other methods because of the expense.

Because there may be an enormous number of people comprising the target market, it would be impossible for a market researcher to obtain data from each possible ideal customer. For this reason, researchers work with a **sample** of the target market. There are a variety of sampling procedures that researchers can choose from in order to ensure that the data they collect represent the opinions and behaviors of the designated target market.

Collect Data

Once the research method and sampling procedures have been selected, researchers *collect the data*. Researchers must take care that the data they collect have been gathered using uniform procedures, are accurate, and are complete. Any data that do not meet these criteria must be eliminated from the study.

Organize and Analyze Data

Researchers then *organize and analyze the data*. Software applications have made in-depth analysis of statistical data much less time consuming than it was only a decade ago. Applications that analyze qualitative data, whether in textual, audio, or visual format, have improved in sophistication and enable researchers to expand the use of multiple research methods.

Prepare and Present the Study

The final step is to *prepare and present the study* and to make recommendations supported by the findings of the study. Effective written and live presentations are concise, supported completely by research findings, and highly visual.

Marketing Research Example: Test Screening

A type of marketing research you are probably familiar with is the test screening of movies. The data collected from test screenings is used to promote a film, and frequently the audience reaction is strong enough for the moviemaker to edit the movie. Director Francis Ford Coppola was famous for conducting test screening while still in production and used the input obtained to edit *Apocalypse Now*. The ending of *Fatal Attraction* was radically changed after audiences reacted negatively to the suicide of the main female character. After test screening the ending of *The Bourne Supremacy* was changed two weeks before its release and added 10 points to its ratings in the final test screening. A test audience did not understand the title *3000* so the film was released as *Pretty Woman*.

The test screening follows the market research process. Typically 300 – 400 people who represent a sample of the target market are invited to the screening. The researchers ask about the age, gender, and movie viewing habits of the audience before the screening begins to learn whether these people fit the profile of the target market. After viewing the film the participants complete a survey. The survey questions ask about the title, specific favorite scenes, reaction to the characters, feelings about the endings, and whether the participant would recommend the movie to a friend. The researchers also ask for suggestions. After analyzing the data, researchers make recommendations for changes in the movie, where to release the film first, what to put in the movie "trailer," and where to advertise.

Understanding Consumer Behavior

Consumer behavior is the study of the decision process by which people buy and consume products. Consumers apply different decision-making processes depending on the price of the purchase, the frequency of the purchase, and the conditions under which they make the purchase.

When making a major purchase such as an automobile or a house, consumers will invest weeks, months, and even years in the decision-making process. The process includes *becoming aware of the need, problem, or opportunity*. The consumer may already have this awareness, or advertising may help the consumer define the need more clearly. The consumer then *gathers information*, usually from a variety of sources: friends, owners of the type of product sought, sellers of the product, experts, and from materials such as brochures, magazines, and websites. Often simultaneously with gathering information, the consumer *evaluates alternatives* according to a host of variables of importance. For a major purchase, the *decision to buy* usually comes after the consumer has deliberately eliminated all but one alternative. The decision-making process, however, does not end here. There is also **post-purchase behavior**. The consumer may experience regret about the purchase, also known as "cognitive dissonance" or "buyer remorse," which may prevent future purchases of the product. Companies will often provide disappointed customers a toll-free number to call or ways to easily return the product, called a "reverse channel of distribution," to reduce the negative impact on future sales.

Post-purchase behavior
May include "buyer remorse" or cognitive dissonance which could prevent future purchases.

Types of Consumer Products

Consumers spend little time making decisions to buy **convenience products**. These are relatively inexpensive products that the consumer buys regularly. Their purchase requires no planning and consumers are unwilling to spend significant time shopping for them. Examples of convenience products and services are candy, soft drinks, aspirin, small hardware items, deodorant, fast-food restaurants, and car washes. Consumers know the brand names of popular convenience products. Marketers of convenience products work hard to make sure their brands are among those that consumers think of first.

Convenience products
Relatively inexpensive products that the consumer buys regularly

Shopping products are usually more expensive than convenience products, though not as costly as automobiles. Consumers are willing to invest some effort in shopping for these products, hence the name of this category. There are two categories of shopping products. Consumers perceive *homogeneous* shopping products to be similar to each other. For example, when looking for products such as dryers, washers, TVs, and refrigerators, consumers typically look for the lowest price for a brand that has the desired features. Marketers of products in this category must make an extra effort to differentiate their offerings from those of competitors. Consumers perceive *heterogeneous* shopping products to be different from each other. In this category are furniture, clothing, and computers. Consumers often have trouble comparing these products because the prices, quality, and features vary so much. Marketers of heterogeneous shopping products might use the tactic of showing the consumer how their offerings are similar to other offerings in the category, but at a lower price or at greater convenience.

Shopping products
Expensive products that consumers are willing to spend time shopping for

Examples of **specialty products** include Rolls Royce cars, fine watches, expensive stereo equipment, gourmet restaurants, and highly specialized forms of medical care. Shopping for these products requires consumers to conduct an extensive search. Consumers are reluctant to buy substitutes because of the status that accompanies ownership of these products. Marketers of these products often use selective, status-conscious advertising and limit distribution to a few stores in order to maintain the exclusive image of their products. Brand names and quality of service are very important to consumers of specialty products.

Unsought products are those that the buyer does not yet know of or are products that the buyer is not seeking. New products fall into this category until advertising and distribution increase consumer awareness of them. Unsought products are also those products that consumers do not like to think about or do not want to spend money on, such as life insurance or burial plots. Marketers of unsought products must use aggressive personal selling, going directly to consumers through the sales force, direct mail, or highly persuasive direct-response advertising. Table 11.2 presents an overview of the marketing classification of **consumer products**.

Specialty products
Expensive, highly specialized, brand name products requiring consumers to conduct an extensive search.

Unsought products
Goods or services that the buyer does not yet know of or that the buyer is not seeking.

Table 11.2   A marketing classification of consumer products

Type of Products	Description	Examples	Promotion
Convenience	Buy frequently & immediately with little effort	Toothpaste, magazines, soap	Mass advertising by producer to a relatively unsegmented market
Shopping	Buy less frequently	Computers, TVs, cars, furniture, clothing	Combination of mass advertising and personal selling by producer and resellers
Specialty	Consumers are willing to make special purchase efforts They are reluctant to accept substitutes	Luxury cars or watches, specialized medical care	Status-conscious advertising placed in carefully selected media outlets to preserve exclusive product image
Unsought	Consumers are unaware of Do not consider buying until a need or emergency arises	Life insurance, blood donation	Aggressive advertising and personal selling by producer

APPLY YOUR KNOWLEDGE

Market Segmentation with OCEAN

The psychographic profile model called Values, Attitudes, Lifestyles (VALS) has long been a fundamental basis for market segmentation, helping to explain the preferences and behavior of consumers so that advertisers can hone their marketing messages. OCEAN is another widely used model of personality.

OCEAN stands for the "Big 5" personality traits: Openness, Conscientiousness, Extraversion, Agreeableness, and Neuroticism. The openness trait describes an individual's receptiveness to new experiences, creativity, and curiosity. The conscientious personality is a self-controlled planner, rule follower, task-oriented individual. Extraversion means that a person likes to interact with people and is assertive, enthusiastic, and easily bored. The agreeableness personality trait measures compassion, cooperativeness, helpfulness, and trust. Neuroticism describes the emotional stability of an individual and his or her reaction to everyday situations.

A high score on any of these personality attributes translates into definite consumer traits.

- *Openness*: supports technological innovation, risk-taker, willing to buy online, favors reliability over style
- *Conscientiousness*: prestige and fashion are important, thinks through purchases, interested in health and exercise, concerned about the environment
- *Extraversion*: overconfidence leading to risk-taking, high interest in fun and stress relief, preference for yellow-green color, likes movies but not television
- *Agreeableness*: will go along with the crowd, supports social innovation, not fashion or prestige conscious, willing to buy online, concerned about the environment
- *Neuroticism*: will go along with the crowd, prefers red and purple colors, likes to watch violent media, willing to buy online, compulsive buyer

GutCheck, a market research firm based in Colorado, used OCEAN to develop a consumer profile of likely buyers of a robotic vacuum. Using the results of a survey completed by 2,000 people and "Big Data," the researchers concluded that the audience's primary characteristic was agreeableness, with extraversion a close second. The marketers were then able to develop actionable messaging tactics for the robotic vacuum company. They suggested that their client encourage consumers to write online reviews, appeal to the audience's desire to try something new, and allow them to see how the product works. Another recommendation was "appeal to this audience's tendency to be accommodating and compassionate by using communications that show how the vacuum can be helpful to them and others."

The average small business owner wanting to advertise on the Internet or on social media can take advantage of the OCEAN model by carefully choosing the words used on the firm's website and in social media messages. Each OCEAN personality dimension carries a unique motivation triggered by certain words. Aesthetic and intellectual interests motivate the open person, so the words "innovation," "intelligence," "sophistication," "imagination", and "creative" will appeal to them. Words like "practical," "precision," "achieve," and "efficient" resonate with the conscientious consumer. Extroverts, who like excitement and social rewards, will respond to words like "strong," "outgoing," "active," and "excite." Agreeable people are compassionate and seek to belong. The words "harmonious," "caring," "trustworthy," and "love" will appeal to them. Neurotic personalities see threats everywhere. Words like "safe," security," and "protect" will reassure them that a product or service is made with them in mind. Nathalie Nahai, award-winning author of *Webs of Influence: The Psychology of Online Persuasion*, suggests that advertisers run several versions of the same content using words that will appeal to different personality types.

Knowledge Application Questions

1. Some research has shown that personality traits can be inferred from e-mail addresses. Make a list of the personal (not work-related) email addresses of your friends and family. Assign a primary trait from the OCEAN model to each address or name. Show your list (without the assigned traits) to a classmate who does not know the people on the list and ask him or her to assign an OCEAN trait to each of the e-mails on the list. Have you both assigned the same traits? How accurate are the traits you assigned? Would it be possible to develop an accurate psychographic profile of this group using this method? Describe your findings and explain the conclusions that you can draw.

2. Make a list of the product brands you buy that you really like. Try to list brands in a variety of categories, for example, personal care, food, clothing, and appliances. Then take the Big 5 personality test at the following website, which will organize your traits using the OCEAN model. How does your psychographic profile explain your product choices? https://www.outofservice.com/bigfive/

3. Below you will find links to video advertisements for Secret deodorant. Each has a distinct personality aimed at a different segment of the target audience. Assign an OCEAN dimension to each of the advertisements. Explain how the words, actions, and music express the personality trait that you chose.

   Secret Deodorant Stress Test
   https://www.ispot.tv/ad/AX3a/secret-deodorant-stress-test-namaste#

   Cheer For Each Other: All Strength, No Sweat
   https://www.youtube.com/watch?v=89ZEYCqppCA

   Luxe Lavender: Fresh All Day so You Can Slay
   https://www.youtube.com/watch?v=YG4b7HU4Zrs

Sources

GutCheck. 2018. "Using the Big 5 Personality Traits to Understand Consumers." [Blog]. Accessed November 20, 2019. https://www.gutcheckit.com/blog/big-5-personality-understand-consumers/

GutCheck. 2018. "Good For All Robotic Vacuum: GutCheck Constellation™ Product Innovation Report." Accessed October 31, 2019. https://www.gutcheckit.com/.

Nahai, N. 2015, January 28. "Nathalie Nahai: Make marketing more effective by using the golden standard Big Five personality traits." *Marketing Week*. Accessed October 31, 2019. https://www.marketingweek.com/2015/01/28/nathalie-nahai-make-marketing-more-effective-by-using-the-golden-standard-big-five-personality-traits/.

QUIZ YOURSELF

Without looking back at the chapter, choose the best answer to each of the questions below. Answers are in the back of the textbook before the Index. Review the chapter to find out why you missed any questions.

1. Of the four utilities of a product, the only utility NOT created by marketing is
   a. form.
   b. time.
   c. place.
   d. possession.
   e. convenience.

2. The marketing mix is
   a. competitive advantage, form utility, bundling, and loyalty programs.
   b. shopping products, consumer behavior, services, and transportation.
   c. product, distribution, pricing, and promotion.
   d. convenience, advertising, demographic variables, and pricing.
   e. None of the above.

3. Companies segment their markets into groups of customers that share specific characteristics in order to
   a. discriminate against buyers who can't afford their products.
   b. exploit the segments to achieve maximum profits.
   c. precisely position their products in the minds of members of the segment.
   d. make efficient use of resources.
   e. Choices c and d.

4. Elba sports shoes are advertised as "for serious runners." The brand is known for its poor quality and is sold in discount stores for an average price of $30 a pair. Sales are poor. One way to remedy the situation would be
   a. to reposition the brand as "a budget running shoe."
   b. to declare bankruptcy to save the company.
   c. to change the price to $80 a pair without changing the quality.
   d. to use Walmart for distribution.
   e. All of the above.

5. Juan sells electric motors to manufacturers. Juan is engaged in selling to a/an
   a. flooded market.
   b. mass market.
   c. retailer.
   d. industrial market.
   e. niche market.

6. Understanding consumer behavior helps marketers
   a. design effective advertising that will attract members of the target market.
   b. determine which distribution strategy will provide place utility.
   c. precisely position their products.
   d. choose a price that consumers will find inviting.
   e. All of the above.

7. Cognitive dissonance is an example of a/an
   a. prepurchase behavior.
   b. aftermarket behavior.
   c. customer relationship.
   d. postpurchase behavior.
   e. shopping behavior.

8. The variables of people, process, and physical evidence refer to the
   a. service marketing mix.
   b. product marketing mix.
   c. motivational mix.
   d. segmentation mix.
   e. psychographic mix.

9. Surveys, observations, and interviews are all methods used in
   a. setting prices.
   b. segmenting markets.
   c. marketing research.
   d. decision making.
   e. None of the above.

10. The concept of a smart refrigerator is meant to differentiate this type of refrigerator from traditional refrigerators. Marketers of refrigerators seek differentiation because refrigerators are thought of as _____ shopping products.
    a. heterogeneous
    b. homogeneous
    c. unsought
    d. expensive
    e. status-conscious

ressmaster/Shutterstock

CHAPTER 12

Products and Pricing

The product and the price are the most important components of the marketing mix. They can provide a competitive advantage for the firm. The product with its distinct added value, coupled with a fair and affordable price, can help firms sustain their positions vis-à-vis their competitors. The first part of this chapter discusses the product mix, the product life cycle, branding, packaging, and labeling. The second part of the chapter deals with pricing strategies. The price, as we have said before, results in revenues for the producer of the goods while promotion and distribution, the other two components of the marketing mix, result in costs. In every single industry, firms strive to create a competitive advantage by finding a balance between quality and price. Michael Dell stated, "The best value to the customer is an economic proposition that is valuable in Germany, France, Japan, or Norway. It doesn't matter. People have a sense of value that goes beyond a cultural affinity." The decisions that firms make have an influence over the behavior of its consumers, and pricing is one of them. By carefully studying and researching its market environment, a firm pricing strategy may achieve the desired effect, including discouraging its competitors.

What Is a Product?

In abstract terms, a product is the need-satisfying offering of a firm. The same definition may be used for a service. The Apple iPod, Toyota Camry, or General Electric ovens are all examples of products. Products may be offered as part of a service, for example, Café Mocha at Starbucks. A cafe or restaurant is classified as a service because although these businesses provide products to customers, the primary need of the customer is satisfied through the serving of the food or beverage.

Product mix *All of the products offered by a company, also known as its product assortment.*

All of Arm & Hammer's® products constitute its **product mix**, also known as its product assortment, shown in Table 12.1 below. The product mix has two dimensions. The *breadth* of the product mix offers different product categories called **product lines** that a customer may want. A product line is a group of closely related product items. Many firms offer one or more product lines. Arm & Hammer®, for example, has four major product lines, as shown in table 12.1. These are deodorizing products, fabric care, personal care, and pet care. The *depth*, or line extension, offers different **product items** within a product line. For example, the fabric care product line is made up of seven product items, each one with its own barcode. (There are actually more than seven product items in this product line. The table shows just a few examples for illustration purposes.)

Product line *A group of closely related product items offered by a company.*

Table 12.1 Arm & Hammer® product mix and product lines

	Width of the product mix (Breadth)			
	Deodorizing	**Fabric Care**	**Personal Care**	**Pet Care**
Depth of the product lines (Line extension)	Baking Soda	Essentials Fabric Softener	Mentadent® Advance Breath Freshening	Puppy Pads
	Fridge-n-Freezer® Odor Absorber	Total® 2-in-1 Dryer Cloths	Whitening Booster 3X	Pet Stain and Odor remover
	Fridge Fresh® Refrigerator Air Filter	Laundry Detergent	Advance White® toothpaste	Super Scoop Clumping Litter
	Clear Balance® Pool Maintenance Tablets	Delicare® Fine Fabric Wash	Complete Care® Enamel Strengthening	Cat Litter Deodorizer
	OxiClean® Dirt Fighters Carpet Odor Eliminator	Plus OxiClean® Stain Fighters		
		RainDrops® Water Softener and Detergent Booster		
		Power Gel Plus OxiClean®		

The Product Life Cycle (PLC)

The **product life cycle (PLC)** refers to the stages that products go through from their development to their eventual withdrawal from the market (see figure 12.1). The stages of the product life cycle, after concept and product development, are introduction, growth, maturity, and decline. Anticipating the PLC helps marketers plan effectively. Product life cycles are shorter today because technology and customer tastes are changing more rapidly. The shorter the length of a firm's product life cycles, the greater the need for rapid innovation and marketing processes.

> *Product Life Cycle (PLC) PLCs are shorter today because technology and customers' tastes change more rapidly than in the past.*

During the **introduction stage** of the PLC, sales are low and profits are nearly nonexistent because of the high production and marketing costs necessary for the launch of a new product. There may be little or no competition, so an introductory pricing strategy of skimming, charging the highest price the market will bear, can allow the firm to reap profits before competition appears. A penetration pricing strategy, charging a very low price, can help secure a loyal customer base that will stay with the firm's product after competition develops. Marketing objectives during the introduction stage are to gain consumer awareness, encourage the ideal customer to try the product, and to develop distribution channels. Because competition will start developing toward the end of this phase, it is important to establish the product's competitive advantage.

In the **growth stage**, the product experiences rapid sales growth and profits reach their peak level as a result of high prices and rising demand. Competitors will enter the marketplace, especially if the product seems successful. Marketing objectives during this phase are to get the early adopters to buy the product again and to find new, first-time buyers. The marketing strategy during the growth stage is to maintain product quality, maintain solid distribution channels, provide information to consumers, and maintain profitable pricing.

Stage of the PLC	Product development	Introduction	Growth	Maturity	Decline
Marketing Strategies		• Reap profits ahead of competition • Secure loyal customer base • Develop distribution channels	• Maintain quality, distribution, profits • Provide information to customers	• Re-position • Reduce prices	• Maintain quality and prices • Phase out *Sales curve*
Promotional Objectives	*Investment*	• Awareness • Trial	• New buyers • Repeat purchase • Build brand loyalty	• Remind buyers • Provide incentives	*Profit curve* • Limit spending on promotion

Time

Figure 12.1   Product life cycle

A product in the **maturity stage** of the PLC will reach the peak sales level, but will not experience sales growth. By this time there are many rivals competing for the same target market. Competition puts pressure on prices, increases costs to the product producer, and drives down profit margins. Marketing strategy during the maturity stage is to find new users, to modify the product so that it continues to provide value to the ideal customer, to offer incentives to distributors so that they will continue to carry the product, to reduce prices, and if possible, to reposition the product in the mind of the consumer.

A product in the **decline phase** of the PLC may remain there for some time. A decline in sales volume at reduced prices will limit profits. However, at this stage there may also be fewer competitors, as the weaker ones will have left the market-place. A loyal consumer base keeps buying the product and no longer requires a high level of promotional effort, so spending on this activity may be reduced. Product quality and prices are maintained in order to sustain a sales volume that will yield the desired profits. At some point, it may become necessary to discontinue the product. In sales decline, if it is determined that the product will not contribute to the achievement of the organization's objectives in the future, a phase-out strategy may be necessary. This decision must weigh profitability against product line considerations and customer support obligations.

Product Branding

© solomon7/Shutterstock.com

© Gil C/Shutterstock.com

© tanuha2001/Shutterstock
.com

Marketers use **branding** to distinguish their products from those of competitors. It is the process by which firms create an identity. The **brand name** is the specific name, symbol, or sign a firm uses to distinguish its product from others and to legally protect it from use by others. Examples of brand names are Union 76, NBA (National Basketball Association), 49ers, and McDonald's. Marketers expend enormous resources to achieve **brand loyalty**, a customer's favorable attitude toward a specific brand. Once a consumer demonstrates loyalty to a brand, it is likely that the person will repurchase the brand for years to come and may become its advocate via **word-of-mouth** recommendation. Brand loyalty helps sustain profitability and reduces promotional costs to the firm. The dollar values of the 10 most valuable brand names in the world are shown in table 12.2.

Characteristics of a Good Brand Name

Careful thought goes into the development of a brand name, for it will represent not only the product but also the firm that produced it for years to come. A good brand name is easy to remember and easy for domestic and foreign buyers to pronounce, as in the case of Coca-Cola. A brand name should be distinctive and easy to recognize. It should also describe the product, its uses, and its benefits. Above all, it should have a positive connotation and reinforce the desired product and company image.

Types of Brands

Manufacturer brands are created by producers. These brands are sometimes called **national brands** because of their wide appeal. Some examples of manufacturer brands are Tide, Cheerios, Windex, Nike, Coca-Cola, Sony, and Dell.

Table 12.2   Top 10 Most Valuable Brands in the World

Rank	Brand	Value in $ billion
1	(Apple)	205.5
2	Google	167.7
3	Microsoft	125.3
4	amazon	97
5	(Facebook)	88.9
6	Coca-Cola	59.2
7	SAMSUNG	53.1
8	Disney	52.2
9	TOYOTA	44.61
10	(McDonald's)	43.8

Source: *Forbes The World's Most Valuable Brands 2019 Ranking*. Retrieved from www.forbes.com/powerful-brands/ list/#tab:rank. Logos: © Shutterstock.com

Private brands are also called **dealer brands** or **store brands**. Intermediaries, such as wholesalers and retailers, create these brands. Sam's Choice (Walmart), Costco's Kirkland, and Kroger's Private Selection are examples of private brands. They are not connected to the manufacturer. Dealer brands are primarily used to generate higher margins for middlemen than they can receive by selling the manufacturer brand. Many retailers have expanded the lines of products sold under their store brands, while reducing the amount of space given to manufacturer brands.

Generic brands are products that do not carry the name of the manufacturer or the retailer. These products offer the advantage of lower prices. Generic brands can be important, low-cost alternatives for consumers, such as in the market of prescription drugs, tissues, and cookies.

Brands and trademarks
A brand is a marketing concept and a trademark is a legal designation. Both are protected by the U.S. Patent and Trademark Office as intellectual property.

The term **family branding,** also called **umbrella branding,** refers to an approach to branding in which all of the products in the "family" carry the same brand name. For example, Classic Coke, Diet Coke, and Cherry Coke are all part of the Coca-Cola Company's family brand. The name "Sunkist" appears on all of the company's fresh fruit, juice, vitamins, and soft drinks. **Individual branding** is the branding approach that Procter & Gamble has adopted. For example, Tide, Bold, and Era detergents are all Procter & Gamble products, but each has a distinct brand name and brand image and targets a unique market segment. Individual branding creates competition within the firm to increase sales.

The **brand mark** is the part of a brand not made up of words. These are symbols or designs such as McDonald's golden arches, the Nike swoosh, and the Mercedes star.

The **trademark** refers to the exclusive use of a brand such as Reebok®, Canon® cameras, Windows XP®, Coca-Cola®, Nike® "swoosh," Hewlett-Packard®, to cite a few. The difference between a brand and a trademark is that the brand is a marketing concept and the trademark is a legal designation. Branding and trademarks are the keys to success in any marketplace. A trademark may be registered federally with the United States Patent and Trademark Office (**USPTO**). This registration provides the registrant the exclusive right of use within the states and other countries. The federal registration symbol ® is a notice of a legally registered ownership to warn the public of unauthorized use of that trademark. Businesses can apply to register online in less than 90 minutes, without requiring legal assistance. An easy way to register is on the USPTO's website (www.uspto.gov). A corporation, a partnership, or individuals should make sure that their mark has not been registered or being used by others by checking the Trademark Electronic Search System ("TESS") database.

A **trade name** or business name is the name under which a company, a partnership, or an individual does business. If the owner wants to protect his or her trademark but does not want to register, then the owner may elect to unregister the trademark and use the "TM" **symbol** instead. Using the "TM" symbol indicates that the owner has not registered the mark but is giving a notice of the intellectual property common law trademark rights under consideration.

Brand equity refers to the marketing and financial value of a brand associated with the degree of loyalty of its consumers.

Product Packaging

Packaging, which includes a container for the product, labeling, and graphic design, is considered part of the product. Packaging serves, first and foremost, to protect the product from damage that may occur during shipping or storage. Packaging should prevent spoilage or breakage, make the product easy to handle when stocking or merchandising, and be tamper proof. Packaging that is reusable and disposable is highly desirable.

In addition to these protective environmentally friendly functions, packaging promotes a product by communicating its features, uses, benefits, and brand image. When customers confront a supermarket shelf of similar products, they expect the packaging to help them identify different product brands, to list the ingredients or materials in the product, describe its features, provide directions for its use, and provide clues as to why a certain brand might be more suitable to the buyer's needs than another.

When designing packaging the producer takes into account its cost. Depending on the product, consumers may or may not be willing to pay for better packaging.

For example, when purchasing perfume or cosmetics, consumers are quite willing to pay for beautifully presented goods because attractive packaging communicates the beautifying benefits of the product. On the other hand, when buying a baguette, which will likely be consumed immediately, the consumer is not likely to be willing to pay anything for packaging.

The producer will also consider how to package all of the firm's family of products similarly, so that the packaging exhibits a common design element. This can be challenging when the family of products includes a variety of forms, for example, gardening tools and gardening supplies that may come in bags and bottles.

The information found on product labels is often legally required. Under the Fair Packaging and Labeling Act of 1966, labels on consumer products must identify the product, indicate the name and location of the manufacturer or distributor, and state the net quantity of the product in both metric and in U.S. customary units, based on English units. Starting in 1990 the Nutrition Labeling Act gave the Food and Drug Administration the authority to require foods to carry labels listing their contents and that manufacturer health claims meet FDA regulations.

Fair Packaging and Labeling Act of 1966
Law that requires package labelling to identify the product, show the name and location of the manufacturer, and state the quantity in metric and U.S. units.

Examples of product labels

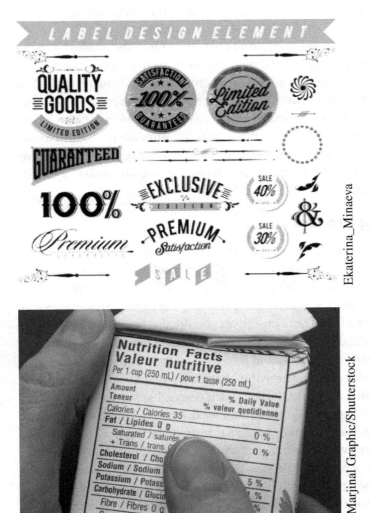

Ekaterina_Minaeva

Marjinal Graphic/Shutterstock

Labels also inform consumers of where a product was made (known as "country of origin"), as in "Made in the U.S.A." Labels support promotion by offering coupons, discounts, and descriptions of product features. Labels may explain legal information, warranties, or product limitations.

What Is Price?

Price as value Perceived benefits must always be greater than the cost of a product or service to retain value to customers.

Price is what the customer gives in exchange for a good or service. From the customer's perspective the price is the cost of something. Since the price that firms charge for their wares impacts the frequency of the sales, it should not be too high. Neither should the price be so low that it does not cover the costs of production, distribution, and marketing. The price of a product or service reflects its perceived **value** to the target consumers when compared with perceived benefits. The relationship of value, cost to the customer, and perceived benefits is often expressed as a ratio.

value = perceived benefits/perceived cost to acquire the product

According to the ratio, perceived benefits must always be greater than the costs in order for a product or service to retain its value for customers. Cost represents the price of the product plus the time and effort customers put into the shopping process. Therefore the formula is personal. Should the perceived benefits decrease, perceived value will decline and the price will have to be adjusted in order to maintain the value.

A wide variety of terms used in different contexts refer to the concept of price as something of value exchanged for the receipt of a good or service. Lawyers, doctors, banks, and consultants charge **fees**. Taxis and airplanes demand **fares**. You pay **rent** for an apartment or a house. An insurance **premium** represents the price of the policy. Home buyers pay real estate brokers a **commission**, as do purchasers of stock from stock brokers. The price of a loan is the **interest** you must pay for the use of the money. Government will ask code violators to pay **fines** for speeding or for infringements of pollution control laws. Even a **donation** made to a charity could be considered a price.

The Price-setting Process

Setting the price of a good or service can be explained as a six-step cyclical process, shown in figure 12.2. Examples of **pricing objectives** include increasing sales, volume (quantity) sold, matching competitors' prices, increasing the company's share of the overall market, securing brand loyalty, or following social/ethical objectives, to name just a few. These objectives should also be consistent with the purpose of the product and the strategic objectives of the company.

As illustrated in chapter 1, the **demand** for a product has significant influence on the price. As you have also seen earlier in this chapter, a product in the decline phase of the product life cycle—the phase during which demand lessens—will be priced differently than it was earlier in the cycle. To estimate demand, you need a clear idea of the characteristics of your target market and how many members of your target market are present in the geographic location where you will sell your product or service.

In step 3 of the price-setting process, costs related to the production and marketing of the product or service must be estimated. Probably the most common method of **using costs to set a price** is to total the direct costs of production per product unit and add a "markup" to cover overhead or operating costs and a profit.

The first three steps of the process will yield a price that can be compared with competitors' prices in step 4, taking into consideration special offers or discounts that competitors may be offering. If your pricing objective was to match competitors' prices and your calculations at this point yield a price that achieves your objective, you have completed the process and you may set your initial price (step 5). If not, then you will have to return to the previous steps, perhaps modifying profit objectives or identifying areas where costs can be cut.

Frequently, a competitor will cut its price and the firm must decide whether to lower its own prices for the same or similar product or service. (See step 6. Change price as needed.) The firm may first conduct a **break-even analysis** to determine the price at which it can still cover its costs and make a profit. The break-even point is where revenue equals costs. The equation below describes the break-even point.

breakeven point = fixed costs/(unit selling price – variable costs)

The firm must ask itself whether a lower price will have a negative effect on its market share and profits. If the answer is yes, the firm may consider the following actions:

- Lower the price of its product or service
- Improve the customer's perception of the quality of the product or service while maintaining the price
- Improve the quality of the product or service and raise the price
- Launch a low price version of the product

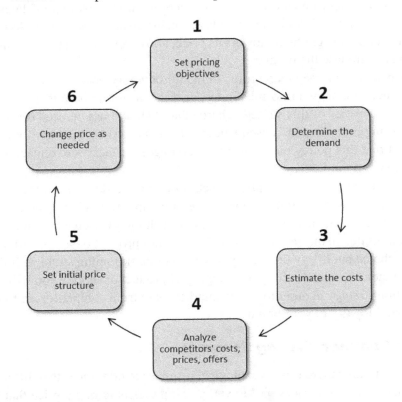

Figure 12.2 Six-step price setting process

As indicated in the product life cycle in figure 12.1, a firm will have to engage in the price setting process multiple times as pricing objectives change.

Price-level Strategies

Two of the major market-entry price-level strategies are price penetration and price skimming. They are most frequently used in the introductory stage of the product life cycle.

Price penetration and price skimming are price-level strategies often used during the introductory stage of the PLC.

Price penetration tries to secure considerable market share by achieving volume at a low price. A penetration strategy typically aims at setting a price low enough to discourage competition. With this strategy, the initial price of the product is set relatively low in hopes of "penetrating" into the marketplace quickly. Hyundai, for example, adopted penetration pricing strategy to enter the U.S. auto industry. The company offers customers value in the form of reliability, a 10-year warranty, and well-furnished interiors at prices far below those of Toyota's, Honda's, or Nissan's. Penetration pricing strategy requires extensive planning since the firm must get ready to mass produce and then implement mass marketing coverage. This strategy is very expensive and can result in high losses if the firm ends up with a huge inventory that no one wants. P&G very successfully employed the price penetration strategy when it rolled out its Crest Spin-Brush toothbrush in 2000. Consumers compared its US$5 price to $50 for the existing battery operated brands and voted with their wallets.

Price skimming is used for high-prestige or otherwise unique products with superior customer value. The firm charges a high, "premium" initial price for a product with a view to "skimming the cream" off the market. This strategy attempts to recover promotion, research, and development costs. For example, a cell phone company might launch a new cutting-edge product at a high price knowing that there are consumers who are willing to pay a premium for owning the latest technology. The company "skims" this highly profitable layer off the market. As demand slows, the company gradually lowers its price, until even the most price-conscious consumers purchase the product.

Price skimming may reap profits in the introductory phase of the product life cycle if there are a few or no substitutes, or if the customer base is not price sensitive. Some critics of this strategy charge that it should not be used for products that have important social consequences such as prescription drugs. Conversely, the profit that this policy may generate encourages businesses to engage in other innovation opportunities.

Deciding whether to use a price penetration or price skimming strategy with a new product depends entirely on the nature of competition. If, like the cell phone company you are the first to market with a new technology, there is no competition. If consumers desire the value and benefits that your product or service offers, they have no choice but to pay the price you set—a price skimming strategy. If there is already much competition for your category of product or service you will use the penetration strategy in order to "steal" market share from competitors or to secure consumers' loyalty to your brand.

Other Common Pricing Schemes

Marketers assume there is a psychological response to odd prices that differs from the responses to even prices. **Odd-even pricing** means setting a price that is just below a whole number to give the impression of a lower price. For example, stating a price as $199.99 seems remarkably lower than $200. Of course it is lower, but by just one penny! This method is also known as **psychological pricing**.

Most prices are stated as "list price," "retail price," "MSRP" (manufacturer's suggested retail price), or "sticker price." The idea of a **discount** subtracted from the retail price is attractive to consumers. Kohl's department store chain relies on frequent sales, discounts, and allowances to maintain its customer base. Other retailers depend on **everyday low pricing (EDLP)**, offering low list prices. Walmart pricing is the most well-known example of the EDLP approach.

J.C. Penney experimented with eliminating discounts in the form of traditional sales, moving to an **everyday low pricing strategy** in 2012. The company nearly went out of business. The following year, J.C. Penney started offering discounts again, this time in the form of "gifts" of 15% to 20% off the retail price. It seems clear from this experience that marketers should research their target markets carefully beforehand in order to determine the approach that will work best for the firm.

Discounts are also offered in business-to-business (B2B) marketing. A cash discount may be offered to a firm that pays its supplier quickly, for example, in cash. Another common discount is "2/10," meaning 2% will be taken off the net—the face value of the invoice—if the bill is paid in full in 10 days.

Almost everyone is familiar with **bundle pricing**, which is the practice of selling two or more products or services at a single package price. The success of this strategy depends on the degree to which consumers value the package over the individual items. The bundle price is less that purchasing the items separately. It is more convenient for consumers and lowers the marketing costs to sellers.

Cost-plus pricing is the most commonly used pricing method in B2B sales. It involves adding a specific amount to the cost of a product or service. The seller may compute the additional amount as a percentage of the total cost of the product or service or by adding a fixed fee or percentage of the cost. For example, a building contractor might add a fee that is 20% of all materials and labor costs.

Standard markup pricing is a method that adds a fixed percentage (known as the **markup**) to the price of all items in the same product category. Hypermarkets and other retailers that offer a large variety of items use this method because it is easier than estimating costs to make a price for each product.

Loss-leader pricing means that a price has been set below its usual level, perhaps not covering its cost to the seller. The purpose is to draw customers into the retailer so that they will buy other items that have high markups. Grocery stores frequently use this strategy.

APPLY YOUR KNOWLEDGE

Innovation Drives the Product Life Cycle (PLC)

As you can see from the product life cycle (PLC), firms must regularly replace mature products and services with new ones in order to maintain and increase revenue. There are two types of new products. A product that has a brand or a category new to the company is considered a new product. For example, when Arm & Hammer™'s introduced deodorizing cat litter, it was a completely new type of product for the baking soda company. Companies will often come up with variations on existing products or services, like a different package size or level of service, called line extensions. Academic research shows that roughly half of all new product/service introductions succeed in meeting the financial objectives set by the company.

Innovation is critical to the development of new products and services. Many, though not all, recent innovations rest on ingenious uses of wireless communication, mobile devices, robotics, and artificial intelligence (AI). Here are some of the products and services that made *Entrepreneur* magazine's 2018 list of innovative products and services.

Nike now has a Pro Hijab product line designed for female Muslim athletes. The clothing is made of moisture-wicking polyester and stays securely fastened around the neck.

Bowery grows what it calls "post-organic" food indoors year-round, achieving a yield of up to 100 times the amount that can be grown outdoors on a similar size plot of ground. BoweryOS runs the robotics technology that tracks and manages production.

Kairos, a company that helps young entrepreneurs with its fellowships and business incubator system, switched its focus to fulfilling social needs. Four new companies sprang to life. **Rhino** eliminates security deposits, **Little Spoon** delivers baby food, **Cera** decreases the cost of elder care, and **Kinside** offers childcare management tools.

FIN is a personal assistant service that integrates AI and human input to book flights, suggest gifts, and do research projects, all accomplished via e-mail, text, or voice input, for $1 per minute.

Tetra, Heatworks' countertop dishwasher, won Consumer Electronics Show 2019 Best of Innovation Award and helps small households save 1,500 gallons of water a year.

Inc. magazine compiled a different list, illustrating once again that a new product or service must fulfill a genuine customer need. Among the list of the *unnecessary* product innovations of 2018 are the following:

Modobag's battery-powered go-kart suitcase, which holds enough clothing to fill a duffel bag and for $1,500 allows the seated owner, weighing up to 260 lb, to race to an airport gate.

Myant utilizes its SKIIN Textile Computing platform to create smart underwear with built-in sensors that track your heart rate, breathing, and sleep to connect with smart devices, warm the wearer's body, and light up at night.

Samsung's 146" MicroLED TV screen (over 12 feet wide) called "The Wall" that can simulate shelves, a fireplace in a stone wall, windows, and other room features or furniture for business and "luxury living."

Knowledge Application Questions

1. Try your hand at new product innovation by completing this sentence: "I wish someone would invent a product or service that would ...." Try to come up with at least three wishes. Share your ideas with a classmate. Identify one or more specific target markets for your ideas using segmentation variables listed in Table 11.1 Common segmentation variables.

2. What change would you make to each of the following products to extend the product line? Try to come up with more than one extension per product.
    - Cascade dishwashing soap
    - Veet hair removal creams
    - Nabisco Zwieback crackers for babies
    - Nestlé baking morsels

3. Specify the most efficient and economical way(s) in which each product line extension above could be promoted. Consider the reputation of the brand, the characteristics of the target market, and how consumers usually obtain the product. Refer to Figure 11.1 The four P's of the marketing mix.

Sources

Briody, B., B. Farrow, J. Feifer, J. Keohane, M. Rhodes, K. Rockwood, S. Schomer, and C. Zulkey. 2018, June. "100 Brilliant companies." *Entrepreneur* 46(5): 34-61.

Ryan, K. 2018, December 17. "The Most Unnecessary Product Innovations of 2018." Accessed October 31, 2019. https://www.inc.com/kevin-j-ryan/worst-innovations-2018.html.

QUIZ YOURSELF

Without looking back at the chapter, choose the best answer to each of the questions below. Answers are in the back of the textbook before the Index. Review the chapter to find out why you missed any questions.

1. Fabric care, baby care, oral care, and hair care products are part of Procter & Gamble's
    a. distribution mix.
    b. product mix.
    c. promotion mix.
    d. supply chain.
    e. packaging mix.

2. Branding is an important marketing activity because it
    a. helps people remember your product or service and the value it delivers.
    b. builds trust with customers that your product or service is worth paying for.
    c. motivates employees and makes them feel proud to work for your company.
    d. is the foundation of word-of-mouth advertising, which generates new revenue.
    e. All of the above.

3. Procter & Gamble offers eight different fabric care products. Kelly Klean, a start-up company, only offers two fabric care products. P&G's _____ _____ is deeper than Kelly Klean's.
    a. product mix.
    b. product assortment.
    c. product line.
    d. product life cycle.
    e. product brands.

4. More and more people are buying the Tesla Model S, while the Ford Focus has been near the top of the automobile market for years and is still popular. In terms of the product life cycle, the Tesla Model S is in the _____ stage, and the Ford Focus is in the _____ stage.
    a. product development, decline
    b. maturity, decline
    c. repositioning, decline
    d. growth, maturity
    e. None of the above

5. Kroger's "Simple Truth" brand and Meijer's "True Goodness" brand are examples of _____ brands.
   a. private
   b. manufacturer
   c. generic
   d. individual
   e. name

6. The new iPhone X Max has a starting price of $1100. When Apple introduces a new phone, millions of buyers seek to own one, no matter the price. This is an example of a successful implementation of
   a. price gouging.
   b. price collusion.
   c. price penetration.
   d. bundle pricing.
   e. price skimming.

7. All of the following are functions of product packaging, EXCEPT
   a. protecting the product.
   b. communicating the features, benefits, and instructions for use.
   c. communicating the company's brand.
   d. providing advice as to how the product satisfies buyers' needs.
   e. making the product seem larger than it actually is.

8. Kroger often offers bananas at a price lower than other stores. Meijer often sells ten items for $10. These are examples of
   a. bundle pricing.
   b. everyday low pricing.
   c. loss leader pricing.
   d. cost-plus pricing.
   e. standard markup pricing.

9. The price at which a company can cover its costs and still make a profit is called the
   a. variable price.
   b. price point.
   c. fixed price.
   d. breakeven price.
   e. None of the above.

10. An insurance premium, the interest rate on a loan, or the commission paid to a realtor are all examples of
    a. fees.
    b. fines.
    c. taxes.
    d. cost-plus pricing.
    e. prices.

CHAPTER 13

Promotion and Distribution

In this chapter you will learn how businesses communicate their marketing message through media channels to current and prospective customers. Promotion is frequently referred to as marketing communications. Promotion strategies attempt to inform, persuade, and remind consumers and stakeholders about a company's wares. Based on the characteristics and behaviors of the target customers, firms select the appropriate promotional mix to promote products or services that the target market will value. The **promotional mix** consists of advertising, personal selling, sales promotion, and public relations. Using promotion, the producer pushes the product toward the wholesaler who in turn promotes it to retailers who promote it to the customers.

The fourth element of the marketing mix is **distribution (place).** You will learn more about the journey the product takes as it moves from its manufacturer or provider, in the case of services, to its end user. Marketing intermediaries have the resources to bridge the gap between production and the product's or service's point of sale (POS). They provide several benefits to both manufacturers and customers, such as improved efficiency, a better product assortment, customer service, delivery, and availability. By carefully selecting marketing intermediaries, firms can create a significant competitive advantage in the marketplace, while ill-chosen ones can bring misfortune to an outstanding product or service.

What Is Promotion?

Promotion *Informs customers, persuades them of the value of a product or service, and reminds them to buy it.*

Promotion is used to inform customers about the attributes of products, to persuade them of the product's value, and remind them to buy. Firms use more than one method to communicate to customers about their products, in order to ensure that members of the target market receive the marketing message. In addition to customers, promotion is geared toward wholesalers, retailers, and the firm's sales force. As mentioned earlier in the text, it is important for marketers to stay close to their customers in order to learn their needs and wants. Part of this research effort is devoted to learning how best to communicate with and persuade the target market. Firms develop a **promotional mix**, which is comprised of several carefully selected promotional methods: **advertising, sales promotion, publicity** and **public relations**, and **personal selling**. Marketing managers utilize different promotional strategies at each stage of the product life cycle, discussed in Chapter 12, to extend the life of a product.

Advertising *Paid, nonpersonal promotion of goods and services through media such as radio, television, newspapers, magazines, billboards, and the Internet.*

Advertising is the paid nonpersonal promotion of goods and services by an identified sponsor using mass media to inform a target audience about products and services offered by an organization. The second objective of advertising is to persuade consumers to purchase products by using the right message with the right language and imagery that effectively convey the value of the product and service. The third objective of advertising is to remind the target audience of the product or service in order to establish a presence in their minds. Advertising media include *radio, television, newspapers, magazines, billboards, context-specific Internet ads,* and *online banner ads*.

Sales promotion *Nonpersonal persuasive efforts designed to boost sales immediately.*

Sales promotions are nonpersonal persuasive efforts designed to boost sales immediately. Examples of sales promotions are coupons, discounts, rebates, free samples, displays, product demonstrations, sales contests, and trade shows.

Publicity/public relations (known as "PR") is the practice of conveying messages to the public through the media to influence their opinions about the firm and its products. A firm receives "good PR" for publicizing the good things it does, for example, sponsoring community events, donating to a cause or a charity, or community service performed by its employees.

Publicity/Public relations *Conveys messages to the public through the media to influence their opinions about the firm and remind them to buy.*

The most commonly used publicity tools are the *news release* and the *news conference*. A news or press release is an announcement that the company sends to newspapers, radio stations, or other media to suggest an idea for a news story. The company invites media representatives to a news conference to make product announcements or to counter negative publicity. The firm's public relations department will usually send information materials in advance of the conference. Though companies have control over the announcements sent to the media, they do not have control over how the media uses the announcements.

Personal selling *Direct, face-to-face communication with existing and potential customers to promote a firm's products.*

Personal selling is the direct, face-to-face communication by salespeople with existing and potential customers to promote a firm's products. For personal selling to be effective as a promotional strategy, salespeople should first of all have in-depth knowledge of their own products and that of all competing products in the marketplace. Salespeople must thoroughly understand the needs and values of customers. Customers want salespeople to be honest, respectful, trustworthy, ethical, good listeners, and to exhibit a professional attitude. Aggressiveness, presumption, poor follow-through, and inflated claims are likely to lose sales. Because sales-people are a company's front-line representatives, sales training is vital. Today's sales representatives must not only sell products and services, but must also have the skill, ability, and desire to build long-term customer relationships critical to a company's continued success.

The strength of the **sales force** is one of the competitive advantages that rival firms cannot copy. Salespeople equipped with the right technology participate in forecasts, collect information from the field about competitors, survey products, and build relationships with intermediaries, customers, and other stakeholders as part of relationship marketing. Firms, thanks to well-trained representatives, are able to create better profiles of their customers, preparing them to meet the challenges of new and potential needs through new product or service development.

Sales force A good sales force is a competitive advantage that rival firms cannot copy.

The ideal promotional mix should be efficient and effective. It should communicate a message that emphasizes product awareness, stimulates demand, and promotes product trial while not incurring needless expenses. The ultimate goal is to retain loyal customers, who can become a firm's advocates. Satisfied customers speak for the firm by talking about the company's wares to family members, friends, and relatives. **Word-of-mouth (WOM)** is a powerful though uncontrollable promotional tool. Word-of-mouth can bolster the reputation of organizations, enhance awareness of their wares, and create a profusion of opportunities, thus increasing sales, often at little or no cost to the organization. In a sense, word-of-mouth is "free advertising." WOM can, however, swiftly devastate the reputation of an organization if it falls short on the promises of its products or services.

Viral marketing Word-of-mouth that spreads via the Internet.

When word-of-mouth spreads via the Internet, it is called **viral marketing**. Consumer opinions that formerly might have taken days, weeks, or months to reach consumers are now relayed worldwide in minutes or hours via social media. **Social media** are online platforms that allow users to publish comments, photos, and videos and enter into conversations on topics of mutual interest with others in their social networks. Examples of social media are: Facebook, Twitter, LinkedIn, Instagram, YouTube, Flickr, Pinterest, and Reddit. Social media is sometimes referred to as "consumer-generated media." The world witnessed the power of "viral" messages during 2011's Arab Spring when the social media and the Internet helped topple Egypt's dictatorial leader, Hosni Mubarak. Likewise, businesses cannot ignore the impact of social media.

Social media Online software that allow users to publish comments, photos, and videos and enter into conversations on topics of mutual interest.

Product Life Cycle and Promotion

Because a product is new to the market in the **introductory phase** of the product life cycle, firms should make use of promotional tools to *inform* customers and *create awareness* of the new product. Advertising may be used to communicate the existence of the product and encourage customers to try it. Some firms use billboards, newspapers, TV, radio, magazines, or Internet advertisements. Other promotional efforts may involve personal selling and publicity. Building and maintaining product awareness, gaining customer trial, and eventually repeat purchase, requires sustained commitment of significant resources. The advertising budget for a product should be large enough to handle the phases the product goes through and to sustain market share.

PLC and promotion Promotion strategies change at each stage of the PLC in order to sustain profitability and minimize loss.

Buying Behavior and Promotion

When a product or service is introduced for the first time, buying behavior of consumers guides the choice of promotional strategies that will be used. Consumers pass through different stages of involvement with a product or service as they move from awareness to purchase. Marketers use each stage to specify promotional objectives. These stages and corresponding objectives are shown below in table 13.1.

Table 13.1 Stages of customer involvement and promotional objectives

Stage	Description of Stage	Promotional Objective
Awareness	When the consumer sees the product or hears the name, the consumer can identify the product type, or some other fact about the product.	Make sure that the consumer sees frequent advertisements.
Interest	The consumer actively seeks out information about the product.	Make sure that information about the product is easy to find, complete, and clear.
Evaluation	The consumer forms an opinion about the product or brand.	Information should help the consumer distinguish the product from competitors' products, highlighting its features and benefits. Make the consumer feel safe by providing samples, test drives, etc.
Trial	The consumer buys and uses the product or service.	Make purchasing simple, for example, by offering different payment options or simplifying payment process.
Adoption	The consumer buys the brand again and again based on a positive trial experience.	Prompt repeat purchases, for example, through coupons in the product package or a "rewards" program.

After the marketer has achieved the goal of consumer trial and adoption, the product or service enters the **growth stage** of the product life cycle where advertising and sales promotion are paramount. These promotional tools inform and persuade new adopters to try the product. It may also convince potential resellers to carry the product and be part of its success by stimulating the demand for the product. This strategy tries to broaden the market share by focusing on brand awareness to encourage loyalty.

At the **maturity stage** of the product life cycle, advertising may be more persuasive if it convinces new customers of the uniqueness of the product such as new features, benefits, and other differentiating product characteristics, and of its value for the money. Firms may also use personal selling, publicity or public relations, and sales promotion tools like samples and rebates in order to build customer loyalty and attract defectors from competing products.

At the **decline stage** of the product life cycle, sales begin to fall since more innovative products are introduced to the market or consumer tastes and preferences have changed. Some companies may use advertising as a way to emphasize product differentiation or to inform customers that a new and improved version will be launched. Other firms may focus on profitability through cost reduction by being more efficient in production and distribution and by reducing promotional expenses.

Integrated Marketing Communications (IMC)

Integrated marketing communications (IMC) means that the promotional mix elements are synchronized in a marketing strategy. The goal of IMC programs or campaigns is to communicate consistently with one voice all the time and every time to inform, persuade, or remind target audience customers directly or indirectly about the value of the products or services the company carries. IMC, if effective, may contribute to brand equity by evoking the brand in the customer's memory and by linking it to some unique and favorable associations. When developing an IMC campaign, firms need to know their target audience through marketing research to be able to fine-tune their promotional mix. Firms also need to be aware of the product's stage in the PLC in order to design an effective campaign. IMC, however, requires a significant amount of funds to be able to coordinate all the marketing efforts.

Integrated Marketing Communications (IMC) Promotional mix elements are synchronized in a marketing strategy.

Increasingly, IMC relies on low-cost social media and websites to reach a wide audience. Social media such as Twitter, Facebook, YouTube, Pinterest, and Instagram present opportunities for firms to inexpensively pursue their IMC strategies in a number of ways. See Figure 13.1 for a demographic breakdown of social media users.

- **Blogging** – A blog is a web site where a company places content that will be useful to members of its target market. The blog increases the exposure of a brand and builds brand equity. Through content-related discussion forums customers and potential customers interact with each other and the company. Blog visitors may also contribute content to the blog, thereby increasing their engagement with the brand.
- **Tweeting** – Twitter is a service that allows users to send short messages of 280 characters or less, called "tweets." These short messages help advertisers keep their offerings in front of customers and help drive business to the advertiser's products and services on a web site or at a retail store. Tweets can help remind customers of the product or service.
- **Sharing** – All social media can be shared. For example, a YouTube video can be shared with no fewer than 13 other social media services! It takes only a click to "re-tweet" a company's original tweet to a new set of followers. Sharing builds "buzz" and word of mouth and is the foundation of viral marketing mentioned earlier.
- **Interaction with customers** – Social media facilitates a company's response to customer feedback, and if handled skillfully, negative feedback can be publicly neutralized. Customers feel valued and engaged when their feedback is solicited, even if it is just a click on the "Like" button.

- **Paid social advertising** – Social media services like Facebook, Twitter, and LinkedIn offer paid advertising solutions that link advertising to audiences that have a specific interest in a company's offerings.
- **Monitoring the promotional mix** – Companies can utilize analytics software built into most social media in order to learn about the volume of traffic on their web sites, frequency and length of visits, customer profiles, and other audience data that will help a company to adjust its promotional mix.
- **Coordinating online and offline strategies** – For example, a firm may use direct mail to send samples to current or prospective customers, recommending that they consult a website for more information or to order the product. The Walt Disney Company uses mass advertising of its film and video entertainment as well as its live destination venues. At the same time, it uses its website to offer free services such as games and coloring for children in order to develop deeper customer relationships.

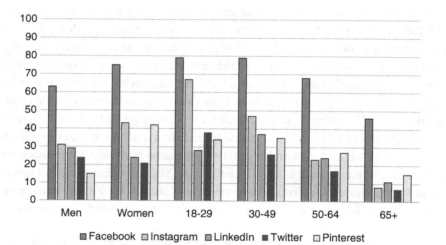

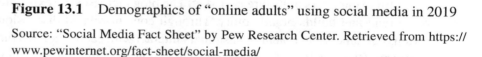

Figure 13.1 Demographics of "online adults" using social media in 2019

Source: "Social Media Fact Sheet" by Pew Research Center. Retrieved from https:// www.pewinternet.org/fact-sheet/social-media/

What Is Meant by Place (Distribution)?

Distribution Channel through which the customer receives a product or service. Often called the "Place" variable of the marketing mix.

The fourth "P," place, refers to how a product or service is distributed to the customer, known as the **distribution channel**. Another way to think about distribution channel is to answer the question, "How will our products be made available to our customers?" Distribution channels provide the means by which the firm quickly moves the goods and services it produces to the ultimate users of the goods and services. In the majority of cases one or more intermediaries, or "middlemen," will be involved in distribution. These intermediaries—wholesalers, distributors, agents, or brokers—help link the producer of a product or a service provider to the end user (see figure 13.2). Note that "direct distribution" moves goods and services directly from the manufacturer or provider to the end user without an intermediary. Other distribution channels involve one or more intermediaries.

Along with the growth of the Internet have come increased opportunities to use **direct channels of distribution**, making it more feasible to distribute goods and services directly from a producer's factory to the consumer. The direct channel has no levels, therefore no intermediaries. Time and inventory costs are saved and may be passed along to the buyer. Dell™ pioneered in direct distribution. Customers ordered a personal computer over the Internet that was custom-built to their specifications and later delivered to their home or business. Advances in technology such as shipping logistics, telecommunications, call centers, etc., are helping to accelerate innovations in the ways in which customers receive products and services, allowing businesses to use distribution to gain that competitive edge.

Reverse channels of distribution retrieve products that customers no longer want. The reverse channel is very important to customer satisfaction and helps build customer confidence in a brand. Examples of reverse channels include the recall of unsafe products, acceptance of returned products that are under warranty, and the return of products and packaging for recycling. Retailers will also return products from incorrectly filled orders, whether the mistake was made by the retailer or by the customer.

Reverse channel of distribution When customers return a product they do not want. The firm thus "retrieves" the product.

To sum up, distribution adds value by providing time, place, and ownership utilities. Distribution depends on interrelationships with organizations outside of the company which competitors cannot emulate, and thus creates a competitive advantage that can expand the reach of the products or services far beyond its current markets.

Marketing Intermediaries

Merchants are intermediaries that buy goods from several suppliers and thus become owners of the products (also known as assuming title). Merchants then resell those goods. An **agent** is a "middleman" whose job is to bring together buyers and sellers *without* assuming ownership title or physical possession of the goods they help distribute.

Wholesalers are firms that manage the flow of products from the manufacturer to the retailer. They provide useful services to both manufacturers and retailers. Wholesalers serve the producers of the goods by providing the following important functions:

Wholesalers warehouse and deliver products, assume financial risk, provide market information, and promote products.

Warehousing

Wholesalers buy items in bulk and store them in their own warehouses. This reduces inventory carrying costs associated with maintaining inventories to make products available to retailers when needed.

Delivery

A manufacturer ships products in bulk to the wholesaler, who in turn breaks up the bulk shipment to make it readily available to retailers. This enables retailers to order in small quantities regularly.

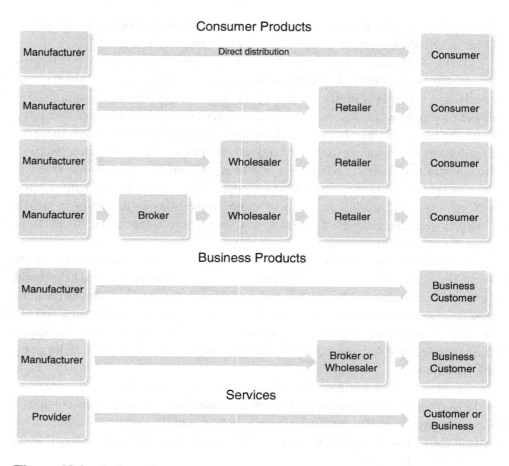

Figure 13.2 Intermediaries involved in common distribution channels

Credit risk

Due to the relationship built over time, a wholesaler may sell goods to retailers on credit as a form of short-term financing.

Market information

Wholesalers are frequently in contact with many retailers. The information they receive about competitors, new products, special offers, pricing, and promotion can be a vital source of feedback to manufacturers.

Promotion

Wholesalers often promote the products they distribute in the form of point-of-sale materials, such as brochures and cash-back cards. Wholesalers will also often set up displays. Wholesalers' promotional activities can help retailers generate a higher level of sales. The role of wholesalers has been reduced in recent years, as large chains such as Walmart and Kroger's are linked directly to suppliers using IT, and are able to use their size and power to negotiate better terms.

Retailers are marketing intermediaries who deliver products directly to final customers. These are the gatekeepers to end users. Retailers can be classified on the basis of several characteristics: number of outlets, nature of the service offered, variety of products offered, and whether the retailer is a store or non-store.

An **independent** retail store has only one outlet, while a **chain** has more than one outlet. Fred and Rita's Pizza Parlor is an example of an independent retailer. Do It Best Hardware is an Indiana chain of hardware stores. A **full-service** retailer offers customers help with purchasing a product. An example of a full-service retailer is a men's clothing store that has a tailor available to make alterations. **Self-service** stores offer little or no sales assistance. U.S. consumers are accustomed to buying clothes, food, and a multitude of other items "off-the-rack" or "off-the-shelf." Self-service cafeterias originated in the United States. These products require little expertise to sell.

Specialty retail stores focus on a narrow range of related products. Examples include stores that sell only cameras and photographic equipment, bookstores, furniture stores, and stores that specialize in automotive parts. While these stores focus on a narrow range of products, they may offer a wide selection of brands. In contrast to specialty retailers, **variety retail stores** offer a wide range of goods. Discount stores such as Target and department stores like Macy's and J.C. Penney, offer clothing, furniture, sporting goods, towels and linens, and many other categories of goods. Both specialty and variety stores have advantages. Specialty stores offer a certain degree of prestige and often have more knowledgeable salespeople, but variety stores offer more convenience because the customer can shop for several types of products in one location. Shopping centers and malls provide customers with both the convenience of variety stores and the prestige of specialty shops by providing a location where many specialty stores are close to each other.

While most retailers sell their products in stores, others use mail order, vending machines, telemarketing, direct selling, or the Internet. These are called **non-store retailers**.

Non-store retailers Companies that sell via mail-order, television, vending machines, and online.

Mail-order retailers receive orders by mail or over the phone and ship products through the mail. This type of retailing has become very popular in recent years because busy consumers with limited time find it more convenient to shop by phone than to visit retail stores. This approach works best for standardized items that are easily shipped and require little or no servicing. Home shopping networks like the QVC Channel are a different approach to mail order that has become popular.

Automatic vending machines can be placed in many locations and are often accessible at all hours, thus providing great convenience. This approach was originally used for cigarettes, candy, and soft drinks, but has been expanded to include other items such as travel insurance, nonprescription medicines, personal grooming items, DVD movies, and electronic devices.

Telemarketing involves the use of the phone to sell products and services directly to consumers. Despite FTC regulations and a generally negative perception of telemarketing among consumers, annual revenue from telemarketing totals US$424 billion.

Direct selling is the in-person presentation of products to customers away from a retail location. Examples of direct selling are door-to-door sales and in-home parties at which products are sold by the host.

Online retailing continues to grow. For example, Amazon.com has become a major seller of books, videos, and other items without having any storefronts. The U.S. Census Bureau reported that by mid-2019 online retail sales accounted for 10.7% of all U.S. retail sales.

Distribution Coverage Strategies

Marketers should be very careful as to the number of intermediaries to involve when deciding on the level of distribution coverage. The key factor in choosing a strategy is whether the costs of distribution can be recovered through sales of the product or service. Some of the costs, such as shipping costs, can be passed along to the customer but others such as paying additional salespeople to handle more distributors cannot. In general, intensive, exclusive, and selective distribution strategies are discussed in the context of goods. They match the classification of convenience, specialty, and shopping products categories, as discussed in chapter 11.

The **intensive coverage** strategy, also known as **mass coverage**, seeks to distribute products in nearly all available channels in a variety of locations. An intensive distribution strategy is usually only feasible for relatively low-priced products with wide appeal. Shampoo, chewing gum, soft drinks, candy bars, newspapers, popular magazines, and many other low-priced *convenience* products are distributed using intensive or mass coverage.

The **selective coverage** strategy attempts to distribute a product through only a limited number of channels in a particular geographic location. Selective distribution strategies appeal to smaller and more focused target markets whose consumers are willing to spend time visiting different retail outlets to compare product attributes such as price, quality, and service. This distribution coverage is suitable for *shopping* products such as home appliances, furniture, electronic equipment, and computers.

Companies choosing the **exclusive coverage** strategy use one wholesaler or one retailer to distribute a product in a specific geographical location. This kind of distribution coverage is typically used with high-end and prestige products. *Specialty* products are suitable for this kind of coverage. Luxury car manufacturers such as Rolls Royce, Jaguar, and Bentley are good examples of an exclusive coverage distribution strategy.

Table 13.2 Comparison of distribution coverage strategies

	Intensive Coverage	Selective Coverage	Exclusive coverage
Description of strategy	Also known as mass coverage, distributing through all available channels in a variety of locations.	Limited number of distribution channels in a specific geographic location	One wholesaler or one retailer in a specific geographic location
Types of products best suited to strategy	Low-priced convenience products like gum, shampoo, magazines.	Shopping products such as appliances, electronics	High-end, prestige, specialty products
Purpose of the strategy	Reach a large audience to achieve maximum sales. Less risky than other types of coverage if products have broad appeal.	Control over brand image, service, lower costs than intensive coverage.	Control and enhance brand image.
Examples of brands sold via the strategy	People magazine, Wrigleys gum, Herbal Essence shampoo	Whirlpool and General Electric sell through dealers and selected retailers	Luxury brands like Gucci, Rolls Royce, Rolex

APPLY YOUR KNOWLEDGE

21st Century Integrated Marketing Communications (IMC)

In the 21st century, if a company doesn't have a website, it doesn't exist. And if a company doesn't implement its integrated marketing communications (IMC) through digital delivery of its promotional mix, its competitive advantage will suffer.

Blue Corona, a Maryland-based digital marketing and analytics company, claims that 70-80 percent of potential customers (B2C) visit a company's website before visiting the local store or purchasing a product. Therefore, first impressions are quickly formed and critical to successful digital marketing. According to Blue Corona, nearly half of users decide on the trustworthiness of a company based on how the website looks. Almost forty percent of the 2,000 adult consumers Adobe surveyed said that they leave a website if it takes too long to load. For every second of delay, sales fall by 12 percent, according to Google, which has developed a "speed scorecard" to help businesses calibrate their websites. Once a website has loaded, consumers form an opinion in .05 seconds, adds Kinesis Inc., a Portland, Oregon marketing firm.

Most small businesses have an annual marketing budget of less than $10,000, and 71 percent do their own digital marketing instead of hiring a marketing consultant. The top three tools used by small businesses are e-mail, websites, and social media. Social media is an inexpensive way to implement an IMC, but it takes planning, skill, and dedication of resources. Small business owners can learn much from examining the work of successful online marketers.

One low-cost way to engage customers with a brand is to encourage user-generated content (UGC)—posts, photos, and videos that customers place online themselves and then share with others. Cupshe is a trend-setting swimsuit company that relies almost entirely on Instagram posts by happy customers to drive orders to its website, designed with Shopify Plus (e-commerce software) at a monthly cost of $300. The Cupshe Instagram account has 829,000 followers. On Instagram, the company combines its promotional mix of free trials, contests, influencer marketing (paid endorsement), and direct sales. Cupshe generates about 35 percent of its annual $50 million in sales from social media.

A common approach is to flood as many social media and Internet platforms as possible with the company's content, known as cross-channel, or multichannel, marketing. The reasoning is that customers use multiple media channels, so it's a good idea for a company to do likewise. Customers can access an advertiser's message using their preferred platform.

An efficient way to populate several platforms with content is to publish the same content on different networks. Casper, the mattress company, uses a Facebook page, Twitter, and Instagram to engage current and potential customers. It recently created a set of sounds, meditations, and bedtime stories called the Casper Sleep Channel and posted them to three different social media platforms: Spotify, YouTube, and Instagram TV (IGTV). At the same time, Casper posted "teasers" announcing new Sleep Channel episodes on the other platforms to "cross-promote" the content.

Digital cross-channel marketing is not just about computers and mobile phones, though. A USA TouchPoints study reveals "media double acts"—media channels like TV, radio, mobile, and computer—that work well together. The study found that "computer" paired with "mobile" was the most popular among adults during work hours, while "TV" paired with "mobile" was preferred in the evening. When the Bravo channel learned that 1/3 of Twitter users tweet about TV shows, it started promoting specific hashtags during shows. Many TV advertisements now include hashtags.

Though managing six or more media channels may seem overwhelming, social media management tools like eClincher, Sprout Social, and Hootsuite, which run from $60 to $400 a month, make the task much easier, enabling even very small businesses to take advantage of multichannel marketing. The key to successful multichannel marketing, though, is to know where the target audience spends most its time and focus efforts there.

Knowledge Application Questions

1. Using Table 13.1 Stages of customer involvement and promotional objectives, identify the online marketing channel that would be the best choice to accomplish the promotional objective for each stage of customer buying behavior: awareness, interest, evaluation, trial, adoption.

2. Develop a digital marketing promotion plan for a local sports team. Use Twitter, Facebook, and other social networking media to promote ticket sales for next season's schedule. In your plan, provide specific details and ideas for the content you would use on the sites. Also, describe how you would encourage fans and potential fans to go to your site. How would you use digital media to motivate sports fans to purchase tickets and merchandise and attend games?

Sources

Cupshe. 2019. Accessed October 31, 2019. https://www.instagram.com/cupshe/.

Horvath, T. 2016, October 20. "51 Insane Web Design Statistics 2018 [Updated]." [Blog post]. Accessed October 31, 2019. https://www.tytonmedia.com/blog/51-insane-web-design-statistics-2016/.

Imeality. 2018, May 17. "From $3M a Month to $50M+ a Year: How Cupshe Breaks the 'Curse' of Growth." [Blog post]. Accessed October 31, 2019. http://www.imeality.in/from-3m-a-month-to-50m-a-year-how-cupshe-breaks-the-curse-of-growth/.

McLeod, B. 2018, October 2. "60+ Small Business Statistics to Help Your Digital Marketing Strategy (2018)." [Blog post]. Accessed October 31, 2019. https://www.bluecorona.com/blog/29-small-business-digital-marketing-statistics.

Think with Google. 2018, March 2018. "The Mobile Speed Scorecard and Impact Calculator." [Blog post]. Accessed October 31, 2019. https://www.thinkwithgoogle.com/marketing-resources/experience-design/mobile-speed-scorecard-impact-calculator/.

West, C. 2019. "6 Standout Social Media Marketing Examples for 2019." [Blog post]. Accessed October 31, 2019. https://sproutsocial.com/insights/social-media-marketing-examples/.

QUIZ YOURSELF

Without looking back at the chapter, choose the best answer to each of the questions below. Answers are in the back of the textbook before the Index. Review the chapter to find out why you missed any questions.

1. The primary aim(s) of promotion is/are to
    a. provide information about a product or service to customers.
    b. convince customers that the product or service will be valuable to them.
    c. cause customers to remember to buy the product or service.
    d. Choices a, b, and c
    e. Choice c only

2. Integrated marketing communications (IMC)
    a. is the synchronization of the promotional mix in a marketing strategy.
    b. communicates to the target market with one voice.
    c. is fairly costly, though social media can reduce the expense.
    d. contributes to brand equity.
    e. All of the above.

3. What kind of utility does promotion provide to the customer?
    a. Form utility, because market research must be done to determine which products customers will like
    b. Possession, because promotion communicates the value of owning the product or using the service
    c. Time, because promotion must be executed at the optimal time to increase sales
    d. Place, because advertising must appear in the media most seen by the target market
    e. All of the above, for the reasons provided.

4. Factors involved in choosing a distribution channel include all of the following, EXCEPT
    a. whether the product is a convenience, specialty, or shopping product.
    b. the ability of sales to cover the costs of distribution.
    c. consideration of the advantages and disadvantages of each type of channel.
    d. consideration of the channels used by competitors.
    e. whether the CEO has a good relationship with a large wholesaler.

5. Factors involved in choosing a promotional mix include all of the following, EXCEPT
   a. where the product is in the product life cycle.
   b. the buying behaviors of the target audience.
   c. consideration of research on social media use by the target audience.
   d. household income of the target audience.
   e. the ability of sales to cover the costs of promotion.

6. Services that wholesalers provide to producers include
   a. point-of-sale promotional materials.
   b. market information.
   c. short-term financing.
   d. choices a, b, and c.
   e. none of the above.

7. Amazon.com is an example of
   a. a brick-and-mortar retailer.
   b. a wholesaler.
   c. direct distribution.
   d. a non-store retailer.
   e. none of the above.

8. Distribution is a competitive advantage because
   a. no two entities can occupy the exact physical location at the same time.
   b. it depends on a complex set of relationships with external organizations that cannot be copied.
   c. it provides only the possession utility to customers.
   d. the flow of products is bidirectional.
   e. None of the above.

9. What type of distribution coverage would be suitable for AA batteries?
   a. Shopping coverage
   b. Intensive coverage
   c. Selective coverage
   d. Exclusive coverage
   e. Intermediary coverage

10. Helen owns a business selling designer handbags and shoes in a mall located in a city where several small colleges and a state university are located. She is deciding on a low-cost integrated marketing communications strategy. Which of the following sets of choices makes the most sense for her?
    a. Facebook page, Pinterest, writing a fashion blog
    b. Selling through a cable shopping channel, advertising on an afternoon TV talk show, posting YouTube videos
    c. Posting product photos in Flickr, joining LinkedIn, and distributing flyers at the mall
    d. All of the above
    e. None of the above

CHAPTER 14

Managing Accounting Information

What Is Accounting?

Accounting refers to the systematic recording and analyzing of a firm's financial transactions. It is the "language" of business. It was created to track money in trade and taxation. The earliest references to accounting can be found in histories of Mesopotamia and Egypt.

Modern accounting began in Venice in 1494 with the Luca Pacioli's invention of **double entry bookkeeping**, based on the concept of debits and credits. Pacioli drew on ideas that had been established over centuries, but he was the first to put these ideas into a coherent set of procedures expressed in writing. Today firms prepare financial statements for financial analysts, banks, shareholders, and the Securities and Exchange Commission (SEC), relying on the fundamental concepts of double entry bookkeeping, now over five centuries old.

Reporting Principles

All the reports emanating from financial transactions must comply with the guidelines set forth by the **Generally Accepted Accounting Principles (GAAP)**. These principles govern how firms should report their financial information and permit stakeholders to perform their own analysis since there is a

Generally Accepted Accounting Principles (GAAP) The GAAP provides consistency across a variety of contexts including providing a format for financial disclosure to the SEC, and to internal or external auditors.

consistency in the format. They can study financial statements, compute financial ratios, and compare reports across the industry. This way they can make a sound "apples-to- apples" comparison of a business entity across the industry in which it operates. The **U.S. Securities and Exchange Commission (SEC)** regulates the financial disclosures and operations of publicly-traded companies. The SEC requires publicly traded and regulated companies to follow GAAP for the purpose of financial reporting. The SEC has charged the **Financial Accounting Standards Board (FASB),** a non-profit organization, with the primary responsibility for improving financial reporting under the GAAP. The Financial Accounting Standards Advisory Councils (FASAC) advises the FASB on all matters that may influence GAAP rules.

Types of Accounting

Managerial accounting focuses on internal stakeholders, such as top executives, management, and administrators within organizations. Managers rely on financial information to be able to make sound decisions that may add value to the organization. Financial information tells a story about a company's strengths and weaknesses. It also depicts a firm's competitive advantage or disadvantage vis-à-vis the opportunities and threats in its external environment. Managerial accounting, in other words, is interested in the performance of the firm. Based on the financial information, these managers are able to control the firm's expenses by departments and by individuals.

Financial accounting focuses on external stakeholders. These stakeholders are interested in the performance of the firm. Others, for example, creditors or suppliers, want to know the creditworthiness of the firm.

The major difference between managerial and financial accounting has to do with the users (internal or external) of the information. However, the financial reports must be prepared in compliance with GAAP.

To make sure that the financial reports are accurate and taxes are paid properly and in a timely fashion, firms **audit** them. **Internal auditors** apply GAAP when analyzing financial reports. These auditors appraise the business divisions to ensure that they are functioning efficiently, that the firm has minimized its financial risks, and that it is complying with its own rules and the law. Internal auditors, like external auditors, must have a comprehensive understanding of the firm's operations. **External auditors** provide an independent outside opinion about a firm's financial statements. Their review is done on an annual basis. External auditors want to know if the statements accurately reflect the company's financial health and whether the statements conform to GAAP. External audits are performed by public accounting firms, by certified public accountants, and sometimes by government agencies.

Financial Statements

Financial statements consist of written reports that shed light on the financial activities of a firm. They evaluate the firm's condition in terms of its financial strengths and weaknesses at any given point in time. Decision-makers study them in order to turn unforeseen threats and opportunities in their favor. These financial reports, as mentioned above, should adhere to the GAAP. They should be consistent and accurate. Companies generate financial statements monthly to help the management make decisions that support the overall strategic planning. The three main types of financial statements are:

- Balance sheet
- Income statement
- Cash flow statement

Balance Sheet

The balance sheet is the cornerstone of financial management. Table 14.1 shows the traditional format of a balance sheet and figure 14.1 is an example of an actual balance sheet. The relationship between the items on a balance sheet is described by the **basic accounting equation:**

$$\textbf{assets = liabilities + owners' equity}$$

Both sides of the accounting equation must always be equal to each other, or "in balance." If we know two of the main components of the accounting equation, we should be able to get the third one.

Example 1:

$$\textbf{Calculating Assets = Liabilities (\$300) + Owners' equity (\$200)}$$
$$\textbf{Assets = \$500}$$

Example 2:

$$\textbf{Assets (\$800) = Liabilities? + Owners' equity (\$400)}$$
$$\textbf{Calculating Liabilities = \$800–\$400}$$
$$\textbf{Liabilities = \$400}$$

Table 14.1 Traditional Format of a Balance Sheet

Total Assets =	Total Liabilities +	Owner's Equity
Current assets	Current liabilities	Paid-in capital
Fixed assets	Long-term liabilities	Retained earnings
Intangible assets		

Assets

Assets are things of value that the company owns. See table 14.2 for examples of what may be considered assets. Assets fall into three categories:

- Current assets
- Fixed assets
- Intangible assets

Current assets are expected to be converted into cash or used up within one year. Examples of current assets, listed in order of liquidity (how easy it is to convert to cash) are:

- Cash
- Marketable securities (e.g., stocks, bonds, commercial paper)
- Accounts receivable (money owed by clients or customers)
- Inventory
- Prepayments (e.g., insurance, rent)

See table 14.3 for terms found in accounts receivable and payable.

Fixed assets are physical items that are expected to last more than a year. These assets are subject to **depreciation**, which represents a reduction in the value of a fixed asset to reflect its wear and tear, obsolescence, as well as market conditions. Depreciation is an income tax deduction. Examples of fixed assets, listed in order of permanence, from most to least, are:

- Land
- Buildings
- Equipment

Intangible assets Copyrights, patents, brand names, trademarks, franchises, and goodwill are all examples of intangible assets.

Intangible assets are things of value that you are not able to touch, see, and feel. **Intellectual property—copyrights, patents** (product and process), **trademarks,** and **brand names**—is a form of intangible asset. **Franchises and licenses,** which entitle a company to sell a product or service are other types intangible assets. **Goodwill** consists of the firm's relationship with stakeholders, the firm's reputation, and location—to name a few elements of goodwill. A firm's goodwill mirrors its competitive advantage. This competitive edge is another important type of intangible asset.

Liabilities

Liabilities "Current" refers to a debt that is payable within one year while "long-term" refers to an obligation that will be carried for more than a year.

Liabilities are debts or obligations the company is expected to pay (see table 14.2). The company, for example, has to pay back financial institutions, creditors, and suppliers for the money it borrowed to finance its venture. The company also has payroll and tax obligations. There are two categories of liabilities—**current liabilities** and **long-term liabilities,** which include **noncurrent liabilities** or **fixed liabilities.**

Table 14.2 Examples of balance sheet items

Current Assets	Current Liabilities	Additional Paid-in Capital
✓ Cash	✓ Accounts payable	✓ Common stock
✓ Marketable securities	✓ Notes payable	✓ Preferred stock
✓ Accounts receivable	✓ Wages payable	
✓ Inventory	✓ Taxes payable	
✓ Prepayments (e.g., rent, insurance)		
Fixed assets	**Long-term liabilities**	**Retained earnings (RE)**
✓ Land	✓ Bonds	Beginning RE
✓ Buildings	✓ Bank loans	+ net income (or – net loss)
✓ Equipment	✓ Deferred taxes	– dividends paid
		= ending retained earnings
Intangible assets		
✓ Trademark/trade name		
✓ Copyrights		
✓ Patents		
✓ Goodwill		

Current liabilities are debts that are expected to be paid within one year. These short-term liabilities are:

- Accounts payable (money the company owes to suppliers)
- Salaries payable
- Taxes payable
- Notes payable (loans)
- Interest payable
- Working capital loan

Long-term liabilities are debts that are carried over for more than a year. These long-term obligations are:

- Bonds payable
- Bank loans
- Deferred taxes
- Mortgage payable

Owners' Equity

Owners' equity is also known as **shareholders' equity** or **net worth**. It refers to the amount of money left when the company sells all its assets and has paid off all its liabilities (see table 14.2). The leftover money goes to the owners of the company who are entitled to it. We think of equity as that part of a company's assets financed by its owners rather than creditors. Mathematically, it is the difference between a firm's assets and its liabilities. Owners' equity categories include:

- Additional paid-in capital from the purchase of common stock or preferred stock issued
- Retained earnings

Table 14.3 Trading terms

Terms	Explanations
"Net"	The full amount is due for payment.
"Net 10"	The full payment is due in 10 days.
"EOM"	The customer must issue payment within a certain number of days following the end of the month.
"Net EOM 10"	The full amount must be paid within 10 days following the end of the month.
"2/10"	2% discount can be taken if payment is made within 10 days.
"2/10 Net 30"	You take 2% discount if you pay in 10 days, otherwise 100% of the account debt is due in 30 days.
"2/10 Net 60"	You take 2% discount if you pay in 10 days, otherwise 100% of the account debt is due in 60 days.
A/P (Accounts)	The amount you owe your suppliers/ other businesses. Accounts payable do not include interest if they are paid on time. They usually are paid within 30 to 60 days.
A/R (Accounts Receivable)	The amount owed to you by your customers/other businesses.
Notes Payable	Promissory notes to pay your creditor the amount borrowed (principal), including interest payments.
Notes Receivable	The amount your customers owe you for their purchases. It is a promissory note from your customers spelling out the date of maturity, the interest rate, and other credit terms.

Balance Sheet		
Assets		
Current assets		
Cash in bank	$20,000	
Inventory	$41,000	
Prepaid expenses		
Insurance	$2,000	
Rent	$14,000	
Accounts receivable	$40,000	
	Total current assets	*$117,000*
Fixed assets		
Machinery & equipment	$25,000	
Furniture & fixtures	$10,000	
Real estate / buildings		
	Total fixed assets	*$35,000*
	Total assets	**$152,000**
Liabilities & net worth		
Current liabilities		
Accounts payable	$8,000	
Taxes payable	$3,000	
Notes payable (due within 12 months)	$3,000	
Salaries payable	$2,000	
	Total current liabilities	*$16,000*
Long-term liabilities		
Bank loans payable (greater than 12 months)	$50,000	
Less: short-term portion		
	Total long-term liabilities	*$50,000*
	Total liabilities	*$66,000*
Owners' equity (net worth)		*$86,000*
	Total liabilities & net worth	**$152,000**

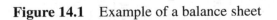

Figure 14.1 Example of a balance sheet

Income Statement - 12 months

Period starting:	Month 1	Month 2	Month 3	Month 4	Month 5	Month 6	Month 7	Month 8	Month 9	Month 10	Month 11	Month 12	Totals
Sales													
Sales	12,000	10,000	8,000	8,500	15,000	13,000	10,000	12,000	10,000	9,000	11,000	10,000	128,500
Other	500	0	0	400	0	0	0	0	200	400	300	200	2,000
Total Sales	12,500	10,000	8,000	8,900	15,000	13,000	10,000	12,000	10,200	9,400	11,300	10,200	130,500
Less Cost of Goods Sold													
Materials	5,000	4,000	3,000	3,100	6,500	5,500	4,000	5,000	4,000	3,000	4,500	4,000	51,600
Labor	500	500	500	500	500	500	500	500	500	500	500	500	6,000
Overhead	500	500	500	500	500	500	500	500	500	500	500	500	6,000
Other	0	0	0	0	0	0	0	0	0	0	0	0	0
Total Cost of Goods Sold	6,000	5,000	4,000	4,100	7,500	6,500	5,000	6,000	5,000	4,000	5,500	5,000	63,600
Gross Profit	6,500	5,000	4,000	4,800	7,500	6,500	5,000	6,000	5,200	5,400	5,800	5,200	66,900
Operating Expenses													
Salaries and wages	2,000	2,000	2,000	2,000	2,000	2,000	2,000	2,000	2,000	2,000	2,000	2,000	24,000
Employee benefits	600	600	600	600	600	600	600	600	600	600	600	600	7,200
Payroll taxes	120	120	120	120	120	120	120	120	120	120	120	120	1,440
Rent	1,200	1,200	1,200	1,200	1,200	1,200	1,200	1,200	1,200	1,200	1,200	1,200	14,400
Utilities	300	300	300	300	300	300	300	300	300	300	300	300	3,600
Repairs and maintenance	300	50	50	50	50	50	50	100	50	50	50	50	900
Insurance	200	200	200	200	200	200	200	200	200	200	200	200	2,400
Travel	100	0	0	0	500	0	0	0	0	0	500	0	1,100

													Total
Telephone	150	150	150	150	150	150	150	150	150	150	150	150	1,800
Postage	0	0	0	0	0	0	0	0	0	0	0	0	0
Office supplies	50	50	50	50	50	50	50	50	50	50	50	50	600
Advertising	500	0	0	500	0	0	500	0	0	500	0	0	2,000
Marketing/promotion	0	0	0	0	0	0	0	0	0	0	0	0	0
Total Operating Expenses	**5,520**	**4,670**	**4,670**	**5,170**	**5,170**	**4,670**	**5,170**	**4,720**	**4,670**	**5,170**	**5,170**	**4,670**	**59,440**
Operating Income	**980**	**330**	**(670)**	**(370)**	**2,330**	**1,830**	**(170)**	**1,280**	**530**	**230**	**630**	**530**	**7,460**
Interest income (expense)													
Other income (expense)													
Total Nonoperating Income (Expense)	**0**	**0**	**0**	**0**	**0**	**0**	**0**	**0**	**0**	**0**	**0**	**0**	**0**
Income (Loss) Before Taxes	**980**	**330**	**(670)**	**(370)**	**2,330**	**1,830**	**(170)**	**1,280**	**530**	**230**	**630**	**530**	**7,460**
Income Taxes	**200**	**0**	**0**	**200**	**0**	**0**	**200**	**0**	**0**	**200**	**0**	**0**	**800**
Net Income (Loss)	**780**	**330**	**(670)**	**(570)**	**2,330**	**1,830**	**(370)**	**1,280**	**530**	**30**	**630**	**530**	**6,660**
Cumulative Net Income (Loss)	**780**	**1,110**	**440**	**(130)**	**2,200**	**4,030**	**3,660**	**4,940**	**5,470**	**5,500**	**6,130**	**6,660**	**6,660**

Figure 14.2 Example of an income statement

Retained Earnings (RE)

Retained earnings are accumulated after-tax profits or losses that are not paid out in dividends. Firms use retained earnings strategically. Rather than financing projects through borrowing, firms use their own funds. These funds can be reinvested in research and development, to upgrade the firm's technology, for relocation, and to acquire other companies, and similar strategic purposes. Retained earnings are calculated by adding net income to (or deducting a **net loss** from) beginning retained earnings and then subtracting any dividends paid to the shareholders. The formula is:

retained earnings = beginning retained earnings + net income
(or minus net loss) – dividends

If the resulting retained earnings turn out to be negative, the term used is "retained deficit." Based on the formula above for RE, the income statement and the balance sheet must be prepared before the Retained Earnings Statement. We need to know the net income or net loss in order to figure out the ending balance of retained earnings. Also the balance sheet must be prepared after the RE statement in order to know the ending balance of Retained Earnings.

Income Statement

This financial statement indicates the revenue, expenses, and profits (or losses) of a firm over a period of time (see figure 14.2). This financial statement, also known as the bottom line statement, tells us if the company is making profits or incurring loss. The format for an income statement is:

revenues – expenses = net income

The components of an income statement are as follows:

- **Net sales**
  Total sales adjusted for any discounts.
- **Cost of goods/services sold (COGS)**
  COGS is the cost of all materials that were used to produce the goods that were sold. If your book-store buys your *Principles of Business Administration* textbook for $50 and then sells it for $80, the bookstore's COGS is $50.
- **Gross profit**
  Gross profit equals *net sales minus the cost of goods sold.*
- **Operating expenses**
  These are composed of *selling expenses* as well as *general and administrative expenses.*
- **Earnings before interest and taxes (EBIT)**
  EBIT are calculated by *subtracting* a firm's *operating expenses* from its *gross profits.*
- **Earnings after taxes (EAT)**
  Earnings after taxes, sometimes referred to as **net income (NI)**, equal **earnings before taxes** *minus taxes.*

Figure 14.3 shows the order in which the statements discussed so far are prepared.

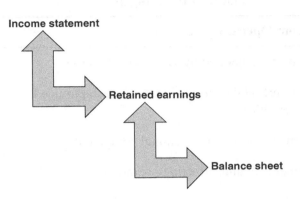

Figure 14.3   Statement preparation order

Cash Flow Statement

The purpose of this statement is to provide relevant information about a firm's cash receipts and its cash disbursements for a particular period of time. The statement shows the exchange that takes place between the firm and the environment where its business takes place (see figure 14.4). The firm's executives need to know if the cash the firm generates will be adequate to support its future plans as outlined in its strategic planning. The shareholders need to find out if the firm is going to be able to pay dividends. The employees of the firm want to know if they are in a secure environment where they will develop their skills and get promoted. Investors need to know if there is a growth potential to be able to capitalize on their investment. Creditors as well as suppliers want to know if the firm is capable of paying its bills if they were to extend credit.

Cash flow statement
Cash flow statements list cash from operating activities first, cash from investing second, and cash from financing last.

The statement of cash flows is organized into three activities:

- Cash from (used for) operating activities
- Cash from (used for) investing activities
- Cash from (used for) financing activities

Operating activities are cash inflows and outflows from operations. They result from activities undertaken to earn income, for example, the sale of goods or services (receipts) and the purchase of inventory (disbursements).

Investing activities result from cash inflows and outflows from fixed assets. The firm acquires these assets in order to operate the business. The firm can purchase or sell property and equipment. It can also purchase or sell investments.

Financing activities are cash inflows and outflows from long-term liabilities and equity. A firm can obtain funds from outside sources. A firm can borrow (debt financing) from banks or investors by debt securities and can also issue stocks.

Statement of Cash Flows for Company ABC Fiscal Year ending June 30, 2xxx	
Cash Flow from Operating Activities	
Net Income (profit generated by sales to customers)	$50,000
Adjustments to reconcile net income to net cash provided by operating activities:	
Depreciation & amortization - capital equipment	$15,000
Changes in other accounts affecting operations:	
(Increase)*/decrease in accounts receivable	$2,000
(Increase)/decrease in inventories	$1,500
(Increase)/decrease in prepaid expenses (rent and insurance increased)	($2,400)
Increase/(decrease) in accounts payable	$600
Increase/(decrease) in taxes payable	$1,200
Net cash provided by operating activities	**$67,900**
Cash Flow from Investing Activities	
Capital expenditures	(0)
Proceeds from sales of equipment	$1,000
Net cash provided by investing activities	**$1,000**
Cash Flow from Financing Activities	
Payments of long-term debt	($24,000)
Purchase of treasury stock	($5,000)
Net cash provided by financing activities	**($29,000)**
Increase (Decrease) in Cash	**$39,900**

Figure 14.4   Example of a cash flow statement

* Parentheses signify a negative dollar amount.

Financial Ratios

A *ratio* refers to the mathematical relationship between two quantities in the form of a fraction or percentage that can be compared or measured. To do this, we simply divide one number by another to illustrate their relationship. The purpose of the analysis of financial ratios is to identify the *strengths and weaknesses* of the firm. Financial ratios can tell an investor, for example, if his or her money is safe with that particular firm. The ratio communicates a level of risk. For examples of the financial ratios of three well-known companies, see table 14.4.

The ratios provide useful information to *benchmark* a company's performance to study changing financial health over time and to compare a company to its competitors in its industry. Managers use financial ratios to understand how profitability will be affected by decisions about pricing, product development, and human resource management policies.

Financial ratios classifications include measures of:

- liquidity
- financial leverage
- profitability
- efficiency (activity ratios)

Measures of Liquidity

Liquidity ratios measure a company's ability to pay its short-term debts (bills) as they come due.

The **current ratio** tests a firm's ability to pay its current liabilities. It illustrates the relationship between current assets and current liabilities. The larger the current ratio, the greater the liquidity. The current ratio formula is:

Liquidity A liquidity ratio of 1 means that the firm is able to cover its liabilities.

current ratio = current assets/current liabilities

It is important to note that:

- A ratio of 2:1 means the firm has sufficient liquidity to cover its liabilities twice over.
- A ratio of 0.75:1 would suggest that the firm is unable to meet its liabilities and could be in a weak financial position.
- A ratio below 1 does not mean the firm will collapse, but it will be in a vulnerable position.

The **quick ratio**, also called the "acid-test" ratio, measures the ability of a firm to meet its debt payments on short notice. It is a more stringent test, hence the name acid-test. (Long ago, acid was used to evaluate the purity of gold. If your ore sample did not meet the acid-test, you received little or no cash for your gold.) The quick ratio eliminates inventories and prepaid expenses as a part of current assets.

The ratio tells the firm's suppliers and creditors how much of the short term debt can be met by getting rid of all the company's liquid assets immediately. The quick ratio formula is:

quick ratio = quick assets*/current liabilities

*quick assets = total current assets *minus* inventories and prepaids

As a general rule, a quick ratio of 1:1 (one-to-one) is satisfactory. It represents the margin of safety accessible to the firm's creditors and suppliers.

Table 14.4   Comparison of Financial Ratios of Three Companies

	Apple	Walmart	Vera Bradley
Gross profit margin	37.9%	24.91%	56.73%
Earnings per share (EPS)	$2.74	$2.43	$0.59
Current ratio	1.5	0.76	2.15
Quick ratio (acid-test)	1.47	0.21	0.91
Inventory turnover	34.63	9.03	1.7
Asset turnover	0.77	2.35	0.93
ROE from total operations	51.65%	18.81%	5.56%
Debt/equity	88.06%	75.54%	0%

Source: Reported as of September 2019. Retrieved from www.investing.com/

Measures of Financial Leverage (Debt)

Leverage refers to the use of borrowed funds to generate returns for stockholders. For example, borrowing at 4% and creating returns of 8% is using leverage effectively. Leverage creates additional returns, but also commits the firm to future cash obligations. Leverage ratios indicate the extent to which a firm relies on debt financing rather than equity financing.

The **debt-to-equity** ratio indicates what proportion of equity and debt the company is using to finance its assets. The formula is:

debt-to-equity ratio = total liabilities/stockholders' equity

It is important to note that:

- If the ratio is greater than 1, the majority of the assets are financed through debt.
- If it is smaller than 1, assets are primarily financed through equity.
- Investing in a firm with a higher ratio may be riskier, especially in times of rising interest rates due to the additional interest that has to be paid out.

Measures of Profitability (Performance)

Earnings per share (EPS) and **return on equity (ROE)** indicate management's ability to generate profits for the owners of the firm. ROE and EPS tell managers and investors how much profit a company has earned for each share of its stock.

Earnings per share is the key ratio used in determining share prices.

Earnings per share (EPS) This measure of profitability is the ratio that results in the share prices you see listed on stock exchanges.

earnings per share = net income/total number of shares

The higher the **return on equity**, the more a company's managers are adding to the value of its owners' investment.

return on equity = net income/owners' equity

Measures of Efficiency (Activity Ratios)

These measures indicate how well management is employing the firm's assets to generate revenue.

Inventory turnover measures how quickly the firm's inventory is shipped and sold in a given period of time. Ideally, management is holding just enough inventory to satisfy consumer demand. A decline in inventory turnover indicates slowing sales and/or excess inventory.

inventory turnover = cost of goods sold/inventory = _____ times/year inventory has been completely sold

Asset turnover measures how well a company's assets are utilized to produce sales. Higher sales means the company's assets are put to good use. Ideally, the firm's asset turnover ratio is larger than that of its rivals.

asset turnover = sales/total assets

Accounts receivable turnover shows how effective the company is in collecting the debts owed by its customers after they have been extended credit. A high ratio indicates that the company is operating on a cash basis or that it is good at collecting money owed. A low ratio might prompt the company to review its policies toward extending credit.

accounts receivable turnover = net sales/accounts receivable= _____ times/year the company collects its average accounts receivable

APPLY YOUR KNOWLEDGE

The Soaring Value of Intangible Assets

The value of tangible assets such as real estate, inventory, and machinery is easy to compute, but the shift to a "knowledge-based" economy built on technological advances has drawn increasing attention to the value of "intangible assets." Intangible assets include intellectual property like patents, trademarks, trade secrets, proprietary technology, and copyrights, as well as brand equity and "goodwill." In preparing their balance sheets, some companies are expanding the intangible asset category to include spending on research and development, employee expertise, and customer data. There are two problems, though, with accounting for intangible assets: it is difficult to place a true value on them, unless the company has purchased the asset, for example, by paying a specified amount to use a patent; and they are considered expenses rather than part of a company's revenue-producing capital investments.

Technology companies, in particular, believe that traditional accounting methods do not accurately measure their financial health and performance. According to Bloomberg, spending on research and sales as a percentage of revenue had risen in 2017 to 14 percent of the revenue of Standard and Poor's 500 (S & P 500) stocks, compared with 7 percent only ten years earlier. Standard accounting rules do not treat these internal investments as assets. Bloomberg reporter Justina Lee observes, "It's a hallmark of American accounting that the value created by things such as advertising or research and development go largely unrecognized when counting up net worth, while eating into earnings." For example, when Autodesk included the spending on its 2018 research and development program in its assets, it was able to add $3.6 million in assets to its balance sheet, significantly reducing the losses it reported.

Intangible assets are classified as "long-term assets" on the balance sheet and are not used in computing the current ratio, which measures the ability of the company to pay its short-term liabilities. They are typically reported on separate lines as "goodwill" and "other intangible assets."

The "goodwill" category represents the purchase of another company along with its brand equity and customer loyalty. The purchase price must exceed the target company's net worth in order for the goodwill to have a positive asset value. Goodwill has an indefinite useful life and cannot be separated from a business, while other intangible assets (patents, proprietary software, domain names, etc.) can be bought, sold, and lose value over time. Goodwill cannot be amortized (marked down in value over time), but other intangible assets can be.

Industries with high levels of intangible assets include technology, entertainment and media, consumer products and services, and health care. The table below shows the amount of intangible assets owned by a company representing each of these industries and the ratio of intangible assets to the total assets possessed by each company. (All figures are from 2018 *Marketwatch.com*)

	Goodwill	Other Intangibles	Total Assets	Total Intangibles/ Total Assets
Oracle Corp.	$43.76 billion	$6.67 billion	$137.26 billion	37%
Walt Disney Co.	$31.27 billion	$6.81 billion	$98.6 billion	39%
Coca-Cola Co.	$10.26 billion	$7.01 billion	$83.22 billion	21%
Amedysis Inc.	$329.48 million	$44.13 million	$717.12 million	52%

If you think that expanding the definition of an intangible asset sounds like an invitation to "fudge" balance sheets, you are not alone. Investors and market analysts are finding it difficult to determine the true market value of a company because up to 80 percent of the average stock valuation of S & P 500 companies now comes from intangible assets. This situation is driving development of new, complex measurement formulas such as calculated intangible value (CIV) and return on assets (ROA) to determine a company's financial health and performance.

Knowledge Application Questions

1. Use the NASDAQ Company Financials page at https://www.nasdaq.com/quotes/company-financials.aspx or investor relations page on the company website to find the most recent balance sheets of these publicly traded Indiana companies: Cummins Inc. (CMI), Steel Dynamics (STLD), Vera Bradley (VRA), and Zimmer Biomet Holdings, Inc. (ZBH). What is the ratio of intangible assets (goodwill plus other intangible assets) to total assets for each company? Construct a table like the one presented above to show your work.

2. Enter the phrase "goodwill impairment" and each company's name above in Google to search the Internet for any losses suffered due to negative goodwill. What do you find?

3. If you were to make a personal balance sheet, what items would you include under Current Assets, Fixed Assets, and Intangible Assets? What value would you give to each item? Justify your estimates.

Sources

Cokins, G. and N. Shepherd. 2017, May 1. "The power of intangibles." *Strategic Finance Magazine*. Accessed October 31, 2019. https://sfmagazine.com/post-entry/may-2017-the-power-of-intangibles/.

Kenton, W. 2019, April 19. "Calculated Intangible Value (CIV)." Accessed October 31, 2019. https://www.investopedia.com/terms/c/civ.asp.

Lee, J. 2018, June 6. "Bubble-Like Stock Valuations Miss $3.4 Trillion in Hidden Assets." Bloomberg. Accessed October 31, 2019. https://www.bloomberg.com/news/articles/2018-06-06/what-s-a-stock-worth-in-new-economy-accounting-has-its-critics.

Maverick, J. B. 2018, May 29. "How Do Intangible Assets Show on a Balance Sheet?" Investopedia. Accessed October 31, 2019. https://www.investopedia.com/ask/answers/013015/how-do-intangible-assets-appear-balance-sheet.asp.

Murphy, C. 2019, May 8. How Do Tangible and Intangible Assets Differ? Accessed October 31, 2019. https://www.investopedia.com/ask/answers/012815/what-difference-between-tangible-and-intangible-assets.asp.

QUIZ YOURSELF

Without looking back at the chapter, choose the best answer to each of the questions below. Answers are in the back of the textbook before the Index. Review the chapter to find out why you missed any questions.

1. Double entry bookkeeping is important because
    a. it is the language of business.
    b. financial statements rely on its fundamental concepts.
    c. it shows the liquidity of a company.
    d. it provides the basis for computing the interest on loans.
    e. None of the above.

2. Which of the following describes the purpose of the generally accepted accounting principles (GAAP)?
    a. Provide the necessary data to the firm's bookkeepers
    b. Illustrate the difference between financial and managerial accounting
    c. Certify the accuracy of a firm's financial statements
    d. Provide for more consistency in the reporting practices of businesses
    e. Comply with the laws and regulations of the federal government

3. _____ is the field of accounting that serves internal users of a company's financial information.
    a. Managerial accounting
    b. Government accounting
    c. Financial accounting
    d. Stock market accounting
    e. None of the above

4. Why would a firm need the services of both internal and external auditors?
    a. To control for external threats to the company's growth
    b. To prevent too much whistle-blowing
    c. To make sure that the company is not exaggerating its success or failure
    d. To provide continued business to certified public accountants
    e. To provide gainful employment to graduates of accounting programs

5. How is an income statement different from a balance sheet?
   a. An income statement focuses on a period of time, but a balance sheet focuses on a certain point in time.
   b. An income statement shows revenue, costs, and profits, but a balance sheet focuses on assets and liabilities.
   c. An income statement is usually prepared before the balance sheet.
   d. The inventory turnover ratio is based on the income statement, but the "acid test" is based on the balance sheet.
   e. All of the above.

6. The accounting equation shows all of the following, EXCEPT
   a. a company's financial position at a specific point in time.
   b. how much money will be left when a firm sells all its assets and pays all its debts.
   c. which of the company's assets are intangible.
   d. the owners' net worth.
   e. how much the company owes to creditors.

7. The major types of assets are
   a. current, fixed, and intangible.
   b. current, long-term, and deferred.
   c. long-term, paid-in capital, and retained.
   d. current, noncurrent, and owners' equity.
   e. None of the above.

8. The major types of liabilities are
   a. current, fixed, and intangible.
   b. current and long-term.
   c. accounts receivable and land.
   d. dividends paid and net loss.
   e. None of the above.

9. The difference between a current ratio and a quick ratio is that the
   a. quick ratio does not count inventory and prepaid expenses as part of the company's assets.
   b. current ratio shows the ability of the firm to pay its debts on short notice.
   c. quick ratio can determine the gold content of a rock sample.
   d. current ratio shows owners' equity but the quick ratio does not.
   e. None of the above.

10. Financial ratios show investors
    a. how easily a company can pay its short-term debts.
    b. the profitability of company.
    c. how secure the investor's money will be.
    d. how efficient the company is in using its funds to generate revenue.
    e. All of the above.

CHAPTER 15

Managing Business Finances

What Is Finance?

Finance is the business function of planning, acquiring, and managing a company's funds in order to accomplish its objectives efficiently and effectively. Simply put, finance is that function of business that transacts money and markets.

Financial Management

The financial manager is largely concerned with where to obtain funds and how to use them effectively and efficiently. The **chief financial officer (CFO)** is the head of a firm's financial operations. The CFO may also be known as a comptroller, controller, or finance controller. The chief financial officer reports directly to the chief executive officer (CEO) or the chief operations officer (COO) and to the board of directors. The CFO is often a member of the board of directors.

Why Must Businesses Acquire Funds?

Funds are needed both to start a business and to keep it going. Financing may be needed to run day-to-day operations, to compensate employees and hire new ones, to pay for inventories, to acquire a new subsidiary or expand an existing one, to name a few uses of funding. The job of a financial manager is to continuously evaluate a firm's need for funding and communicate the financial status of the firm in informing business decisions. Poor financial management often leads to bankruptcy, with a poor economy as a contributing factor. A firm, small or large, can file for bankruptcy under Chapter 11 or 13 of the U.S. Bankruptcy code as a way of staying in business. According to the American Bankruptcy Institute, there were 5,480 bankruptcy filings in 2018, about half the number filed in 2010 as a result of the Great Recession.

Raising Funds for Business

Capital refers to the long-term funds a firm needs to acquire fixed assets, such as land, factories, vehicles, buildings, and equipment, in order to carry on its operations. Firms acquire funds in the form of debt financing or equity financing. The most beneficial mixture of debt and equity financing will lower the cost of capital, which will boost the value of the firm.

Debt Financing

Debt financing
Acquiring funds by borrowing money and promising to pay interest to the lender for use of the funds.

Debt financing refers to the act of borrowing funds. The most common practice is when a firm borrows from financial institutions such as commercial banks, savings banks, credit unions, pension funds, and life insurance companies. **Collateral** is a legal asset of value that may be appropriated by lenders in case of nonpayment. A building, equipment, vehicles, or computers are assets that are often accepted as collateral, for example. Collateral reduces the risk of default in favor of the creditor. Terms of a loan from financial institutions spell out the amount borrowed, maturity, collateral, and rate of interest. A borrower may be required to pledge collateral.

The **loan rate** of interest is often based on the **prime rate** of interest. The prime rate is the interest rate financial institutions charge on loans to the most creditworthy businesses. If a company is less creditworthy, a risk premium is added to the prime rate. Most financial institutions offer the option of a **fixed rate** loan versus a **variable rate** loan (also called a **floating rate** loan). A fixed rate remains constant throughout the duration of the loan agreement while a variable rate moves up and down depending on the market. The benefit of one of the rates over the other is contingent upon the expectations of the future direction of interest rates, which are always under a great deal of uncertainty.

Secured Loans and Unsecured Loans

- **Secured Loans**
  These loans, backed by collateral, are ones that the creditor can claim if the borrower does not repay the debt. For example, a bank or other creditor can repossess a vehicle purchased with a loan or foreclose on a house, if the mortgage is not paid as agreed.

- **Unsecured Loans**
  Unsecured loans are supported only by the reputation and previous credit rating of the borrower.

Bonds

Large firms may opt to raise money by issuing **bonds**. Bonds are long-term debt obligations that are sold to investors. Bonds can be *secured* or *unsecured*. **Secured bonds** are backed by collateral, which consists of a specific asset that must be given up to the bond investors in case the issuing firm fails to pay. **Unsecured bonds**, also called **debentures**, are not backed by a specific asset but simply by the issuing firm's creditworthiness. In other words, based on its past reputation, the firm is likely to be able to make good on the bond. Because unsecured bonds are considered to be riskier than secured bonds, they pay higher returns.

Potential bondholders may try to limit the risk of default on a bond by demanding a **protective covenant**. The covenant is a loan agreement that restricts the borrowing firm from undertaking certain financial policies during the term of the loan. For example, a covenant may limit a firm's additional debt and its payment of dividends until the existing bonds are settled. This way, the covenant protects the interests of the bondholders. Bond ratings performed by rating companies such as Moody's and Standard and Poor's, help investors anticipate the level of risk that they will be exposed to through their purchase of a bond offering (table 15.1.).

Table 15.1   Bond ratings

Moody's Bond Ratings	Standard & Poor's Bond Ratings	Description
Aaa, Aa, A, Baa	AAA and AA	High-credit quality investment grade
	AA and BBB	Medium-credit quality investment grade
Ba, B, Caa, Ca, C	BB, B, CCC, CC, C	Low credit quality (non-investment grade), or "junk bonds"
	D	Bonds in default for nonpayment of principal and/or interest

Note: Any bond with a C rating or below is currently in default. This means that the bond is not paying interest or repaying the principal. A "junk bond" is a bond issued by a company that is considered to be a higher credit risk. The credit rating of "junk bonds" is considered "speculative grade" or below "investment grade." This means that the chance of default with these types of bonds is higher than those of other bonds.

Firms issue a bond certificate as proof of indebtedness to investors. The certificate spells out the name of the issuing firm, the par value, the interest rate (also known as coupon rate), the maturity, and the payment schedule when the interest will be paid. The legal written agreement, which describes the firm's obligations to its bond investors, is known as an **indenture**. Besides the protective covenant stated above, an indenture spells out the following:

- The **par value** is the amount that bondholders receive when the bond matures. For example, bondholders owning a bond with a par value of $1000 and an interest rate of 7.5% will receive $75 in interest each year until the bond matures.

- A **call feature (provision)** provides the issuing firm with the right to repurchase its bonds before they mature at a **call price** (predetermined price).

Short-term Financing

Most often firms seek short-term funds rather than long-term ones. Short-term financing is usually needed to run day-to day operations, which include payments for payroll, inventory, supplies, and other expenses when the firm does not have adequate cash on hand. Short-term financing has a maturity of less than a year, but the debt is usually settled in less than 180 days. Short-term financing can be unsecured or secured.

Unsecured Short-term Debt Financing

Unsecured financing carries no obligation for the borrower to provide collateral against the loan. The creditor relies on the relationship and creditworthiness of the borrower. **Short-term financing** may come from trade credit, banks, and commercial paper.

- **Trade credit**
  The seller simply does not require immediate payment after the merchandise has been delivered. However, it is customary that the credit terms be expressed with a discount for timely payment. For example, the seller may state that if payment is received within 10 days of the date of the invoice, a 2% cash discount will be allotted to the account. If the firm does not take advantage of the discount, the payment for the merchandise comes due 30 days after the date of the invoice (terms commonly referred to as Net 30).

- **Commercial banks**
  The firm may also seek additional funds from commercial banks. To obtain the funds the firm usually signs a conventional **promissory note**. A promissory note is a written pledge to pay, in a lump sum or in installments, money to a creditor throughout the life of the loan. Unlike trade credit, a promissory note usually carries interest and is legally binding. Another way that a commercial bank may help a good client to obtain funds is by negotiating a **line of credit**. A line of credit is a maximum loan balance that the bank will allow a customer to maintain. The customer may draw down on the balance at any time as long as the maximum is not exceeded.

- **Commercial paper**
  Firms in good financial condition can obtain unsecured short-term debt through issuing **commercial paper**. Commercial paper is a short-term, unsecured promissory note. It is generally issued by well-established businesses like **blue chip** companies, such as AT&T, Kellogg's, General Electric, Coca-Cola, McDonald's Corp, and Procter & Gamble. (These companies are called blue chip because, in a poker game, the blue-colored chip is the most valuable one.)

Secured Short-term Debt Financing

The most common types of collateral that businesses pledge for secured short-term debt are inventories and accounts receivable.

- **Inventory**
  Loans can be secured by inventory that the firm can pledge as collateral. The lender takes over the title to the inventory and has control over it until the loan is repaid, while the borrower pays for the storage and insurance.

- **Accounts receivable (invoices)**
  The sum of money owed the firm in the form of accounts receivable from trade credit given to customers can be used as a form of debt financing. Accounts receivable can be pledged as collateral for a loan. In this instance, the firm retains its ownership of the receivables. Another way to use accounts receivable for financing is to sell them at a discount, a practice known as **factoring**. A **factor** is a business entity that specializes in the buying of accounts receivable of other firms. The factoring firm buys the receivables outright at a discount in order to compensate for the risk of not being able to collect. The profit the factoring firm generates is the difference between the face value of the receivables and what it paid for them.

When a firm uses a factor to obtain financing from its receivables, the firm gives up its ownership of the receivables. The quality of the receivables is based on the level of confidence in the customers' payment of the credit extended. The lender may seek payment from the borrowing firm if the receivables used to secure the loan are difficult to collect. To make the receivables very attractive, some firms fastidiously monitor them to avoid any excessive buildup of unpaid invoices.

Equity Financing

Equity financing refers to the act of raising money from the owners of the firm or from other investors. One source of equity financing is **retained earnings**. Rather than distributing earnings to the **shareholders** in the form of **dividends**, many firms retain a portion of the earnings to reinvest in future activities, such as paying off debt, relocation, research and development, purchasing plants and equipment, or introducing a new product. Another source of equity financing is selling **common** or **preferred stocks**. In return for the funds raised from the issuance of the stocks, the investors receive ownership interests in the firm.

Equity financing Raising money from owners and investors, by retaining earnings rather than paying dividends, or by selling stock.

Common stock, also called **common share**, is an equity security that represents an ownership in the issuing firm. A common stockholder participates in the election of the board of directors and votes on the firm's corporate policies. In case of liquidation, the common stockholders will not receive payments until the lenders and preferred stock owners receive theirs. As a matter of fact, dividends are not always paid to common shareholders.

Preferred stock, also called **preferred share,** offers specific priorities over common stock. Preferred stockholders receive dividend payments before they are paid to the common shareholders.

The most popular stock markets include the New York Stock Exchange (NYSE), the American Stock Exchange (AMEX), over-the-counter (OTC), Nasdaq, and the Chicago Board of Trade. Examples of stock quotes on the NYSE and the Nasdaq are shown in table 15.2.

Table 15.2 How to read stock quotes

Hi	Low	Stock	Exchange	Ticker Symbol	Div.	Yield %	Avg 10 day Volume	Prev. Close	Net Change
$173.54	$120.61	IBM	NYSE	IBM	$ 0.75	1.79%	5,053,491	167.18	$0.30
$ 52.36	$ 22.00	Vera Bradley	Nasdaq	VRA	-	-	247,612	49.61	$0.16
$642.96	$433.63	Google	Nasdaq	GOOG	-	-	2,285,273	518.13	$2.81
$ 68.77	$ 49.47	Coca Cola	NYSE	KO	$ 3.47	2.82%	6,509,652	66.7	($0.13)
1		**2**	**3**	**4**	**5**	**6**	**7**	**8**	**9**

Notes:

1. These are the highest and lowest prices paid for a share of stock in the previous 52-week period.
2. The name of the issuing company. When followed by "pf" the stock is preferred stock.
3. The market in which the stock is traded. NYSE is New York Stock Exchange. NASDAQ stands for National Association of Securities Dealers Automated Quotations. Major technology stocks are traded on the NASDAQ.
4. The "ticker tape" symbol for the stock.
5. The annual cash dividend paid out to stockholders. Under some conditions dividends may not be paid.
6. The dividend return on one share of common stock.
7. Average number of shares traded daily for the previous 10 days.
8. The price of a share of stock as of the close of the previous day's business.
9. Change in the price per share after a day of trading.

Firms may decide to issue stocks to venture capitalists or angel investors. Venture capitalists and angel investors are similar. They both provide capital to potentially profitable businesses.

- **Angel investors**
  These investors are wealthy individuals determined to undertake high financial risks by investing relatively small amounts of money in the early stages of a local business venture. These investors also offer advice and support to help the new firm achieve adequate growth to be subsequently able to draw in other investors. In return, angel investors want to have some form of control and involvement in the running of the business.

- **Venture capitalists**
  Once a business entity is up and running, a firm may seek funding from venture capitalists. These investors anticipate more control and involvement over a business venture than angel investors. **Venture capital** is a substantial

Table 15.3   Biggest IPOs of 2018 (in U.S. $).

Company	Description of Business	Ticker Symbol	Funds Raised (billion)	Opening Share Price	Share Price as of 12/07/18
Spotify	Music streaming	SPOT	9.2	165.90	136.19↓
AXA	Insurance	EQH	2.7	20.00	20.04↑
PagSeguro	Mobile payment service (Brazil)	PAGS	2.3	21.50	22.17↑
iQiyi	Video streaming service (China)	IQ	2.3	18.00	20.12↑
Pinduoduo	Social ecommerce service (China)	PDD	1.6	19.00	21.80↑
Elanco	Animal Health	ELAN	1.5	24.00	33.01↑
ADT Inc.	Electronic security	ADT	1.5	14.00	7.73↓
StoneCo Ltd.	Financial services (Brazil)	STNE	1.2	24.00	22.58↓
VICI Properties Inc.	Gaming and hospitality real estate	VICI	1.2	20.00	21.81↑
World Gold Trust	Gold investment	GLDM	1.0	12.98	12.22↓

Sources: "The top 26 largest company IPOs of the year," *USA Today*, December 7, 2018. Retrieved from www.usatoday.com/story/money/business/2018/12/07/top-ipos-2018-26-biggest-companies-went-public-year/38611947/

pooled investment fund that comes from several wealthy investors. To be able to obtain funding, a business has to prepare a sound business plan. To learn more about venture capitalists, you may visit the National Venture Capital Association's website at www.nvca.org.

Initial Public Offering (IPO) When a private company offers stock to the public for the first time in order to raise funds.

When a privately held corporation wishes to raise additional funds to expand its business, it may consider an **initial public offering (IPO)** of stock. The first sale of common stock to the general public is known as "**going public**." Venture capitalists have used IPOs to realize a return on investments from those successful firms that they assisted. In 2018 there were 190 IPOs, about the same number as in 2017. Compare this number with the 489 IPOs at the height of the "dot com bubble" in 1999 and the 31 offerings in 2008 at the start of "the Great Recession." The ten most successful offerings of 2018 are shown in table 15.3.

The advantage of an IPO is that the business can generate capital without increasing its debt burden. The firm gains credibility in the industry where it operates and also has access to financial markets and information. One disadvantage of IPO is that the firm must disclose financial information to the investing public. This implies that the firm's competitors may learn valuable information too. The firm may have difficulty persuading its local investors of its potential profitability and success. This may affect the fair market price for the firm's stock. In an IPO, ownership is diluted since the firm will have new added investors.

The IPO process is very expensive. The firm has to pay significant legal fees, accounting fees, and marketing costs. Investment banks and brokers charge high fees for professional advising and for placing IPO stocks in the securities markets or stock exchange.

Capital Structure

The term **capital structure** is used to describe the composition of debt versus equity financing. The most favorable capital structure of a firm is the mix of debt and equity financing that reduces the cost of acquiring the necessary funds for the firm. Firms adjust their capital structure by monitoring the conditions of the economy. For example, when interest rates go down in a recession, to boost investment, the firm may raise its debt level. However, debt provides the firm with **tax-deductible** interest payments. Further, excessive and unwarranted debt may increase the risk of default. Equity funding offers no tax deduction because it is an investment by the owners.

In figure 15.1 the capital structure of well-known companies in a variety of industries is shown. Notice that debt financing in all but two companies is 50% or more. This could be due to low interest rates over a period of years, making it fairly inexpensive to borrow money and take advantage of tax-deductions. The structures shown have held constant over the past several years except for Starbucks, which increased its debt financing by over 30% in 2018.

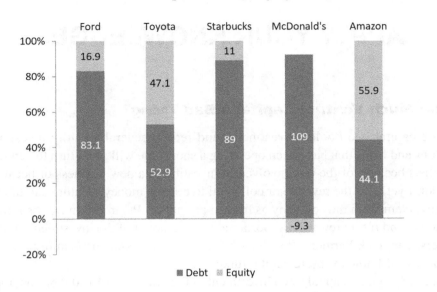

Figure 15.1 Capital structure of firms in a variety of industries

Source: Morningstar.com

APPLY YOUR KNOWLEDGE

Is Too Much Venture Capital a Bad Thing?

Venture capital is a pooled investment fund fed by several wealthy investors. Start-ups and firms that have been operating a short time will often turn to venture capitalists because of the risk involved in investing in a new business or because they don't yet have the revenue or collateral to borrow money. Venture capitalists seek involvement in the company as limited partners (LPs) in return for assuming a high risk and future rewards proportional to the amount of the investment. Accel Partners, Greylock Partners, Benchmark Capital, and Bessemer Venture Partners are some well-known venture capital funds.

In 2018, venture capital (VC) investment in U.S. firms was $130.9 billion, topping the record set in 2000 at the height of growth in Internet-based companies—the "dot-com" era. The National Venture Capital Association (NVCA) predicted that investment in 2019 would match or exceed this figure. This should be good news, but a closer examination of trends in VC investment reveals some troubling facts, according to experts.

Companies engage in different types of "rounds" of investing, depending on what stage of development the company is in. Newer companies with great ideas and a strong strategy go through a Series A round, usually seeking a maximum of $15 million. Companies that want to grow the company to meet demand engage in a Series B round, asking for $30 million to $60 million. In Series C rounds, the goal is to fund expansion into new products and new markets or buy another company. Series C funding is usually in the $100 million range.

According to the NVCA, the once rare $100 million rounds have become "a daily occurrence." Only the wealthiest of venture capitalists can afford to invest so that the number of deals struck has been decreasing. Some investors see sharpening of the divide between the "haves and the have nots." Competition to be the first in line may also mean that investors are less thorough in their analysis of companies seeking venture capital. As a result, they could be losing more money than they should, money that could have been more safely invested elsewhere.

A growing concern is that highly successful companies like Uber and Lyft, for example, are staying private longer, meaning that the private investors—the venture capitalists—are the ones benefiting from the company's gains. Thus, by the time of the company's initial public offering (IPO), the stock price is already high, discouraging public investors. Many say that companies and analysts exaggerate the value of a firm, as in the case of Snap, Dropbox, Spotify, Pinterest, Uber, and Lyft. The stock prices of all of these enterprises fell after their IPOs.

For example, Lyft opened at $72 a share on the first day of its IPO in March 2019 and was valued at $24 billion. The share price rose by 9 percent by the end of the trading day, and the Uber rival raised $2.3 billion. The share price dropped by 40 percent over 6 weeks and was still falling by midyear, hovering around a little less than $60 per share. Soon after the IPO, the company was devalued by $9 billion.

Though a few experts have predicted the "death of the IPO," 2019 was on track to see more IPOs than ever before. Slack, the workplace messaging service, valued at $17 billion; Airbnb, renting and leasing broker, valued at $38 billion; Palantir Technologies, a data analytics firm valued at $26 to $30 billion; and WeWork, the shared office space company valued at $47 billion, were among the young companies scheduled for IPOs in 2019.

Knowledge Application Questions

1. If you had purchased $10,000 worth of shares in each of these companies on the date of their IPOs, how much money would you have made, or lost, if you sold your shares today? (Figure out how many shares you could have bought, then multiply by today's share price. Use Nasdaq.com to obtain the current share price.)

Company Name	Symbol	Date of IPO	Opening Share Price
Spotify	SPOT	April 3, 2018	$165.90
Elanco Animal Health Inc.	ELAN	September 20, 2018	$24
ADT Inc.	ADT	January 19, 2018	$14
Dropbox, Inc.	DBX	March 23, 2018	$21

2. Based on their balance sheets dated December 31, 2018, the capital structures of Spotify, Elanco, ADT Inc., and Dropbox, Inc. are summarized below. Given this information, relevant financial ratios, and the balance sheets, which of the companies would represent the least risky investment? Explain your answer.

Company Name	Debt (percent)	Equity (percent)
Spotify	26	74
Elanco Animal Health Inc.	40	60
ADT Inc.	74	26
Dropbox, Inc.	52	48

3. Dell Computers, Burger King, H. J. Heinz, and Panera are all public companies that decided to become privately owned. What are the reasons why a company would return to private ownership, also known as "delisting" from a stock exchange?

Sources

Divine, J. 2019, May 17. "10 Major upcoming IPOs to watch in 2019." *US News & World Report.* Accessed October 31, 2019. https://money.usnews.com/investing/stock-market-news/slideshows/best-stocks-ipo-this-year?onepage.

Investopedia n.d. "6 Wealthy Venture Capitalists." Accessed October 31, 2019. https://www.investopedia.com/slide-show/venture-capitalists/?article=1.

Levy, A. 2019, May 20. "Uber, Lyft and Pinterest Prove that Private Investors are Sucking Up all the Value." Accessed October 31, 2019. https://www.cnbc.com/2019/05/18/uber-lyft-pinterest-ipos-proving-private-investors-suck-up-the-value.html.

Reiff, N. 2019, February 8. "Series A, B, C Funding: How It Works." *Investopedia.* Accessed October 31, 2019. https://www.investopedia.com/articles/personal-finance/102015/series-b-c-funding-what-it-all-means-and-how-it-works.asp.

Seth, S. 2018, October 5. "10 Most Famous Public Companies that Went Private." *Investopedia.* Accessed October 31, 2019. https://www.investopedia.com/articles/active-trading/073015/10-most-famous-public-companies-went-private.asp.

Venture Monitor: 1Q 2019. 2019. Accessed October 31, 2019. https://nvca.org/wp-content/uploads/2019/05/1Q_2019_PitchBook_NVCA_Venture_Monitor.pdf.

QUIZ YOURSELF

Without looking back at the chapter, choose the best answer to each of the questions below. Answers are in the back of the textbook before the Index. Review the chapter to find out why you missed any questions.

1. The main goal of the financing function of a firm is to
    a. produce income statements and balance sheets.
    b. make sure that invoices are sent in a timely fashion.
    c. collect payment from customers who are delinquent.
    d. plan, obtain, and manage the firm's funds to achieve its mission.
    e. None of the above.

2. All of the following are main sources of funding for a company, EXCEPT
    a. loans.
    b. bonds.
    c. selling shares of stock.
    d. angel investors.
    e. current assets.

3. On April 18, 2019, Pinterest, a social media platform, began trading on the New York Stock Exchange for the first time. This is an example of a/an
    a. limited liability company.
    b. initial public offering (IPO).
    c. acquisition.
    d. taking the company private.
    e. horizontal merger.

4. Meena purchased $1,000 in office supplies for her company from Office Depot. Her invoice says that she may pay within thirty days from the date shown. This is an example of a type of unsecured short-term debt financing called
    a. commercial paper.
    b. a factor.
    c. a promissory note.
    d. a line of credit.
    e. a trade credit.

5. Blanchard Trucking Inc. has sold its accounts receivable to RTS Financial because it needs $50,000 immediately in order to stay in business. RTS will give Blanchard Trucking $50,000 less $2,500 and keep the money it will collect directly from Blanchard's customers. This is an example of a type of secured short-term debt financing called
   a. equity financing.
   b. debentures.
   c. loan sharking.
   d. line of credit.
   e. factoring.

6. Preferred stock is different from common stock in that
   a. preferred stockholders receive dividends before holders of shares of common stock.
   b. only preferred stockholders have ownership in the company.
   c. preferred stock is a type of equity financing and common stock is not.
   d. common stock is sold over the counter and preferred stock is sold only by brokers.
   e. holders of common stock do not vote on corporate policies, but preferred stockholders do.

7. Collateral is
   a. a specific asset that must be given to investors or lenders should a company fail to pay back a bond or loan.
   b. a film about business.
   c. a protective covenant.
   d. a line of credit.
   e. an unsecured debt.

8. Standard & Poor's has given Vanguard bonds an AA rating. This means that the bonds are
   a. high risk.
   b. "junk" bonds.
   c. "investment grade."
   d. to be avoided.
   e. too expensive for the average investor.

9. A firm's ability to meet short-term obligations is a financial test of its
   _____.
   a. liquidity
   b. long-term obligations
   c. debt-to-equity position
   d. cost of goods sold
   e. asset turnover

10. The amount of money borrowed by a company in issuing a bond that it must repay at some time in the future is called the
    a. maturity premium.
    b. par value.
    c. risk premium.
    d. dividend amount.
    e. collateral.

QUIZ YOURSELF ANSWERS

CHAPTER 1
1.c
2.b
3.b
4.b
5.a
6.e
7.c
8.a
9.d
10.e

CHAPTER 2
1.a
2.c
3.c
4.b
5.e
6.c
7.a
8.d
9.e
10.e

CHAPTER 3
1.e
2.e
3.c
4.b
5.a
6.e
7.a
8.c
9.c
10.e

CHAPTER 4
1.e
2.e
3.c
4.d
5.c
6.c
7.c
8.b

9.e
10.d

CHAPTER 5
1.b
2.d
3.c
4.c
5.b
6.c
7.d
8.a
9.c
10.c

CHAPTER 6
1.a
2.e
3.e
4.d
5.d
6.c
7.a
8.e
9.a
10.b

CHAPTER 7
1.e
2.e
3.e
4.d
5.d
6.c
7.c
8.a
9.b
10.b

CHAPTER 8
1.b
2.c
3.b
4.e
5.d

6.d
7.e
8.a
9.c
10.e

CHAPTER 9
1.c
2.e
3.e
4.d
5.e
6.e
7.e
8.d
9.a
10.a

CHAPTER 10
1.a
2.a
3.a
4.e
5.c
6.e
7.b
8.e
9.e
10.b

CHAPTER 11
1.a
2.c
3.e
4.a
5.d
6.e
7.d
8.a
9.c
10.b

CHAPTER 12
1.b
2.e

3.c
4.d
5.a
6.e
7.e
8.c
9.d
10.e

CHAPTER 13
1.d
2.e
3.b
4.e
5.d
6.d
7.d
8.b
9.b
10.a

CHAPTER 14
1.b
2.d
3.a
4.c
5.e
6.c
7.a
8.b
9.a
10.e

CHAPTER 15
1.d
2.e
3.b
4.e
5.e
6.a
7.a
8.c
9.a
10.b

INDEX

Off-the-job training, 170
"Off-the-rack" products, 239
"Off-the-shelf" products, 239
Office of Whistleblower Protection
    Program, 51
OIC (Organization of the Islamic
    Conference), 76
Oldham, 189
Oligopoly, 6
Olive Garden, 204
Online advertising, 55
Online retailing, 239
Online training, 170
OPEC (Organization of Petroleum
    Exporting Countries), 77
Open-source software, 153
Operating activities listed in the cash
    flow statement, 257
Operating expenses, 254
Operations control, 135–141
Operations management, 129–142
    capacity planning, 131–132
    defined, 129
    layout planning, 133
    location planning, 132
    operations control, 135–141
    quality control, 137–138
    scheduling, 136–137
    service providers and
        manufacturers, similarities
        between, 131
    supply chain management,
        141–142
Operations managers, 130
Ordering costs, 135
Organization, defined, 111
Organization of Economic
    Cooperation and Development
    (OECD), 74–75
Organization of Petroleum Exporting
    Countries (OPEC), 77
Organization of the Islamic
    Conference (OIC), 76
Organizational goals, 90–91, 96
Organizational objectives, 90
Organizational rites, 121
Organizational structure, 111–112

changing, 120
corporate culture, 121–122
by customer, 114
defined, 111
by function, 112
hybrid, 116
informal, 120–121
by location, 114
matrix, 115–116
by process, 115
by product or service, 122
span of control, 118–119
Organizational vision, 91
Organization's mission, 91
Organizing in the management
    process, 89, 93–95
Orientation for new employees, 169
Ouchi, William, 184
Outsourcing, 135, 149
Over-the-counter securities
    market, 271
Owner's equity, 253

P

P2P (peer-to-peer), 154
Pacioli, Luca, 247
Packaging, product, 220–222
Page, Larry, 27
Palmer House Hilton, 62
Par value, 270
Paraguay, MERCOSUR membership,
    76
Pareto, Vilfredo, 138
Paris Agreement, 51
Participative leadership style, 95
Participative management, 189
Patents, 250, 252
Patheo, 151
Pay for time not worked, 173
Peak state of the business cycle, 6
Peer-to-peer (P2P), 154
Penetration pricing strategy, 217
Pension programs, 173
Pepsi-Cola, 35
Perfect competition, 5
Performance evaluations, 171–172
Performance feedback, 130

Permission-based marketing, 55
Personal selling, 232–233
PERT (program evaluation and review
    technique), 136
Pew Research Center, 44
Pharmaceutical firm licensing, 81
Philippines, ASEAN membership, 76
Phishing, 154
Physiological needs, 182
Pizza Hut, 117
Place (distribution), marketing
    mix, 197
Place utility, 196
Planned economies, 3
Planning in the management process,
    89–95
Plans of action, 91–92
PLC (product life cycle), 217–218,
    233–235
Point of sale (POS), 231
Point-of-sale materials, 238
Political-legal environment, 8
Polo, Marco, 69
POS (point of sale), 231
Positioning, 203–204
Positive balance of trade, 71
Positive reinforcement, 185
Possession utility, 196
Post-it Notes, 121
Post-purchase behavior, 208
Preferred share, 271
Preferred stock, 271
Premium, insurance, 222
Prepayments listed in the balance
    sheet, 250, 252
Pressure on co-workers as unethical
    behavior, 44–46
Prevention through Design (PtD), 58
Price
    bundle pricing, 225
    collusion, 54
    competition and, 224
    cost-plus, 225
    defined, 222
    demand and, 222
    discounts, 225
    discrimination, 54

CPSIA information can be obtained
at www.ICGtesting.com
Printed in the USA
LVHW100419211219
641255LV00002B/2/P

9 781792 408656